Anime and Memory

ALSO BY DANI CAVALLARO
AND FROM MCFARLAND

The Art of Studio Gainax: Experimentation, Style and Innovation at the Leading Edge of Anime (2009)

Anime Intersections: Tradition and Innovation in Theme and Technique (2007)

The Animé Art of Hayao Miyazaki (2006)

The Cinema of Mamoru Oshii: Fantasy, Technology and Politics (2006)

Anime and Memory

Aesthetic, Cultural and Thematic Perspectives

DANI CAVALLARO

McFarland & Company, Inc., Publishers
Jefferson, North Carolina, and London

LIBRARY OF CONGRESS CATALOGUING-IN-PUBLICATION DATA

Cavallaro, Dani.
  Anime and memory : aesthetic, cultural and
thematic perspectives / Dani Cavallaro.
      p.   cm.
  Includes bibliographical references and index.

  ISBN 978-0-7864-4112-9
  softcover : 50# alkaline paper ∞

  1. Animated films — Japan — Themes, motives.
       2. Memory in motion pictures.
                I. Title.
NC1766.J3C37   2009   791.43'340952 — dc22   2009014117

British Library cataloguing data are available

©2009 Dani Cavallaro. All rights reserved

*No part of this book may be reproduced or transmitted in any form
or by any means, electronic or mechanical, including photocopying
or recording, or by any information storage and retrieval system,
without permission in writing from the publisher.*

On the cover: Poster art for the 2001 film *Millennium Actress
(Sennen joyû)* directed by Satoshi Kon (DreamWorks/Photofest)

Manufactured in the United States of America

*McFarland & Company, Inc., Publishers
Box 611, Jefferson, North Carolina 28640
www.mcfarlandpub.com*

To Paddy,
with love and gratitude

Contents

Preface 1

1— Theoretical Perspectives   5
2— Memory and Desire   13
3— The Archaeology of Memory   31
4— Memory as Quest   51
5— Split Memories   69
6— Memory and the City   90
7— Memory as Worldbuilding   109
8— Submerged Memories   133
9— Haunted Memories   155

Filmography   177
Chapter Notes   183
Bibliography   188
Index   191

It's a poor sort of memory that only works backward.
— Lewis Carroll, *Through the Looking-Glass, and What Alice Found There* (1871)

Preface

> When I was younger, I could remember anything, whether it had happened or not.
> —Mark Twain in G. T. Couser, *Alter Egos* (1989)

> The difference between false memories and true ones is the same as for jewels: it is always the false ones that look the most real, the most brilliant.
> —Salvador Dalí, *The Secret Life of Salvador Dalí* (1942)

The topos of memory has often played a significant role in anime but its impact has grown exponentially over the past decade. Anime's handling of memory is multifaceted and brings it into collusion with diverse symbolic and diegetic motifs. This study aims to provide a detailed analysis of a range of titles wherein different aspects of this cultural phenomenon are articulated. In seeking to offer an original contribution to the burgeoning field of Anglophone anime scholarship, the book does not presume to delve into every possible production in which the memory theme is invoked, since this would inevitably impair intellectual penetration. It endeavors instead to supply in-depth assessments of an appropriate selection of films and series, chosen in accordance with the following criteria:

- they highlight the prominence of memory with reference to specific philosophical, artistic and historical contexts;
- they exemplify the distinctive signatures placed by particular directors and animation studios on their treatment of the topic;
- they are popular in Western countries as well as on home turf and are therefore likely to attract prospective readers of this study.

In its engagement with the memory theme, anime embraces a distinctively Eastern perspective on time that posits incessant becoming as that dimension's most salient trait. Within the unpredictable eddies of this current, there are no universally reliable data, only bundles of provisional intuitions; no neatly parceled facts, only ephemeral remembrances. Thus, the art form assiduously points to the radical impermanence of what we call our world by underscoring the highly subjective and lacunary nature of the stories we construct to keep that world in place. Concomitantly, it rejects the notion of a transparent master history presumed to chart the unfolding of truth and offers instead a pluralization of histories issuing from inevitably skewed and tentative mnemonic fragments. These messages are rendered especially poignant by their couching in a deliberately unpretentious — at times even restrained — fashion, in keeping with Japanese art's proverbial preference for allusiveness over direct statement, subtly nuanced implication over bold explication.

Chapter 1, "Theoretical Perspectives" evaluates a range of theoretical views pertinent to anime's engagement with memory. The chapter consists of two parts. The first concentrates on the relationship between memory and the five linchpins of Japanese aesthetics (*mono no aware, yugen, sabi, wabi, kire/kire tsuzuki*). All of these aesthetic tenets are deemed profoundly relevant to the theme of memory insofar as they invariably point to philosophical preoccupations with the mysteries of time. The second part expands the book's frame of reference to address memory's implication with temporality at large, its inscription in recorded history, its material embodiment and its inextricability from technology.

The aesthetic and broadly theoretical concepts addressed in the first chapter are revisited in the case studies to follow in order to demonstrate their direct pertinence to specific titles. The case studies consist of eight chapters, each of which explores one particular facet of the collusion of anime and memory by means of close analysis of one primary title and additional reference to a selection of ancillary productions spanning the early 1970s to the present. This approach is intended to maximize the book's historical breadth. The amount of space apportioned to each subsidiary title varies according to relevance and appeal.

Cursory reference is also made, both in the main body of the book and in the chapter notes, to additional titles worthy of inspection by readers eager to pursue particular aspects of the memory theme. This strategy allows for a comprehensive contextualization of the primary titles in relation to further areas of critical inquiry that transcend the book's contingent purview. Chronological range is matched by generic variety, the titles selected for inclusion having been drawn from areas as diverse as action adventure, romance, science fiction, steampunk, the epic, the supernatural, mystery, horror, crime, historical drama, domestic drama and slice-of-life drama (with tangential forays into other anime categories).

Chapter 2, "Memory and Desire" looks at a selection of anime whose narrative trajectory is shaped by the yearning to fulfill an objective fueled by memories of the protagonists' first discovery of romantic longing. Chapter 3, "The Archaeology of Memory," Gilgamesh explores anime's ideation of varyingly revisionist, legendary or antiquarian versions of history through a focus on the explicitly material dimension of the past and its mnemonic reservoir. In Chapter 4, "Memory as Quest," the emphasis is placed on the extent to which memories, both full-dress and inchoate, are responsible for triggering journeys of self-discovery and self-actualization. The titles discussed in Chapter 5, "Split Memories," dramatize eminently schizoid situations in which memories are carved up and distributed across distinct characters, on the one hand, and brought into play in order to establish powerful bonds between them, on the other.

Chapter 6, "Memory and the City," investigates the inscription of memory on ceaselessly mutating urban environments and the impact of this phenomenon on their inhabitants and their changing perceptions of both themselves and others over time. In Chapter 7, "Memory as Worldbuilding," the focus is on anime's deployment of the memory topos as a means of generating meticulously detailed and coherent universes underpinned by specific styles, customs and world views that render them emphatically credible despite their fictitious status. Finally, Chapter 8, "Submerged Memories," and Chapter 9, "Haunted Memories," concentrate on the impact of latent, repressed or submerged memories on both individual characters and their familial or societal milieux, drawing attention to those memories' penchant for irreverently eroding the boundary between reality and dreams.

The discussion is supplemented by a detailed filmography consisting of three sections (Primary Titles; Secondary Titles; Additional Titles Cited), as well as chapter notes, bibliographical references, and an index.

Chapter 1

Theoretical Perspectives

> Harvest moon:
> around the pond I wander
> and the night is gone.
> — Matsuo Bashou (1644–1694)
>
> The moment two bubbles
> are united, they both vanish.
> A lotus blooms.
> — Kijo Murakami (1865–1938)

Chapter 1 examines the relationship between memory and key concepts in Japanese aesthetics in order to illustrate ways in which anime is imbued with time-honored indigenous values even as it persistently absorbs contemporary global influences. It then considers the extent to which, in dealing with memory, anime concurrently grapples with broader issues regarding the concept of temporality and the recording of the passage of time in textual form.

Anime is deeply influenced by Japan's traditional aesthetic principles, and to appreciate it fully, some grasp of those values is highly beneficial. Insofar as several of the concepts underlying Japanese aesthetics allude to metaphysical issues inextricable from a keen awareness of the passing of time, their specific relevance to the memory topos can hardly go unheeded. Particularly important, in this respect, is the notion of *mono no aware*, the "sadness of things": namely, the pathos associated with sensitivity to the transience of beauty and pleasure. As observed in the entry for "Japanese Aesthetics" in the *Stanford Encyclopedia of Philosophy*, "the feeling of *aware* is typically triggered by the plaintive calls of birds or other animals."

Auditory effects of this kind are often deployed in anime and can work very powerfully in evoking both memories and the longings to which memories notoriously give rise. As the concept of *mono no aware* is broadened in order to embrace the "affective dimensions of existence in general" ("Japanese Aesthetics"), one frequently finds that it is through seemingly inert objects — rather than human motions and expressions — that pathos is most effectively communicated. Anime repeatedly focuses on static entities drawn from both the world of Nature and interior design (such as rocks and shells, screens and pots) to convey dramatic density economically, thereby bringing out the inner aliveness of the apparently inanimate and the body of memories that such objects host.

If *mono no aware* points to ineluctable perishability, the notion of *yugen*, conversely, designates the unfathomable timelessness of cosmic infinity. As David Pascal notes, *yugen* "is not the presence of, but the hint, the glow, of the eternal, the incorruptible." The notion of ineffable grace is intrinsic to *yugen* and serves to throw into relief the ultimate impenetrability of the world we inhabit: a dimension never to be conquered but only, at best, to be imaginatively approximated through a suspension of both belief and disbelief.[1] In terms of *mono no aware*, memory functions as the faculty that strives to salvage durable impressions from the ephemeral. In those of *yugen*, it is a reaching towards the vastness of time: a level of reality to which no individual life cycle can aspire, yet sympathetic participation in the remembrance of other people and epochs might at least evoke.

Overtly entangled with temporality is the aesthetic tenet known as *sabi*: "pleasure in that which is old, faded, lonely ... a love of imperfection. *Sabi* differs from *aware* in that one does not lament for the fallen blossom, but loves it, and from *yugen* in that the flower does not (or rather need not) suggest greater eternities" (Pascal). According to the *Stanford Encyclopedia*, the poetic mood of *sabi* is typified by the haiku of the seventeenth-century poet Matsuo Bashou — for example: "Solitary now —/ Standing amidst the blossoms / Is a cypress tree." As the article points out, the spirit of *sabi* is characteristically captured not by "the colorful beauty of the blossoms" but by "the more subdued gracefulness of the cypress" ("Japanese Aesthetics").

The concept of *wabi* also commends the beauty of the aged and the flawed, but specifically to honor the spiritual richness to be found in the materially imperfect as opposed to pristine goods. When applied to the domain of memory, *wabi* would seem to suggest that greater beauty can be ultimately located with the frayed tatters of a person's — or a group's — inner treasurehouse of recollections than with bounded dates and data. Such beauty will always, given memory's legendary elusiveness, be understated and unpretentious. Glamour is resolutely ostracized.

Taken in tandem, *sabi*'s and *wabi*'s acceptance of transience and elevation of the imperfect are rooted in Buddhist ideals. These regard lacunary states not as defects but as fertile grounds for growth. After all, it is the existence of gaps that stimulates thought, encouraging the mind and body to devise ways of provisionally filling them, whereas sealed scenarios of completeness stultify both perception and creativity. Just as an image of the moon or of the sun partially obscured by clouds or fog is more beautiful — in the logic of *sabi-wabi*— than an unblemished view, so the very fallibility and fragmentariness of memory are the qualities that make it appealing. However, the courting of imperfection intrinsic to the ideas discussed above is pertinent to anime at large and not merely to anime engaged with the theme of memory. Indeed, Japanese art's preference for the approximate and the incomplete is mirrored by anime's own passion for "faces half-sketched" and "backgrounds half-done," as well as a tendency to leave "things critical to the story never explained" (Pascal).

The materials supplied by the works here examined stylistically reflect the aesthetic criteria examined in the foregoing paragraphs by capitalizing on the inveterate Japanese passion for the allusive and the inconclusive, for suggestion rather than assertion. At times, they accomplish that goal by recourse to graphic flourishes that render their images intentionally incomplete. At others, they adopt the opposite approach, jam-packing the visuals with a profusion of details and making them indefinite by means of exaggerated repletion. Lack and fullness are construed as germane rather than adversarial, which is quite consonant with anime's impatience with stark binary oppositions. Thematically, viewers are invited to engage with shards and shreds of memory and evaluate their reliability in the face of a rampant mood of ambiguity. Distinguishing empirical knowledge from paranoid delusion, lived experience from hallucination, and science from magic is thus positioned as the axial—and never-ending—interpretative act.

The picture emerging from this body of thought is an intrinsically unstable world view that matches Japanese philosophy's grasp of reality as constant flux, as impermanence (*mujou*). As we have seen, Japanese aesthetics is capable of both lamenting and upholding that fundamental condition. Either way, however, it emplaces it as the *only* reality that presents itself to the senses. This proposition carries considerable weight when it is assessed specifically in relation to the phenomenon of memory. Indeed, it intimates that the worlds constructed by memory are never anchored to a Platonic substratum of unchanging truths but actually partake at all times of interminable cycles of birth, death and rebirth.

The Japanese preference for allusiveness over explicitness is typically suggested, in anime of the kind here explored, by recourse to panoramas and to background art. These find a vivid correlative in the type of landscape presented by Nancy G. Hume in her assessment of Japanese art's fascination with the inconclusive and inexplicable facets of the aesthetic experience: "When looking at autumn mountains through mist, the view may be indistinct yet have great depth. Although few autumn leaves may be visible through the mist, the view is alluring. The limitless vista created in imagination far surpasses anything one can see more clearly" (Hume, pp. 253–254).

Another pertinent characterization of the lure of allusiveness is provided by the thirteenth-century author Kamo no Choumei: "It is like an autumn evening under a colorless expanse of silent sky. Somehow, as if for some reason that we should be able to recall, tears well up uncontrollably" (quoted in "Japanese Aesthetics"). An analogous mood pervades Italo Calvino's description of the imaginary city of "Diomira": "the special quality of this city for the man who arrives there on a September evening, when the days are growing shorter and the multicolored lamps are lighted all at once at the doors of the food stalls and from a terrace a woman's voice cries ooh!, is that he feels envy towards those who now believe they have once before lived an evening identical to this and who think they were happy, that time" (Calvino 1997 [1972], p. 7). In both Choumei and Calvino, memory plays a major part in conveying the feeling of ineffability as the perceiver senses the urge to remember something profound yet just beyond his grasp.

One additional aesthetic principle deserves attention in this context: the *kire* ("cut") or *kire tsuzuki* ("cut continuity" or "cut continuation"). Like live-action cinematography, anime uses the cut as a versatile technique. One of its most distinctive strategies is the employment of cuts to move quite sharply from one shot to the next (which allows studios to economize in the creation of frames), yet also evoke a sense of continuity by retaining certain formal elements across discrete shots, such as a natural or architectural detail. This ploy reflects closely the principle of *kire*. At the same time, the concept echoes the Zen teaching: to look at the world with eyes unclouded by contingent desires and thus perceive its underlying beauty, the self must let go of its hold on the here-and-now and cut itself off from the pressures of the moment.

By consciously embracing a state of rootlessness, the self may thereby harmonize its actions and affects with the impermanence of the world at large. Additionally, in presenting motion as a corollary of the sequential arrangement of distinct, albeit adjacent, scenes (a defining trait of all animation as a frame-by-frame construct), cut continuity underscores the episodic character of life. Applied specifically to the topos of memory, the concept delineated above indicates that what we think of as recollections, be they reflections of actual events or pure imaginings, can be released from their putative roots in empirically quantifiable facts and allowed to take off unfettered into parallel universes.

The principles of *kire* and *kire tsuzuki* also suggest that it is possible to appreciate the beauty of each single component of a large constellation of interconnected entities without losing sight of the beauty of the overall ensemble. Calvino advances this proposition in the segment of his novel *If on a winter's night a traveler* titled "On the carpet of leaves illuminated by the moon," which is set in a traditional Japanese context, where the narrator observes the ginkgo leaves falling from the boughs and coming to rest on the lawn below, and reflects on the possibility of distinguishing "the sensation of each single ginkgo leaf from the sensation of all the others." His host and mentor Mr. Okeda assures him that this is feasible. The secret is to concentrate on an individual leaf first and then gradually proceed to reconstruct the wider scenario: "If from the ginkgo tree a single little yellow leaf falls and rests on the lawn, the sensation felt in looking at it is that of a single yellow leaf. If two leaves descend from the tree, the eye follows the twirling of the two leaves as they move closer, then separate in the air, like two butterflies chasing each other, then glide finally to the grass, one here, one there. And so with three, with four, even with five; as the number of leaves spinning in the air increases further, the sensations corresponding to each of them are summed up, creating a general sensation like that of a silent rain..." (Calvino 1993 [1981], p. 194).

This process requires at once the ability to isolate each of the individual elements from its companions, which entails a cut or series of successive cuts, and the ability to still grasp the interconnectedness of the various elements by focusing on the continuity that brings them together. Memory often operates in an analogous fashion. A comprehensive, albeit inevitably provisional, appreciation not only of the beauty of memory but also of the pain (and indeed the terror) inherent in its contents demands sensitivity to both the building blocks and the entire edifice. Hence, it entails both cuts and the orchestration of the isolated components into a continuous flow.

Leaves, incidentally, play an important part in Japanese aesthetics (as do blossom and vegetation generally). This is typified by the Zen anecdote in which a priest in charge of the garden of a famous temple meticulously rakes up and disposes the dry autumn leaves in preparation for the imminent arrival of illustrious guests. When the priest asks his master if the result of his efforts is agreeable, the older man praises him but also opines that there is scope for improvement. He then proceeds to shake the trunk of the tree from which the leaves came in the first place, which triggers a fresh shower of leaves, and instructs his acolyte to arrange them in the pattern of the original layer. The tale underscores the idea that in order to truly appreciate the beauty of Nature, it is necessary to restrain from the desire to tame it and organize it according to human agendas and develop an intimate awareness of the design principles on the basis of which Nature itself distributes and lays out its materials.

This proposition is also pertinent to the processes through which memories are formed, consciously grasped and constelled as an ensemble within the psyche. Where memories are concerned, the kind of procedure commended by the Zen elder with regard to the autumn leaves works as a metaphor for the necessity of achieving a deeper understanding of their import instead of smoothing or glossing over the difficulties arising from their often burdensome bequest. The attainment of awareness is the pivotal factor in this task. The characters portrayed in the anime examined in this book must learn precisely how to become aware of their memories, and internalize their lessons, past the constraints posed by their dominant desires, self-divisions and repressions.

Of all the productions here examined, the ones that articulate most potently the ethos of *mono no aware* are those discussed in Chapter 6, "Memory and the City." This is because the urban setting, as the receptacle of both private and shared remembrances, tends to be presented as an unrelentingly mutating map in which everything is, by definition, ephemeral. The titles addressed in Chapter 4, "Memory as Quest," for their part, partake of the spirit of *yugen* by positing memory as the trigger for daring forays into the unknown and the unknowable. The works covered in Chapter 7, "Memory as Worldbuilding" also invoke *yugen*: in this instance, mainly in the form of a reaching towards cosmic infinity. In both cases, mythological frames of reference are occasionally brought into play to underscore the timeless magnitude of the task at hand.

Sabi is elliptically evoked by the anime studied in Chapter 3, "The Archaeology of Memory," where a bittersweet fascination with the ancient and the crumbling recurrently manifests itself. *Wabi* comes most overtly to the fore in the titles addressed in Chapter 2, "Memory and Desire"; Chapter 8, "Submerged Memories"; and Chapter 9, "Haunted Memories." In Chapter 2, the lure of the imperfect is captured by the very nature of desire as an endlessly self-renewing — and hence insatiable — mechanism that is only capable, at best, of yielding partial satisfaction. In chapters 8 and 9, it is the amorphous character of the memories involved that renders their latent power coterminous with imperfection, as well as an overarching sense of unpretentious beauty. The works explored in Chapter 5, "Split Memories" emplace the principles of *kire* and *kire tsuzuki* as decisive by literally cutting up mnemonic materials and apportioning them to distinct personae. However, insofar as these various characters are portrayed as interdependent, an overriding sense of continuity can also be detected across the fabric of their adventures.

In assessing anime's engagement with the relationship between memory and wider aspects of temporality and history, four interrelated elements deserve close attention: the collusion of past and future; the construction of history; the materiality of memory; and the interplay of memory and technology. Memory pertains to the future no less than to the past: recollections are ineluctably colored by a propensity to project their legacy onto prospective scenarios. The use of fractured timelines and multiperspectival diegesis dramatically enhances this motif. Eastern notions of time based on principles of cyclicality and recurrence are deeply relevant to this scenario. In principle, according to this perspective, everything has already happened for an eternity in the past, and will continue to happen for an eternity in the future. The hourglass of existence is turned over and over, and us with it, mere grains of sand.

Memory does not provide a reliable record of past occurrences but rather edited, and hence arbitrary, versions of history: in so doing, it fabricates both personal and communal narratives by recourse to the mechanisms of repression, sublimation and idealization. All texts are based on the displacement of meaning and presence: any individual element present in a text is only meaningful insofar as it is implicitly related to other elements that are not present but could have been. Meaning is an effect of what is absent no less than what is present, and, by extension, of unvoiced memory traces no less than openly articulated recollections. Writing is inseparable from memory because all texts are tapestries of previous traces. There is no means of reascending the river of time to the first memory, let alone of trying to foresee the ultimate memory. A text is an ensemble of traces which can never totally erase memories of previous texts. We always write over previous writing, and always remember over previous recollections. Concurrently, all forms of language are riddled with aporias, undecidables, slippages and self-dismantling marks.

Although memory is a mental phenomenon, it also takes corporeal form insofar as its contents become embodied in actual people and places. In tandem, these provide the basis for vast ideological and mythological systems. This idea challenges the Cartesian mind-body dualism endemic in the West in favor of a characteristically Eastern perception of balance between spirit and matter. In underscoring the materiality of memory, the works here examined propose that even though memory is often regarded as a fundamentally mental function, the acts of memorization and retrieval actually bring the body into play as a primary agent. At the most basic level, this is borne out by the fact that reminiscences are most frequently associated with sensory experiences. It is not uncommon, for example, for a smell to evoke a memory or indeed a galaxy of memories.

According to Christian Steinbeck, the body can indeed be conceived of as a "medium of memory," and Japanese thought overtly contributes to the validation of this hypothesis. Thus, although the images that reminiscences bring forth pertain to something that is physically absent, memory and corporeality are inseparable. Steinbeck discusses the case of a clinically brain-dead Japanese youth as an apt illustration: "all parts of his brain had permanently ceased to function," yet the patient's body remained sensitive to the presence of close relatives, as attested to by significant fluctuations in "blood pressure and pulse rate" (Steinbeck, p. 4). This, Steinbeck maintains, indicates that even without the brain's support, the body is still capable of processing mnemonic materials and of displaying reactions that reflect a person's "individual past and personal life history.... As long as it is perceived as an individual, living body, it continues to be part of an intercorporeal exchange," which entails that the "flow of memories will be influenced and mediated by the living presence of the brain-dead body" (pp. 4–5).

The corporeality of memory is confirmed by cases of patients who, following organ transplants, exhibit novel personality traits that are presumably passed on to them by the organ donors. These can be regarded as memories literally flowing from one person's body to another's. As Ben Ashford notes, a paradigmatic example is provided by Cheryl Johnson who, in the wake of "a life-saving kidney transplant," found herself transformed into something of "a brainbox." An avid reader of "popular novels" prior to the operation, she subsequently developed a passion for "high-brow writers such as Jane Austen and Russian heavyweight Fyodor Dostoevsky" (Ashford).

A further illustration offered by Steinbeck, also drawn from Japanese culture, consists of the principles of a seventeenth-century strand of Neo-Confucianism advocating a "theory of correspondence" between nature and human society (Steinbeck, p. 6). Its principal exponent, Ogyu Sorai (1666–1728), promulgated the notion that the body plays an essential role in the grasp and assimilation of exemplary behavior — and hence in the fostering of harmony — by means of its "performance," especially of "rites" and "music" (p. 7). It is as though the sense of balance inherent in ceremonial and melodic practices could physically map itself onto the body while this engaged in their enactment, and so communicate to the performer via his or her body the virtuous principles emanating from that concord and the ability to remember them as enduring guides. Sorai's theory therefore connects corporeality and memory unequivocally.

Once certain patterns are firmly imprinted onto the body, the latter is in a position to perpetuate the legacy of the past as a "living symbol" even "without depending on conscious acts of remembrance" (p. 8). Therefore, it should not be regarded as a passive conduit for mental activities and contents but rather as an agent that plays an indispensable role in the genesis and expression of thoughts, feelings and hence memories. Whereas conceptual thinking and its representations tend to marginalize the corporeal dimension of existence in favor of abstract schemata, the body's symbolic function grounds meaning in the concrete realm of matter.

Memory is inseparable from technology. Since prehistory, being human has meant being involved in the development of technologies, not only mechanisms and tools, but also stories, pictures and melodies. As Bernard Stiegler persuasively argues in *Technics and Time* (1998), human evolution and technological development are inextricably intertwined. Human history is a chain of successive transformations of the technologies conceived by diverse cultures, and memory is a record of such transformations — a mnemotechnology.

As an inherently technological phenomenon, animation is ideally equipped to convey this message. Over time, the relationship between technology and animation has repeatedly yielded an intriguing paradox. Indeed, as James Clarke argues, although animation is a "product of the mechanized, modern age," it "often tells stories that play up the usually hapless relationship between humans and their inventions." The irony of this situation is compounded by the fact that "it was by mocking and parodying the modern world of machines that animation really broke into mainstream culture, itself becoming a mass-produced form involving huge numbers of animators, painters, designers and technicians" (Clarke, pp. 2–3). Artificiality, therefore, constitutes the very essence of animation.

Insofar as the cinematic apparatus in its entirety depends on artifice, even though the more realistic film genres tend to ensconce this dependence, it could be argued that animation's procedures form the bedrock of cinema at large. Lev Manovich has promulgated this hypothesis by emphasizing that the inceptive techniques from which cinema evolved "all relied on hand-painted or hand-drawn images." When, at the end of the nineteenth century, "the automatic generation of images and their automatic projection were finally combined," animation was marginalized as a "bastard relative" and cinema "cut all references to its origins in artifice." What cinema opposed most pugnaciously was animation's tendency to proclaim "its artificial character" by explicitly "admitting that its images are mere representations." Conversely, cinema sustained by mimetic priorities "works hard to erase any traces of its own production process.... It denies that the reality it shows often does not exist outside of the film image."

The exponential growth of digital tools and techniques over the past two decades, and their enthusiastic adoption not merely by animation but also by live-action cinema, signals a return to the industry's artificial foundations. Often, methodologies first tested in the domain of animation are subsequently adapted to the requirements of live-action cinema, making the latter something of a by-product. As Manovich comments, "Born from animation, cinema pushed animation to its boundary, only to become one particular case of animation in the end" (Manovich 2001).

As far as anime — as a distinctive form of animation — is specifically concerned, the technological dimension acquires unique resonance. Indeed, anime never induces us to forget its constructedness. According to Donald Richie, anime is "completely presentational.... Everything is designed." In this respect, it could be regarded as the "quintessential" Japanese art in that it fully encapsulates the latter's propensity for the "presentational" — a frank exposure of the work's madeness — as opposed to the "representational" — a striving towards mimetic realism meant to efface artificiality (Richie).

As a mnemotechnology *sui generis*, anime underscores the evolution of animational techniques over time as a markedly material process that entails not only the creation and perfection of tools and methods but also the charting of a body of memories by means of moving images. This involves that in erecting memory as their cardinal theme, the films here studied never lose sight of the technical dimension. As a result, the story's mnemonic contents and the ways in which these are presented are inextricably interrelated. The affective import of the memories mapped out by an anime does not simply depend on their inherent poignancy, but also, perhaps more importantly, on the cinematographical style and format in which they are couched.

The four elements discussed in the preceding paragraphs will be returned to in the body of the book to exemplify their relevance to specific productions and contexts. Be they traumatic or therapeutic, the memories dramatized by anime are intangible experiences that nonetheless succeed in bringing intensely palpable worlds to the screen. Thus, they constitute a correlative for the cinematic apparatus itself as a presence made of absence: a sprawling dreamland in which every frame is a presence dependent for its meaning on the absence of what it evokes or records, and is hence analogous to a fleetingly preserved memory. In the process, anime holds out an intricately woven poetry of remembrance.

Chapter 2

Memory and Desire

Millennium Actress
(feature film; dir. Satoshi Kon, 2001)

> We do not remember days; we remember moments.
> — Cesare Pavese, *The Burning Brand* (1961)

> Fate is like a small sandstorm that keeps changing directions.
> You change direction but the sandstorm chases you. You turn again,
> but the storm adjusts. Over and over you play this out, like some
> ominous dance with death just before dawn. Why? Because this
> storm isn't something that blew in from far away, something that has
> nothing to do with you. This storm is you.
> — Haruki Murakami, *Kafka on the Shore* (2005)

In *Millennium Actress*,[1] desire functions as the trigger of both the protagonist's life story and the cinematographical format imparted on the narrative, thus bringing together the thematic and structural dimensions of the film. At the same time, desire is indissociable from the memories that unrelentingly feed it at each turn of the action.

Millennium Actress's protagonist is the eighty-year-old Chiyoko Fujiwara, a retired actress of high repute. The film chronicles Chiyoko's life history by recourse to intertwined events from her actual experiences and snatches of the countless movies in which she has starred. Chiyoko's memories fluidly unfold, in a stream-of-consciousness fashion, in the course of an interview conducted by Genya Tachibana, a documentary maker who also happens to be one of the *grand dame*'s most loyal admirers, with the assistance of the cameraman Kyoji Ida. The purpose of the interview is to commemorate the studio, now in the process of demolition, to which Chiyoko once contributed her versatile talent. When Tachibana and his associate visit the actress in the secluded mountain lodge where she appears to have spent her thirty-year-long retirement in almost total isolation, and the documentarian presents her with an old key, the door to her memories is literally unlocked. Scenes from both Chiyoko's movies and the real world behind them start welling up and accumulating in a deftly paced crescendo by means of impeccable editing and intercutting.

In this respect, the director's dexterity is most eloquently attested to by the action's transitions between Chiyoko's reality and her on-set reverie, or between any two of her movies, related historical periods and locales. A threshold crossed by the pursuing protagonist in a setting based on ancient Japan may well mark a parallel heroine's entry into a modern scenario. A horse ride through a kaleidoscopic profusion of tumultuous fights and blazing sunsets may transmute into a pleasant carriage trip amidst cherry trees in full bloom. A cursed princess may seamlessly morph into a valiant ninja, a courtesan or a space scientist. At one point, by merely stepping through a door, Chiyoko travels from the historical actuality of war-torn Manchuria to the opulent set of a samurai saga. The list could feasibly stretch over several paragraphs. So could the catalogue of memories summoned by both single situations in themselves and by the charade formed by their agile concatenations and superimpositions.

Satoshi Kon has commented on several aspects of the film's symbolism and diegetic arrangement in a "Q & A" session specifically conducted for the official *Millennium Actress* website. As noted in this context, by "interweaving truth and fiction," the director sought to evoke a "sense of anxiety or intoxication"—a mood with which Kon's oeuvre has become synonymous. In the process, the protagonist's experiences and the historical contexts surrounding them transcend both space and time. While Chiyoko's life trajectory takes us from 1923, the year of the Great Tokyo Earthquake in which she is said to have been born, to the early twenty-first century, her roles span a significantly more protracted temporal scale. This moves from the Warring States Period (fifteenth and sixteenth centuries), to the Edo Period (1603–1868), and thence to the Meiji Period (1869–1912) and the Showa Period (1912–1945). Character design and facial expressions vary subtly as we move from one epoch to the next, seeking to convey economically the passage of time while retaining overall continuity. The mole placed on Chiyoko's face as a distinctive mark enabled Kon to preserve a sense of coherence but the director was well aware that in covering a stretch of seven or eight decades, he could not afford to pay excessive attention to minutiae and should assume instead that "there could be many different Chiyokos" (Kon 2004a).

The story's leading thread consists of the protagonist's longing to find her first and lifelong love, an injured artist and dissident fleeing the government authorities whom she briefly shelters in her family's storage house as a young girl. As Kenneth Turan observes, "At first glance, the plot of *Millennium Actress* sounds so conventional that you wonder why its Japanese creators went to the trouble of making it as an animated film. But first glances can be deceptive.... For what ... director and co-screenwriter Satoshi Kon has in mind is the shredding of the laws of space and time" in a feat of "*trompe l'oeil* or fool-the-eye filmmaking, and animation can fool the eye with the best of them." Moreover, it is the movie's "matter-of-fact, realistic animation style" that throws most memorably into relief the helter-skelter character of its diegesis (Turan).

By consistently interweaving Chiyoko's recollections with her consuming yearning, the film powerfully communicates the coalescence of memory and desire. Although the runaway leaves before Chiyoko has had a chance to discover who he truly is, the man gives her a key destined to sustain her odyssey as something of a talisman. (This is the very key delivered by Genya to the ex-actress in the film's early segment.) From this point onwards, Chiyoko runs unrelentingly, in both her real life and her cinematic parts, in order to meet her love again and find out the significance of the mysterious key.

Parallels between Chiyoko's real-life experiences and her screen incarnations are consistently established by the suggestion that just as the young woman is motivated by the desire for a lost love, so her filmic counterparts vainly pursue the ungraspable objects of their own affection. The two strands are linked by a fabulistic motif steeped in mythological memory: the image of a hag capable of spinning Chiyoko's fate, and indeed the destinies of her celluloid aliases, around a perfidious curse—to burn forlornly in the "flames of eternal love."

The film's portrayal of fulfillment as endlessly deferred, of desire itself as self-perpetuating, and of the memories it generates as correspondingly unlimited is tersely captured by two key moments in the story. One of these coincides with the culmination of Chiyoko's last attempt to trace her beloved (who, we discover at the end courtesy of Genya, has by then been long gone). When the heroine reaches the snowy wastes of Hokkaido, where the dissident once promised he would take her, and finds an easel bearing the painting he had resolved to complete once he could return to his homeland, she is confronted with incontrovertible evidence for the finality of her loss. The picture indeed displays an image of the young man, his back turned to the viewer, receding into the distance amidst melancholy sublimity. When Chiyoko tries to reach out to him, the figure dissolves, leaving only the majestic scenery behind. The other pivotal moment consists of the ex-actress's closing statement, where she avers that it would not truly matter "after all, after all" if she were to fail to see her love again in a possible afterlife, capping this proposition with the climactic admission: "it's the *chase* that I really loved."

In the course of the interview, as Chiyoko takes on a wide array of roles as war nurse, geisha, ninja, princess and cosmonaut, two manifestations of the collision of memory and desire come to dominate the action. On the one hand, we witness Chiyoko's efforts to keep alive and nourish her first embryonic inkling of erotic desire. On the other hand, we see the growth of the character's urge to tell her story as she moves from polite reticence to frank unreservedness. To the former level of desire correspond the recollections associated specifically with the elusive rebel; to the latter, those embedded in both the heroine's life journey and her whole culture's tumultuous history. At the same time, the disclosure of Chiyoko's mnemonic coffers, and attendant yearning for both an emotional destination and a narrative resolution, creates additional memories through her interviewers' own perceptions of the drama, as well as through the theatrical audience's reactions.

Chiyoko keeps running across the changing times and vogues, at each stage confronting the same pair of enemies: a man with a scar—the incarnation of authority—and the rival actress Eiko Shimao, the epitome of experience against the heroine's innocence. Composer Susumu Hirasawa's haunting electronic music works wonders in highlighting the film's atmosphere, and especially the mounting urgency and momentum of Chiyoko's desperate chases. In a filmed interview supplied in the official English-language website devoted to *Millennium Actress* (referred to earlier in this discussion), Kon maintains that Hirasawa's knack of evoking at once "scientific and mythological images" served as a major source of inspiration for the director and his team. "The story of a thousand years," Kon pithily adds, "is complete only with Mr. Hirasawa's music in the ending scene" (Kon 2004b).

It is also noteworthy that Chiyoko is not only repeatedly portrayed in the act of running as a correlative for her desperate quest. In fact, she also persistently appears to be running *away* from various forms of societal confinement, including a prison, a brothel, and the studio system itself as the prime cage. Thus, like Kon's earlier *Perfect Blue* (1998),[2] *Mil-

lennium Actress is no less a critique of the entertainment industry than it is a tale of intermeshed memories. The vagaries of stardom are also exposed by Kon's emphasis on the purely chance route taking the protagonist into acting. Discovered by the head of a prestigious production studio as a schoolgirl, yet strongly discouraged from pursuing a thespian career by her mother, Chiyoko decides to accept a part after all when the opportunity arises for playing in a film set in Manchuria, where the young radical of her dreams is said to have taken refuge. It is at least ironical that these purely personal and contingent factors should lie at the roots of one of the most stellar careers of all times.

The director has commented on the symbolic significance of the action of running, emphasizing the ways in which the imagery progresses from the act as a movement performed by human legs to pictures entailing "a horse, a bicycle, a car, a train, a boat and a rocket." This pictorial trajectory functions as an allegory for the evolution of "modern Western science." However, the underlying message is unsympathetic to teleological celebrations of progress, for Chiyoko's "ultimate destination is somewhere she cannot reach with the help of modern science. The first rocket you see is a symbol of science, but the one that appears at the end ... is not" (Kon 2004a). One belongs to history, the other to fiction.

In pursuing at increasing speed the object of her desire through the ages, and then recording her quest for her interviewers' benefit, Chiyoko weaves a rich mnemonic tapestry in which the process of remembrance itself becomes akin to a race. The key constitutes the nuclear symbol not only in the logic of the story, but also in the shaping of the audience's expectations and responses to the protagonist's recollections: the key, as Chiyoko states at the end, serves essentially "to open up a box of memories." The receptacle is ultimately no less our own than Chiyoko's.

The idea that the container uncovered by the retired star is not just a personal possession but a collective treasure trove is corroborated by the moment where the focus shifts from the heroine's memories to Genya's. The documentarian's own story indeed unfolds in parallel to Chiyoko's throughout the interview, and the film's full perspective only comes into view, therefore, when the two narratives are contemplated in tandem. Moreover, insofar as Genya is depicted as the film viewer par excellence, the character also operates as the audience's intradiegetic avatar. Hence, the surfacing of Genya's memories obliquely invites the emergence of our own personal recollections.

Kon has felicitously described the point in the story where Genya becomes the centre of attention as "acrobatic": this same designation is plausibly applicable to *Millennium Actress* as a whole. Moreover, the director has emphasized that in terms of dramatic import, the fashion in which Chiyoko constellates her narrative construct is far more important than the content of the events it records — which, it is implied, might be real and imagined in equal measures. By the same token, the subjective take on history offered by *Millennium Actress* is far more important than reportorial accuracy: "Historical verification doesn't really matter in this case. We created the film with our own vision of Japanese history." This approach resulted largely from Kon's awareness that "many modern Japanese have specific images" of distinct epochs in their history that have more to do with a consensual imaginary bred by the media than with recorded facts. For example, people tend to harbor certain images of the "Edo Period, which are not necessarily the actual Edo Period. Television and movies have created these particular images" (Kon 2004a). This suggests that the collective memories fostered by a culture often amount to a body of fictions, not a historiographically objective set of dates and facts.

In interweaving Chiyoko's personal experience of unrequited love with her screen incarnations within genres as diverse as melodrama, the costume epic, the war movie and science fiction, *Millennium Actress* does not only provide a telescoped vision of Japanese history but also a panoramic survey of the evolution of indigenous cinema across changing socio-economic contexts. The cinematic apparatus is thus portrayed as a prime technological instrument for the forging of cultural memory: namely, a mnemotechnology of arguably unparalleled appeal.

Michael Arnold has usefully commented on the film's relationship with native film history, while also emphasizing its Western connections: *Millennium Actress* "treats us to a number of parodies of film classics. The story opens and closes with a bang in a setting like *2001: A Space Odyssey* (1968) and it borrows an important scene from Kurosawa's *Throne of Blood* (1957) when the young Fujiwara is cursed by an old lady on a spinning wheel. Later there are glimpses of the Truck Yaro series, action flicks à la Shintaro Katsu and Ken Takakura, and many others" (Arnold). The mnemonic arabesque yielded by the film, therefore, encompasses at once recollections of documented occurrences and memories of their framing by the film industry. The two categories are tastefully harmonized with a *wabi*-like taste for the unglamorous.

By blurring the boundary between past and present, communal and private remembrances, history and spectacle, Kon erodes the line between reality and fantasy with arguably unprecedented gusto. This dimension of *Millennium Actress* is tantalizingly enhanced by the employment of the documentarists themselves as characters in the heroine's narrative, wherein they increasingly feature as filmic extras while the story progresses. In the process, Genya and Kyoji find themselves chasing the ever-running Chiyoko down busy streets, idyllic rural lanes, war-torn cityscapes and snowy wastes. The precipitous passage of time could barely have been evoked with greater sophistication, warmth and, ultimately, sympathetic humor.

A veritable gem is offered by the scene where Genya frantically draws a rickshaw carrying the lovely Chiyoko in a bustling early-twentieth-century setting, while Kyoji films the action from a hired car cruising along the older man and his charge. Moreover, as Amy Harlib points out, "Genya's and Kyoji's reactions seem almost like a Greek chorus and their commentaries frequently add refreshing wit to the proceedings" (Harlib).

Genya, whose fascination with Chiyoko is romantic no less than artistic, becomes so consummately absorbed by the tale unfolding before him that he ends up appearing in attire consonant with the different settings of the movies referred to by the narrator. An especially entertaining instance is the sequence from one of Chiyoko's period dramas in which Genya features as the character of a guard sworn to protect her at all costs, and becomes so wrapped up in the fiction that he steps outside the film's boundaries altogether and finds himself reenacting the sequence with Chiyoko in the context of her present-day abode. (The ex-star's housekeeper obligingly supplies Genya with a horned helmet for the occasion.) Kyoji remains somewhat detached, offering a snarky assessment of events that felicitously counterbalances the immersive pathos exuded by Chiyoko's recollections. This point is tersely underscored by the scene in which a baffled Kyoji asks: "What are we filming? ... Wasn't this supposed to be a documentary?"

As Ed Gonzalez maintains, *Millennium Actress* also constitutes a self-reflexive commentary on the film world to the extent that it "concerns itself with our love affair with women in movies (many of whom are unceremoniously forgotten when they become too old)." Moreover, just as audiences have experienced emotions secondhand through film characters throughout the entire history of cinema, so it is feasible that "Chiyoko knew all along that she was chasing the shadow of a man, and as such the thrill she derives from the chase suggests she's experiencing love vicariously through her acting." This renders *Millennium Actress* something of a "love poem to cinema itself." As "a tale of perseverance," however, the heroine's history can also be read as the director's upholding of "the defiant Chiyoko's power over various manmade creations and destructions in the film" (Gonzalez) — and hence over the mendacity of the film industry itself.

Gonzalez has also compared *Millennium Actress* to David Lynch's *Mulholland Dr.* (2001) as a further movie concerned with audiences' infatuation with celluloid females. It is indeed undeniable that both Kon's anime and Lynch's live-action film blend people's actual experiences and their memories of movies and stars so thoroughly as to render them virtually indistinguishable — in much the same way as they both obfuscate at each turn of their respective narratives the dividing line between waking life and dreams. The protagonists' personal dramas become metaphorical reflections of their cinematic careers, while their professional pursuits, conversely, become allegories for their affective vicissitudes.

The dialogue between these two dimensions remains tantalizing throughout thanks to the employment of a double perspective which, as intimated, progressively interweaves Chiyoko's projection of her romantic travails onto her art with the documentarists' metafilmic strategies for accessing the ex-diva's mnemonic treasurehouse. The interpenetration of reality and fantasy is neatly encapsulated by Kon's unobtrusive suggestion of a mirroring relationship between off-screen women seeking to hinder the heroine's artistic development — namely, her mother and the rival actress with whom Chiyoko performs in numerous productions — and the fictional figure of the witch supposed to have damned one of her onscreen counterparts to the torments of eternal love in one of the period dramas.

For both Chiyoko and the filmmakers, the journey through time is a markedly personal experience underpinned by their own specific memories and by the desire to convey an equally specific sense of time and space. The subjective dimension of *Millennium Actress* thus bolsters the collusion of memory and desire in a candid and unflinching fashion. No claims to objectivity are made at any point, and this effectively communicates the intrinsically slanted nature of any historical record.

Kon has also stressed the emblematic centrality of the image of "rubble," obliquely calling attention to the movie's imbrication with the ethos of *wabi* as a taste for the imperfect. As the director observes, debris abounds in the representations of the film studio provided both at the beginning and at the end of the movie, in the scenes chronicling the aftermath of the Great Tokyo Earthquake, when the protagonist is said to have come into the world, and in the frames capturing the disconsolate atmosphere of the postwar era, offering in each instance a potent symbol of "death and rebirth" (Kon 2004a).

A *wabi*-infused ambience also emanates from the portrayal of the protagonist's remote abode in which the crucial interview takes place. Its distinctive architectural and ornamental features indeed capture both the aesthetic and the ethical underpinnings of that concept down to the seemingly most peripheral minutia, exuding an all-around feeling of calm and composure. Chiyoko's own attitude matches perfectly this mood, conveying a deep sense of quiet contentedness and humble acceptance. Especially relevant, in this regard, is the particular assessment of *wabi* proffered by the architect Tadao Ando: "*Wabi* stems from the root *wa*, which refers to harmony, peace, tranquility, and balance. Generally speaking, *wabi* had the original meaning of sad, desolate, and lonely, but poetically it has come to mean simple ... and in tune with nature. Someone who is perfectly herself and never craves to be anything else would be described as *wabi*.... A *wabi* person ... understands the wisdom of rocks and grasshoppers" (Ando).

Kon himself has an especially fond memory of the film's production concerning the voice actors. An unforgettable moment came at the end of the recording process: by the time the actors had reached the closing sequence, they had finished playing their parts and could simply have left the set but chose to stay behind and observe the action right through to the last shot. This recollection is a potent testimony to the depth of the performers' commitment to the film and to its protagonist's life history in particular (Kon 2004a).

As intimated in this chapter's opening segment, throughout *Millennium Actress* the contents of Chiyoko's recollections — as both personal attributes and fragments of film history — are inextricable from the cinematographical and pictorial moulds in which they are cast. From an aesthetic point of view, Kon's treatment of the interplay of memory and desire with a sustained focus on formal and stylistic considerations encapsulates a distinctively Japanese understanding of "art" as the coalescence of form and design (*katachi*). The main aesthetic tenet at the heart of *katachi* is the value of harmony and simplicity: concepts to be observed in Nature, extrapolated from its processes, and replicated in art through apparently effortless but actually studied economy and candor. Even at its most theatrical, *Millennium Actress* consistently prioritizes an atmosphere of harmonious balance over sensationalism, and a meticulous rendition of both physical and affective situations in a fashion that evokes at each turn a luminous sense of unpretentious limpidity regardless of the toil and artfulness injected into the film's fabric.

It is in the celebration of the aforementioned poetics of *wabi* that Kon's taste for unostentatious and intimate beauty proclaims itself most audibly. Indeed, *wabi* takes the Japanese devotion to the principle of simplicity beyond sheer stylization and elevates the incomplete, the impermanent and the humble to the status of cherished objectives. At the same time, the Japanese preference for allusiveness is cultivated through *wabi* by intimating that no putatively conclusive statement is authentically all-encompassing and that consciously embracing the beauty of the unfinished might therefore be the only way of approximating the world's baffling rhythms.

The collusion of memory and desire succinctly throws these propositions into relief. Indeed, the protagonist's memories and the desire animating their emergence are inexorably incomplete insofar as they stem from selective mental processes, as well as impermanent due to their vulnerability to erosion and displacement by the passage of time, and by the accretion of other memories and yearnings. Concurrently, they partake of the *wabi* ethos of modesty and restraint to the extent that they are not afraid of upholding the value of small-scale private moments even as the historical events unfolding around them carry far-reaching cultural implications.

In its articulation of memory's inextricability from the vagaries of desire, *Millennium Actress* also invokes the principle of *wabi* through its own visual style, as a contemporary product indebted to Japan's traditional arts. To be more precise, the film's emphatically painterly dimension oozes with a specifically indigenous sensitivity redolent of the aesthetic trend associated with the woodblock prints known as *ukiyo-e*. In one scene, *Millennium Actress* offers an explicit reference to this art form by means of a frame overtly based on a famous painting by Katsushika Hokusai, *Beneath the Wave off Kanagawa* (c. 1830). However, the spirit of the *ukiyo-e* pervades the movie's entire fabric, and especially its lovingly executed tableaux capturing the stylistic conventions of specific eras in the guise of a staggering variety of architectural, decorative and sartorial motifs.

As "pictures of the floating world" intent on portraying the transient spectacle of life and its pleasures, *ukiyo-e* focus on scenes from everyday life (including landscapes and townscapes), and on the urban entertainment industry burgeoning at the time of their execution. The epoch in question stretches from the first two decades of the seventeenth century to the 1860s and witnesses the ascent of "an affluent middle class," as Douglas Mannering explains, "with money to spend but no defined social or political role. Consequently its members gravitated towards the Yoshiwara, Edo's [i.e., Tokyo's] redlight district.... This was the milieu which the *ukiyo-e* artists immortalized.... The most popular subject of all was beautiful women most often, though not always, the courtesans" (Mannering, p. 6).

Millennium Actress explicitly invokes this motif in the retrospective snatches documenting Chiyoko's cinematic part as a geisha. Yet, the film as a whole replicates the *ukiyo-e*'s atmosphere by means of its tone and imagery. Particularly notable, in this respect, is Kon's unremitting commitment to the balance of figure and decoration, of corporeal solidity and graphic allusiveness, of palpable mass and swirling linearity. The coalescence of a potent sense of human intimacy and brilliant patterning abets this artistic pursuit to unparalleled degrees. The characteristic sense of dynamism inherent in traditional woodblock prints devoted to the representation of Kabuki actors, sumo wrestlers and other popular performers is simultaneously conveyed by Kon's emphasis on vibrant motion. Grace and elegance are often accorded a pivotal role but never allowed to crystallize into inert icons of beauty of the fashion-plate variety. Landscapes distinguished by a daring use of perspective, attention to the majestic presence of Nature behind and around the urban carousel, and a loving depiction of delicate facets of native flora and fauna likewise mirror the *ukiyio-e*'s predilections.

In addition, *Millennium Actress* can be compared to the *ukiyo-e* specifically in respect of its evocation of the concept of *wabi*. Both the woodblock print and Kon's film expose the incompleteness of the joys associated with the entertainment industry as a metonym for the lack of plenitude befalling any kind of pleasure—and hence the ultimately unfulfillable nature of all forms of desire. Dwelling on the pleasures yielded by the urban environment and especially on the sensual delights dished out by professional entertainers, more typically with an emphasis on elegantly rendered eroticism than on overtly carnal satisfaction, the images immortalized by the *ukiyo-e* foreground the intrinsic imperfection of any worldly or material achievement. Kon's movie echoes this world view in its sustained presentation of the forever inconclusive character of the delights spawned by cinema as contingent phenomena. The systemic displacement of filmic vogues, genres and agendas over time neatly summarizes this message.

In assessing *Millennium Actress*'s encounter with the *ukiyo-e* over a *wabi*-oriented aesthetic terrain, an additional aesthetic concept demands attention: *iki*. Depending on the circumstances of its usage, the term may denote artless sophistication, classy refinement, inconspicuous elegance, a flair for improvisational wit or an aura of casual sensuality. Anything overtly affected, arty, boastful, schmaltzy or maudlin is anathema to the ethos of *iki*. As noted in the *Taste of Japan* webpage published by the Mitsubishi Group, "The word *iki*, both in its noun and adjective usages, conjures up a panoply of aesthetic and moral ideals that developed and became ingrained in Japanese culture and lifestyle over the centuries. Even today, to tell someone he or she has *iki*—whether in reference to behavior, attitude toward life, fashion or whatever—constitutes a compliment of the highest order" ("*Iki*").

In the *ukiyio-e*, this notion is most memorably conveyed by the display of sensuality within tasteful parameters. In *Millennium Actress*, it is Kon's knack of orchestrating an intricate narrative so frankly and lucidly as to make it come across as straightforward even where it strikes its most Byzantine or idiosyncratic chords that encapsulates *iki* with disarming appeal. In the portions of the action informed by the visual codes of costume drama, *iki* is captured by the quintessentially Nippon garment, the kimono, as a subtle fusion of vestimentary simplicity and decorative attributes so sophisticated and nuanced as to elevate the item to the status of a work of art in its own right.

Millennium Actress's interweaving of multiple temporal levels finds an intriguing antecedent in the movie *Belladonna of Sadness* (dir. Eiichi Yamamoto, 1973). As a contribution to the history of cinema at large, this film is most notable as very possibly the only anime to have experimented with the *pinku* genre. This refers to a type of movie permeated by erotic (or even soft-core pornographic) elements. The genre flourished in Japan between the mid–1960s and the mid–1980s, and the majority of its products issued from small independent studios. Although the survival of *pinku* film was seriously threatened by the emergence of the adult video (AV) in the 1980s, the genre never quite disappeared. In fact, *pinku* movies are still being produced today and often deployed as vehicles for the communication of feelings of cultural malaise and insecurity bred by the socioeconomic climate of post-bubble Japan.

Undeniably, *Belladonna of Sadness* is an intensely erotic tale, taking as its sources of inspiration Jules Michelet's novel *La Sorcière* (1862), the story of Joan of Arc (Jeanne d'Arc) and medieval witchcraft lore generally. The film pivots on Jeanne, a peasant woman in fourteenth-century France who is raped by the local lord on her wedding night and hence rejected by her husband. Paradoxically, the depiction of the woman's violation by recourse to metaphorical, stylized and impressionistic images—rather than graphic realism—is precisely what renders it most disturbing. Though horrendous, Jeanne's experience is also epiphanic. Indeed, while the rape and the subsequent awakening of the protagonist's earthy desires eventually lead to grief, their enlightening effect cannot be overestimated.

By turning against the status quo, and thus subverting the mores regulating women's roles in medieval society, Jeanne discovers not only her quiescent libido but also her inquisitive spirit, her hitherto unsuspected self-confidence and an almost magical ability to interact spontaneously with the natural realm. This aspect of the film is faithful to Michelet's own ethos, where the practice of witchcraft is posited as a metaphor for spirited rebellion against the oppressive agencies of Church and State alike.

Concurrently, the film underscores the inextricability of past, present and future across mnemonic terrain by vividly showing that at the same time as its protagonist is haunted by the past in the form of traumatic recollections of her abuse, those same memories also lure her towards a future in which her previously repressed capacities and affects might find satisfactory expression. As seen in the analysis of *Millennium Actress*, Chiyoko's memories of her initial discovery of desire likewise draw her simultaneously towards the past and to the future. Furthermore, Kon's use of changing fashions as a means of epitomizing the heroine's mnemonic journey enthrones style as a principal cinematographical agent in ways that are also foreshadowed by *Belladonna of Sadness*.

The film's most memorable aspect is indeed its graphic style. Illustrator Kuni Fukai's designs deliver a boldly experimental integration of motifs drawn from sources as diverse as Tarot cards, Celtic decoration, Gustav Klimt, Edmund Dulac, Edvard Munch, Audrey Beardsley, Impressionism, and Noh theatre. The measure of the movie's cinematographical adventurousness is instantly declared by the pervasive use of still drawings in the first segment of the story, where the peasant couple's nuptials are dramatized with the accompaniment of a narration sung in the soulful manner of a 1970s rock opera. It is not until the feudal ruler, begged by the groom to decrease the marriage tax he cannot afford, decides to levy his payment in the form of the bride's body that full animation becomes dominant.

While Yamamoto's visual phantasmagoria stands out as an artistic achievement of autonomous value, it also bolsters the film's narrative import insofar as the fragments of color, broken lines and scrambled surfaces to which the screen insistently returns symbolize the tatters of Jeanne's own memories as she struggles to patch them back together into a new motley identity. The notion of beauty thereby upheld is intensely redolent of the spirit of *wabi*.

The associative character of memory is persistently evoked through the use of frames that appear to flow into one another. The genesis of memories, and the accretional processes through which they gain complexity and density over time, is concomitantly mirrored by a self-reflexive approach that literally depicts the evolution of single lines into multidimensional shapes and of monochromatic vignettes into multicolored composites. The elegant transitions between still illustrations and full motion engineered by animation director Gisaburo Sugii, moreover, capture the essence of memory as a faculty by turns reliant on single vivid images and dynamic sequences of interconnected visuals.

Belladonna of Sadness also echoes, in both several individual frames and in its overall graphic mood, the works of Junko Mizuno, a renowned Japanese artist whose drawing style characteristically combines childish innocence and loveliness with elements of terror and monstrosity, gaining the designations of "*Gothic kawaii*" or "*kawaii noir*." (Please note that the word "*kawaii*" loosely translates as "cute.") Capitalizing on bright hues, huge eyes, long and exotically colored locks and highly stylized feminine silhouettes, Mizuno's works evince the influence of *shoujo* manga and anime, while also drawing on other pop-art sources. While these graphic elements also feature in Yamamoto's film, it is in the psychedelic feel exuded by both *Belladonna of Sadness* and by so many of Mizuno's illustrations (and ancillary spin-offs) that the two come most intimately together.

If *Belladonna of Sadness* parallels *Millennium Actress* in the representation of the dawn of desire as a painful revelation, the gentler connotations of Kon's treatment of the topos find an apt correlative in *Ocean Waves* (TV film; dir. Tomomi Mochizuki, 1993). This film offers a touching portrayal of the discovery of desire in adolescence and its translation into memories, both at the time of its occurrence and in later years. In the process, it highlights the interplay between the mind's speculative reconstruction of the past and its projection of that hypothetical dimension onto the future. Dramatizing a gracefully understated love triangle, the film focuses on high-school students Taku Morisaki and Yutaka Matsuno, as their quiet existence in the small town of Kochi, on Shikoku island, is suddenly disrupted by the advent of a transfer student from Tokyo: the attractive, athletic and academically gifted Rikako Muto. Avoided by the vast majority of her peers as a snobbish city girl, Rikako is actually tormented by insecurity and the omnipresent specter of domestic conflict, which results in a contorted and, at times, downright manipulative approach to interpersonal contact.

As Taku becomes unintentionally entangled with Rikako's family life and her predicament, while Yutaka feels increasingly drawn to the girl, the boys' friendship receives a severe blow. Flying back to Kochi for a high-school reunion two years after those events, Taku revisits the past in a dreamlike chain of recollections — partly triggered by his recent sight of a young woman resembling Rikako on a station platform. The frequently corporeal nature of the stimuli that kindle mnemonic association is here explicitly invoked. The entire movie has the flavor of a wistful retrospection, felicitously sustained by the musical accompaniment of desultory piano melodies and by a symbolically poignant visual poetry redolent of the haiku form. In celebrating the lyrical beauty of inevitably frayed recollections, moreover, the movie elliptically invokes the ethos of *wabi*.

Two more recent anime concerned with the interplay of memory and desire deserve closer attention in the present context as illustrations of the treatment of that topos in the realms of romantic drama and experimental cinema respectively, since these two areas are also at the heart of Kon's artistic vision as elaborated in *Millennium Actress*. In the latter, the passage of time in accordance with the unfolding of the protagonist's memories is registered by changes in her physical appearance — at times quite blatant, at others barely perceptible — that intimate that memories are literally written on the body.

This idea is no less central to *Kashimashi — Girl Meets Girl* (TV series; dir. Nobuaki Nakanishi, 2006). An initially semicomical tale of gender reversal that grows increasingly bittersweet as the narrative progresses, the series proposes that memories are encoded in and through people's corporeal forms. In the case of *Kashimashi*'s hero/ine, this is exemplified by the graphic coalescence of memories associated with the initial male self and memories subsequently accrued by the female self in a cornucopia of stylish montages and intercuttings. Blotchy and yet enchanting, the memories embedded in such images appear to partake of the aesthetic principle of *wabi*. The dialectical relationship between the principles of yin and yang is concomitantly enlisted.

As the gentle, nature-loving and timid high-school student Hazumu Osaragi climbs up Mount Kashima in an effort to get over his rejection by classmate Yasuna Kamiizumi, an alien spaceship crashes upon him. Feeling ethically obliged to save the young Earthling, the extraterrestrial crew revive Hazumu and reconstitute his body, unintentionally switching his sex in the process. Although Hazumu's basic psyche has not altered, s/he accepts that s/he has no alternative but to live as a female adolescent. Acquiring the relevant code of conduct proves arduous but Hazumu is loyally assisted by his childhood friend Tomari Kurusu: an energetic and athletic kid who has felt romantically drawn to Hazumu from an early age but sublimated her desires by assuming the role of Hazumu's protector from bullies scornful of his soft-hearted disposition.

Tomari at first finds it hard to come to terms with Hazumu's gender switch, yet gradually discovers that her original attraction to the old friend has not in the least waned in the aftermath of the event. Yasuna, for her part, grows increasingly fond of Hazumu and openly declares her love relatively early in the story. (Please note that in anime and manga, the subgenre of romance dealing with homoerotic relationships involving female characters of the kind articulated through Hazumu and Asuna is designated as *yuri*. Another classic instance is the relationship between Mai Kawasumi and Sayuri Kurata in Tatsuya Ishihara's *Kanon* [2006–2007].)[3]

Through these emotional complications, what could easily have amounted to shallow melodrama had Nakanishi indulged in overwrought cris de coeur, actually turns out to be a profoundly satisfying anime experience, capable of raising serious questions about gender roles and positions. The principal part in this scenario is played by the crisscrossing of the main characters' memories of their experiences and mutually defining interactions both before and after Hazumu's metamorphosis. This simultaneously retrospective and introspective journey, conducted through the artful juggling of multiple perspectives and a delicate portrayal of the characters' churning emotions, elevates the actors well above the limits of standard anime stereotypes and enables the viewer to empathize with each of them from an early stage in the action.

Kashimashi also proposes that whereas a person's memories constitute a continuum wherein past, present and future fluidly intermingle, it is at times necessary to appreciate the value of childhood memories as autonomous experiences that do not unequivocally predetermine later actions and choices. Thus, Tomari must learn to accept that her reminiscences of her childhood relationship with Hazumu should be treasured in specific conjunction with their infantile selves and circumstances, and not be expected to shape the here-and-now. Learning how to recognize the past as past is a crucial part of growing up.

Tomari's response to Hazumu's transformation is not only affected by the tension within her psyche between juvenile memories and recently formed recollections. In fact, it is also influenced by a set of assumptions and values embedded in cultural memory. When she resolves to be the one that will teach Hazumu how to look and behave like a "proper girl," Tomari is pandering to stereotypical gender roles and positions passed onto her by her culture's age-old heritage. Ironically, she does not seem aware of the incongruity between this agenda and her own customary conduct as the perfect tomboy. The humor of the situation is summed up by the scene in which Tomari tersely instructs Hazumu not to jump down the stairs: an option which Hazumu does not appear to have ever entertained even as a boy, whereas jumping down the stairs is precisely the action with which Tomari makes her first appearance in the show.

An especially moving moment consists of the section in which Yasuna, who appears to have seen males as a grey blur from the start, is traumatized by Tomari's betrayal of their friendship and loses the ability to perceive females, too. The depth of her affliction is most effectively communicated by the scenes in which Yasuna struggles to recapture her memories of Hazumu and consigns them to paper in the form of sketches which, alas, remain unfinished and are therefore no less amorphous than her actual visions.

Kashimashi also carries intertextual memories of other anime shows. This is clearly borne out by the portrayal of the alien observers. One of the creatures brings to mind a magnified version of the semiorganic program "Marie" from the TV series *Please Teacher!* (dir. Yasunori Ide, 2002). His pink-haired female companion, for her part, is closely fashioned on the model supplied by Nono in *Gunbuster 2* (OVA series; dir. Kazuya Tsurumaki, 2004–2006). Her tendency to address Hazumu as "*Onee-nii-sama*" ("big sister/brother") echoes Nono's insistent use of "*Onee-sama*"("big sister"). *Kashimashi*'s finale, where a deluge of lights akin to ethereal snowflakes fills the scene, is redolent of an especially poignant moment from the same show. In their all-pervasive solemnity, the lights could be regarded as metaphors for the cosmos' own memories. Furthermore, the clumsy and anachronistically cute homeroom teacher Namiko Tsuki often recalls the lustful teacher Miss Shikijo from the TV series *Mahoromatic — Automatic Maiden* (dir. Hiroyuki Yamaga, 2001–2002).

From a specifically visual point of view, *Kashimashi* is instantly distinguished by a flair for mellow effects, subtly evocative settings and soft palettes. This aspect of the show links it stylistically with *Five Centimeters Per Second* (2007), one of the most impressive elaborations of the interplay of memory and desire recently released that has issued from Makoto Shinkai's unique visual imagination. This is a compilation of three interconnected tales of love and deferred fulfillment. No less cardinal to this work than to Kon's *Millennium Actress* is the yearning for reunion after enforced separation experienced by its young protagonists. This is sustained by fond memories of their shared moments that both draw them back to the past and propel them onwards into the future and whatever promises this might hold out.

The main characters, Takaki Tono and Akari Shinohara, forge a deep connection in their elementary-school days and trust they will never be wrenched apart. Their hopes are dashed when both of their families relocate to remote areas of Japan separated by thousands of miles. In the film's first part, Takaki sets out on a long train journey into the night to meet Akari again a year after their primary graduation, his longing for the reunion underscored by memories of their time together. Slightly anxious at first, Takaki is flung into a mood of intense frustration that gradually escalates into despair as inclement weather delays train connections, leaving him to wait helplessly for motion to resume amidst snow-swept desolation.

The flavor of the boy's recollections grows proportionately bleaker as the hours go by. Apprehension regarding the prospective rendezvous, accordingly, deteriorates into downright forlornness. In the hands of a less inspired director, an image as obvious as that of the unrelentingly ticking clock would have looked intolerably stereotypical. Intercut as this is with exquisitely detailed settings in which prosaic details are no less captivating than sublime panoramas, the icon acquires overwhelming affective resonance.

In the second segment, Shinkai focuses on high-school student and would-be surfer Kanae Sumida and her pathological inability to declare her affection for Takaki — who, having moved to a new town and school, still seems intent on reminiscing about Akari. At the microcosmic level, therefore, the episode focuses on the distance between Kanae and Takaki as the former remains incapable of externalizing her feelings while the latter seems forever absorbed in the contemplation of an unattainable object of desire. This intensely personal drama is mirrored, on the macrocosmic plane, by the characters' reflections on the enormous distances covered by cosmonauts in outer space as they look at the Tanegashima Space Center in the shadow of which they go about their daily routines. Paradoxically, the distances entailed by intergalactic travel are no more an obstacle to physical intimacy than the gulf separating the two kids in the context of their small Earth-based town.

The closing installment returns to Takaki and Akari, offering vignette-like fragments of their separate adult lives and culminating in an array of rapid-cut shots set to a stirring pop theme. The inherently fragmentary character of these frames recalls the principle of *wabi*. At the same time, the image of the cherry blossom explicitly invoked by the episode — five centimeters per second being indeed the speed at which the *sakura* petal falls to the ground — encapsulates the ethos of *mono no aware* with each the plant is traditionally associated. In its deployment of this ancestral symbol, *Five Centimeters* also reverberates with memories of other anime likewise indebted to that motif in thematic and graphic terms. A notable example is the TV show *D. C. ~Da Capo~* (dir. Nagisa Miyazaki, 2003), where the magic of the setting, the crescent-shaped island of Hatsune Jima, is encapsulated by the ubiquitous presence of cherry trees that bloom all year long.

Sakura also feature prominently in *Clannad* (TV series; dir. Tatsuya Ishihara, 2007), where the character of Tomoyo Sakagami devotes herself wholeheartedly to the protection of an avenue of cherry trees in defiance of the authorities. Her objective is to honor the memory of her little brother Takafumi, responsible for averting their parents' divorce and for inspiring the Sakagamis to learn how to live like a proper family at last. These are merely two instances of a widespread tendency to pepper anime's sceneries with images of *sakura* petals drifting on the wind, swallowing the world in a pink haze, beckoning students to the start of a new school year, or symbolically harking back to old Japan and its rich mythology. *Hanami*, namely *sakura*-viewing parties held under the flowering trees, are sprinkled across the anime realm as both substantial settings and cameo appearances. Classic depictions of the event are provided in *Sailor Moon* (TV series; dirs. Junichi Sato et al., 1992–1997) and in the film *Lum the Forever* (here examined in Chapter 6). *RahXephon* offers an intriguing variation on the cherry blossom motif with the introduction of trees whose flowers sport blue petals: the analysis of the show presented in Chapter 7 will hopefully explain this deviation from the norm.

Furthermore, countless anime females are named Sakura as an economical way of emphasizing their gentleness, innocence, simplicity, generosity and purity, or else to foreshadow a sad fate consonant with the flowers' proverbial ephemerality. The heroine of *Tsubasa: RESERVoir CHRoNiCLE*, the main title discussed in chapters 8 and 9, epitomizes both aspects of the name's allegorical connotations, Sakura being at once distinguished by unmatched amiability and compassionateness and by a singularly tragic destiny. Even though *sakura* are an established icon of evanescence and mutability and Shinkai is therefore not alone in deploying them to evoke those ideas, his use of the image does not come across as purely formulaic. As Paul Starr observes, the director's "focus on the *rate* of that change brings a freshness to the concept that is often lacking from more pedestrian invocations" of the topos (Starr, p. 60).

In economically tracing the characters' development from childhood through adolescence to young adulthood over the three episodes, Shinkai illustrates how the perception of time and collateral formation of memories alter as one grows older, becoming more and more compressed. To each stage corresponds a specific experience of desire. "The Chosen Cherry Blossoms" chronicles the slow passage of time over just a few hours: the atmosphere of protractedness is paralleled by the long-term nature of the characters' yearnings at this juncture. "Cosmonaut" spans about a month, conveying a more rapid passage of time that aptly reflects the increasingly intense pressure exerted upon the actors by their social and educational milieux regarding future goals. The final part, "Five Centimeters Per Second," covers over a decade in a highly capsulated cinematographical format, suggesting that the characters' desires no longer allow for either long-term or medium-term action but require immediate steps. This is pithily communicated by the shots in which Takaki and Akari state their decisions concerning familial and professional commitments. The work as a whole is not so much about action as about the absence of action and the mnemonic processes through which people construct their worlds as they are, in turn, constructed by their changing circumstances.

In all of the film's three segments, Shinkai's engagement with the concept of time through a focus on memories and their legacy is complemented by a cinematographically original approach to timing and spacing. Quiet moments punctuated by subtle gestures, barely perceptible changes of expression and lingering glances, allied to still shots of humble props and slow pans across the landscape, abound throughout. However, this preference for static or minimally dynamic scenes does not preclude altogether the use of vibrant sequences in which the meditative tone gives way to energetic action. The scenes in "Cosmonaut" where Kanae endeavors to perfect her surfing skills provide a paradigmatic example, yielding electrifying vibes for characters and viewers alike.

This strategy enables Shinkai to offer a double perspective on memory itself as both a tranquil meditation and an ebullient expression of simmering emotions ready to overbrim at an instant's notice. In the process, the director's achingly beautiful and deeply layered tableaux do not merely operate as external screens onto which the protagonists project their emotions and memories. In fact, the scenery is an actor in its own right and enables the characters to convey their messages, often nonverbally, by bringing out their emotions as they simply look at their surroundings. Thus, it is not a question of attributing human moods to a setting by means of pathetic fallacy but rather of establishing a dialectical exchange between human and nonhuman agencies.

The stories dramatized in the three segments of *Five Centimeters Per Second* are interwoven at the levels of both characterization and imagery, and each of them accordingly reverberates with mnemonic echoes of the others. Throughout the film, memory is emplaced as the cardinal motif. The story unrelentingly highlights the inseparability of the characters' desire for a future that might offer fulfillment from past experiences and recollections thereof. In so doing, it intimates that just as the past cannot be reliably recaptured, so future gratification is bound to be indefinitely postponed. The narrative, simple though it is, oozes with a haunting feeling of unease, as well as a debilitating sense of hindrance: every second, albeit ephemeral, feels like an eternity engulfing the characters' vaporous reminiscences in its flux.

All of the titles discussed in this chapter thus far address the interplay of memory and desire through a focus on individual trials, which imparts their overall import with a poignant sense of intimacy. In charting its heroine's private life story with consistent reference to Japanese history and the history of cinema at large, *Millennium Actress* does stretch its purview beyond the boundaries of purely personal concerns. So do *Ocean Waves* and *Five Centimeters Per Second* in the dramatization of their respective protagonists' coming-of-age vicissitudes as metonyms for a universal Bildungsroman trajectory. *Belladonna of Sadness* also reaches beyond the sphere of the individual drama it depicts by means of oblique allusions to its historical and ideological context. *Kashimashi — Girl Meets Girl*, for its part, deploys the sci-fi dimension to infuse a private romance with an intergalactic flavor. Nevertheless, in all of these productions, priority is ultimately accorded to the personal side of the narrative. With *Origin: Spirits of the Past* (movie; dir. Keiichi Sugiyama, 2006), conversely, the epic repercussions of the collusion of memory and desire come to the fore even as the adventure repeatedly dwells on the inner states of its protagonists.

The heroic scale of the story is instantly asserted by the movie's opening sequence, a sensational ensemble of images endowed with a visceral, almost brutal, palpability. The sequence records a chain of apocalyptic events presumed to have occurred about three centuries prior to the film's setting, in which the "Forest-Beast" erupted from a lunar forest and reached the Earth in the form of a dragon like creature consisting of sprawling tangles of creepers, roots, lianas and tendrils, causing the planet's atmosphere to dissipate and its surface to burn beyond recognition. Having reconstructed a world of sorts from the vine-infested debris left behind by the cataclysm, humans live under the ominous shadow of the mighty Forest that has invaded their habitat and despotically controls the water supply that is key to their survival. Some, namely the inhabitants of "Neutral City," seek a state of mutually tolerant — though precarious — coexistence with the surging jungle, its spirits and its law-enforcers, the leaf-shrouded Druids. Others are hell-bent on dominating the Forest by recourse to cutting-edge military equipment, baffled by a power they cannot even begin to fathom. Most prominent, in this regard, is the character of Colonel Shunack, a recently resuscitated old-world survivor who has joined forces with the bellicose state of Ragna.

Key to the diegesis is the hero Agito's discovery of a girl named Toola in a storage pod where she has been kept, frozen into a comatose sleep, since the time of the disaster. Like Shunack, therefore, Toola comes "from the past." Ironically, even though she belongs to a chronologically older world, the girl finds the Neutral City setup more primitive than her place of origin. This is barely surprising, given Toola's culture was replete with highly advanced technology, whereas Agito's town is a retrofuturistic ensemble of ruinous buildings and scavenged surfaces that appear to be held together by chance rather than by design, exuding an intense atmosphere of *wabi*-like precariousness. In dramatizing this cultural clash, *Origin* implicitly alludes to a conflict between two distinct versions of the past and of the mnemonic traces it carries: namely, the past recorded in Toola's personal memory, on the one hand, and the past embedded in the palimpsest of Neutral City's collective consciousness, on the other.

Unable to adjust to her new environment, Toola decides to cooperate with Colonel Shunack and summon ancient technology invented by her own father to regenerate the environment and return the human planet to its original configuration. Dubbed "Environmental Defragmentation System" (a.k.a. "Estoc"), the device which Toola is enjoined to activate will supposedly bring forth a "new future" from the "ashes of the past." Determined to get Toola back at any price, Agito resolves to merge with the Forest, which endows him with superhuman strength, in exchange for his fealty in the war against Shunack. In surrendering his human nature, the hero follows in his father Agashi's footsteps, having endeavored to emulate his old man's actions since childhood. Agashi was the principal architect behind Neutral City's haphazard construction and has interacted so intimately with the Forest as to have morphed into a man-tree hybrid. His physiognomy instantly brings to mind the "Ents" from J. R. R. Tolkien's *The Lord of the Rings*.

Although Toola is initially quite willing to comply with Shunack's request, she undergoes a drastic change of heart when she realizes that Estoc's goal can only be achieved by incinerating the present world and that the Colonel's first target will be Neutral City: a world which Toola has only experienced as a temporary home but has by now learned to trust and respect. In the film's climax, the complicity of memory and desire is incontrovertibly foregrounded as recollections of the catastrophe responsible for bringing human civilization to its knees are shown to be inextricable from the dynamics of desire — an insane yearning, specifically, to enhance the natural environment by means of extensive genetic engineering intended to breed plants capable of thriving in inhospitable habitats, undertaken on the Moon. Through Shunack's account of his personal reminiscences of the holocaust, it transpires that the research carried out in the lunar facilities led to the trees' acquisition of consciousness as a direct consequence of his personal desire to control Nature out of "foolish pride." For the Colonel, activating Estoc is the sole means of appeasing a guilt-ridden conscience.

As the action unfolds, the power-driven desire leading to the apocalypse symptomatic of human hubris at its most arrant, is increasingly counteracted by Agito's own wish to reestablish a peaceful relationship between humanity and the overwhelming expanse of trees that dominates his culture and its ecosystem. This desire culminates with the realization, informed by quintessentially Buddhist and Shintoist beliefs, that all species — animate and inanimate alike — are intimately interconnected. The powers acquired by the protagonist when he allows himself to be "enhanced" by the Forest belong to the trees no less than to Agito himself, confirming the hypothesis that potent connective threads weave disparate life forms together.

Agito's benevolent desire is eventually fulfilled in one of the most gloriously heartwarming finales regaled by recent anime. Memory is here incontrovertibly emplaced as one of *Origin*'s axial preoccupations, as Agito revisits his childhood by means of a densely atmospheric flashback and is urged by Agashi to return to his world. With the twin encouragement proffered by the memory of his father and by Toola, the boy extricates himself from the womblike interior of the venerable tree in which his body has become encased since his heroic confrontation with Shunack and returns to Neutral City to inaugurate a new era of amicable coexistence between humans and trees. In this dramatic culmination, memory and desire explicitly coalesce, Agito's yearning to go back to his home town and reconcile its human and vegetable inhabitants being inconceivable independently of the flashback that inspires it. Agito's task as the harmonizer of the conflicting interests of humans and trees echoes the "tuning" mission undertaken by Ayato in the climax of the TV series *RahXephon* (please see Chapter 7).

Origin is, among other things, a mnemonic repository of thematic allusions to and visual citations from a plethora of previous anime. The film often echoes Hayao Miyazaki's oeuvre. *Princess Mononoke* (1997), in particular, comes to mind in the depiction of the warmongering Shunack as a villain, yet also someone motivated by potentially noble intentions. Just as Lady Eboshi in Miyazaki's movie seems genuinely to believe that the production of weapons will save humanity from the encroaching forest, so the Colonel is "possessed" by the desire to return the human world to its original state in the conviction that the current state of affairs is an "abomination." *Origin* also recalls Miyazaki's *Nausicaä of the Valley of the Wind* (1984) in the representation of the impressive Ragna uniforms, vividly redolent of the costumes donned by Kushana and her followers. Miyazaki's *Laputa: Castle in the Sky* (1986) is arguably the principal source of inspiration behind Sugiyama's feature, as evinced by its use of the trope of the idealistic youth eager to mimic his father's heroic exploits and committed to the rescue of a trusting but helpless girl from the clutches of a belligerent leader. *Laputa* is additionally invoked by the visuals in the employment of dizzying perspectives, baleful military machinery and sprawling vegetation. At the specifically graphic level, *Origin* occasionally mirrors the TV show *Vision of Escaflowne* (dirs. Kazuki Akane and Shouji Kawamori, 1996), here discussed in Chapter 7—above all, in the portrayal of the natural setting and of various dragon-based motifs.

However, the film is made unique, despite its intertextual borrowings, by its luxuriantly painted and multilayered backgrounds, meticulous blend of manually executed drawings and digital animation, gently nuanced character designs and impeccably paced action sequences. The scenes where Agito's body morphs, at first partially and then totally, into a tree are especially remarkable by virtue of their ability to come across as palpably credible where analogous images could easily have yielded hilarious effects in the hands of less judicious artists.

Chapter 3

The Archaeology of Memory
Gilgamesh
(TV series; dir. Masahiko Murata, 2003–2004)

> The past is never dead; it's not even past.
> — William Faulkner, *Requiem for a Nun* (1951)

> Find beauty not only in the thing itself but in the pattern
> of the shadows, the light and dark which that thing provides.
> — Junichiro Tanizaki, *In Praise of Shadows* (1933)

Anime has frequently engaged with the material vestiges of the past through imaginary temporal scenarios in which time is not remembered in the sense that it is "recalled" but rather in the sense that it is literally *re-membered*: endowed with new members, a new body. In the TV series *Phoenix* (dir. Ryousuke Takahashi, 2004), the "re-membering" strategy is explicitly encapsulated by the titular bird's mythical credentials. A classic symbol for regeneration and recurrence, the phoenix is here deployed to bring together the experiences and accompanying recollections of various characters across time and space. The *Phoenix* anime is quite faithful to the narrative style adopted in its parent text, the massive manga created by Osamu Tezuka between 1954 and 1989 (and appropriately described by the artist himself as his life's opus). Thus, although it cannot presume to capture the entirety of Tezuka's 3,000-page sweeping epic within the breadth of 13 episodes, the show does justice to the original in its subtle juxtaposition of a cluster of adventures which, while apparently disjointed, are subliminally intertwined by philosophical questions regarding birth, death, rebirth and the endurance of mnemonic reverberations across those alternating dimensions.

One of the show's leading threads is the idea that humans are fundamentally incapable of appreciating the phoenix's prodigious gift, let alone its sheer beauty, and are therefore hell-bent on destroying it in order to appropriate its blood, which is held to grant eternal life to those who partake of it. What these acquisitive characters ignore, in the process, is the creature's amaranthine power to be reborn from its own ashes, and thus defy any attempt to possess it conclusively. Concomitantly, *Phoenix* presents immortality either as unobtainable or as a dreadful curse. It is in the Buddhist concept of life as a never-ending cycle that the narrative finds an at least provisional source of comfort. Relatedly, memory is portrayed as the vessel wherein life's cyclicality is treasured as an ongoing collusion of past, present and future. *Phoenix* reverberates with the poetics of *sabi* in the very representation of the mythical creature at its centre. Indeed, the "firebird" acts throughout as a potent reminder of the inseparability of beauty from its ineluctable frailty.

Other anime eager to furnish history with a novel body have taken a pseudodocumentary route, delivering a rich gallery of retrofuturistic narratives. Four productions drawn from different phases in the evolution of anime persuasively illustrate this: *Captain Harlock, Rose of Versailles, Revolutionary Girl Utena* and *Le Chevalier D'Eon*. In *Captain Harlock* (TV series; dir. Rintaro, 1978), the material past invoked by the narrative to construct its alternate history is quite explicitly fictional, its primary point of reference pirate lore. The thoroughly executed spaceships pivotal to legion tantalizing battles clearly recall eighteenth-century galleons worthy of the bravest buccaneers of old. However, the story's depiction of a decadent society in which prosperity has led to either apathy or complacency, and humankind is no longer capable of positive action, elliptically alludes to actual historical contexts afflicted by analogous predicaments. At the same time, the series underscores the material dimension of memory in the guise of literally archaeological traces: namely, sea-bottom pyramids from the era of pre–Columbian civilizations enigmatically connected with the "Mazone," a humanoid race eager to make the Earth their new home.

Moreover, the legacy of traditional codes of conduct of both Eastern and Western derivation is overtly foregrounded by the story's unremitting emphasis on the ethical principles of respect, loyalty and selflessness sustaining Harlock's war against both human and alien opponents. The precepts of both Bushido and Chivalry are thus brought into play. Most touching, in this respect, is the protagonist's recognition that the Mazone are as capable of love and honor as humans are, and likewise plagued by sadness, loneliness and fear. This realization entails that Harlock derives no automatic solace or reprieve from his defeat of the enemy. Resolutely eschewing triumphalism, even his final victory exudes a melancholy, *sabi*-inflected mood.

With *Rose of Versailles* (TV series; dirs. Tadao Nagahama and Osamu Dezaki, 1979–1980), we move into the realm of more overt historical reinvention.[1] The program paradigmatically exemplifies an attraction to old Europe, steadily evinced by both anime and manga, as a synthesis of majestic *yugen* and unpretentious *sabi*. This fascination is related to what the Japanese designate as *akogare no Paris* ("the Paris of our dreams")—namely, a speculative version of that world envisioned through Eastern eyes, akin to the West's imaginary configurations of the East founded upon the figment of the exotic. *Rose of Versailles*, originally a manga by Ryoko Ikeda published in 1972 and subsequently translated not only into an animated series but also into live-action movies, is a crucial bridge between that world view and quasi-historical anime. Loosely based on actual historical personalities and events, and especially on the life of Marie Antoinette (1755–1793) and her interactions with the Swedish diplomat Axel von Fersen and with the effervescent female swashbuckler Oscar de Jarjayes, *Rose of Versailles* ushered Japanese popular culture into the history, etiquette and fashion of late eighteenth-century France and the turbulent backdrop to the French Revolution of 1789. Several programs inspired by that same epoch (seldom based on real figures) quickly followed.

The dueling motif already prominent in *Rose of Versailles* becomes absolutely sustaining in *Revolutionary Girl Utena* (TV series; dir. Kunihiko Ikuhara, 1997)—where basketball, however, also plays a prominent role. Sartorial attributes associated with the French Revolution are also notable. A cross-dressing pupil at Ohtori Academy, Utena Tenjou enters the limelight as she endeavors to protect her friend Anthy—the "Rose Bride"—from an abusive member of the Student Council, and is thereby drawn into a series of duels with other members of that body for the possession of Anthy and, more importantly, what she signifies: a power instrumental to the unleashing of a world revolution. The show also invokes the theme of memory as a diegetic trigger insofar as the heroine's recollection of a kindly prince supposed to have offered her comfort in childhood after her parents' death and attendant decision to become a prince herself (by title and by costume) unflinchingly motivates the ensuing action. Though tenuous and *sabi*-like, this memory capable of shaping Utena's existence as a guiding agent.

Presuming to cover in depth an extensive range of alternate-history anime in the present context would be absurd. It therefore seems apposite, following the cursory delineation of a few illustrative titles supplied in the previous paragraphs, to dwell in greater detail on one further instance of that modality released in recent years in which memory and archaeology come resplendently together: *Le Chevalier D'Eon*. This TV series (dir. Kazuhiro Furuhashi, 2006–2007) stands out as a major accomplishment in the domain of pseudohistorical anime thanks to its masterful treatment of memory as a vehicle for the fabrication of a narrative which, albeit fictional, sheds light onto very real historical and psychological phenomena. On one plane, the adventures of the actual D'Eon de Beaumont—a diplomat and spy in the service of Louis XV in the mid-1700s—are translated into an explicitly fantastic yarn as the protagonist puts his allegiance to king and country to one side to pursue a personal quest for knowledge and vengeance.

This is triggered by the discovery of his beloved sister Lia, seemingly dead, in a coffin afloat on the Seine. Lia, it gradually transpires, is one of the legion victims of a secret sect of aristocrats, well versed in alchemy and various esoteric practices, who deploy their dark knowledge to engender mercury-bloodied zombies known as "Gargoyles." On another plane, however, the fantasy is consistently led back to reality for the purpose of commenting dispassionately on the vicissitudes of a turbulent era and on its pained entry into modernity without overloading the scene with the stuffy rhetoric of typical period pieces. Lace, ruffles and frills abound but never stifle the flow of the action; in fact, their almost ethereal delicateness felicitously intensifies the frantically visceral impact of the swordfighting sequences.

The artistic elegance exhibited by *Le Chevalier D'Eon* in practically every frame is crucially indebted to the singular vision of character designer Tomomi Ozaki—who is also, importantly, the genius behind *Kurau Phantom Memory*'s unique personae. (This series is here examined as the focal case study of Chapter 5.) As Ozaki herself explains in an interview posted on the Production I.G website, "Furuhashi-san told me that characters should not look like manga characters or too real; and not too anime-like ... he wanted the characters to be faithful to historical details including the costumes.... I sometimes referred to the portraits of that age, but I prioritized character images in the script. It was a process of trial and error, through which I tried to come up with suitable characters, for instance differentiating the royal family members from the ordinary aristocrats.... We've paid meticulous attention to the historic and geographic settings. I hope you will enjoy the authentic recreation of XVIII century Europe" (Ozaki).

No less important is the show's psychological credibility as an anatomy of a tormented and splintered psyche. Thus, while harnessing memory to the fictionalized depiction of a macrocosmic historical situation, *Le Chevalier D'Eon* concurrently invokes memory to articulate an intensely personal drama. This dimension of the story is rendered most effective (and, occasionally, overtly disquieting) by Furuhashi's intermeshing of three mnemonic strands. The protagonist is clearly haunted by memories of Lia in the incorporeal guise of flashbacks, hallucinations and reveries. At the same time, however, the memories take on a more substantial status as Lia's very soul fills her brother's body as though this were merely a vessel. More disturbingly still, Lia's own corporeal form periodically possesses the hero, especially at times of extreme danger, as succinctly communicated by the transformation of D'Eon's well-groomed coiffure into an exuberantly unfettered mane. The recounting of the tale by the aged D'Eon in a well-sustained diaristic style enhances the show's historiographical dimension by interweaving the documentary with the memoir.

In quasi-historical anime of this kind, the notion of *sabi* is lovingly evoked by the melancholy lure of the old, and concomitant intimations of imperfection and lack. Even at their most spectacular, these shows call attention to the beauty of an irretrievable past with restrained elegance. When steampunk motifs[2] are also brought into play, as overtly exemplified by *Captain Harlock*, the charm of the old is enhanced by its projection onto an imaginary future.[3]

Gilgamesh offers a unique take on the collusion of memory and archaeology, boldly commingling elements of ancient lore and mythology with scientific concepts grounded in empirical research, on the one hand, and science fictional speculations issuing from the creators' own imagination, on the other. In *Gilgamesh*, memory is imbricated with archaeology at three interrelated levels. First, the story takes as its source of inspiration Babylonian culture and its foundational epic, thus grounding a futuristic adventure in the material substratum provided by a venerable mnemonic inheritance. Second, it posits as diegetically critical the cloning of a team of scientists working on an archaeological site, motivated by their determination to preserve their legacy were they to come to harm. This aspect of the story constitutes a fictional replica of the biological processes governing the transmission of genetic information, and hence the development of genetic memory, across generations. At the same time, it binds memory and technology by presenting the endurance of hereditary memories as a corollary of their technological manipulation. Third, *Gilgamesh* articulates its multilayered mysteries around the protagonists' efforts to recapture the *arché*, or first principle, underlying their current predicament in order to determine their personal roles within a wide web of intrigue.

The audience's own mnemonic faculties are persistently brought to trial by the narrative's sibylline disclosure of its many secrets, requiring us to pay heed to a plethora of gradually accruing clues. It is indeed through the incrementally accumulating hints delivered by both central and ancillary personae in the course of the story that a broad pattern of interconnections comes to the surface. In the process, the characters' buried past, motives and aims are also revealed as strands of a relational fabric. Each episode adds fresh enigmas to the show's diegesis even as it discloses partial answers and clues. Whenever the audience may feel closer to ascertaining who is in the right and whose cause should be favored, new information emerges that throws all provisional certainties into disarray and unsettles the value of the memories produced by prior events. *Gilgamesh* therefore retains throughout the aura of a compelling mystery abetted by suspenseful storytelling.

Alongside Babylonian history and mythology, *Gilgamesh* incorporates myriad mnemonic traces of disparate civilizations and styles in its elaboration of an intricate web of architectural, ornamental and sartorial motifs. The screen's transitions from one locale or atmosphere to the next are at times so smooth as to be hardly noticeable until the change has been effected. At others, they are intentionally abrupt and their impact is correspondingly jarring. Thus, the tenebrous mood of a creepy mansion familiar to any viewer or reader of classic ghost stories may seamlessly give way to a comparably somber urbanscape depicted in the noir vein. Alternatively, the same ambience may be drastically displaced by the appearance of an austerely illuminated edifice of neoclassical derivation (the palace modeled on the Royal Albert Hall and the Versailles-like "Hotel Providence" are cases in point). At the same time, allusions to Renaissance and Manneristic painting abound (with more or less overt symbolic connotations), as do references to Goth fashion, at one end of the vestimentary spectrum, and Mesopotamian fashion, at the other. Finally, through its Gothic fascination with ruins as literal embodiments of the injuries of time, *Gilgamesh* simultaneously recalls the aesthetic concept of *sabi*.

Instantly distinguished by a unique approach to character design that boldly redefines some of anime's most deeply rooted conventions, *Gilgamesh* is set in a not-too-distant future tinged with post-apocalyptic connotations. The opening narrative informs us that a terrorist attack carried out fifteen years prior to the main story by a man known as "Enkidu" (a pseudonym adopted by the scientist Terumichi Madoka) cataclysmically affected the entire Earth, turning the sky into a psychedelic mirror and unleashing horrific waves of war and famine in its wake. Even the technological amenities which generations preceding the catastrophic event could take for granted, such as computers and long-distance communication devices, were relegated by Dr. Madoka's attack to the status of flimsy archaeological memories. The act took place in a huge scientific base known as "Heaven's Gate," located in the archaeological zone corresponding to the ancient Mesopotamian city of Uruk, with the Tomb of Gilgamesh at its core. The tomb itself was first discovered by Dr. Madoka, who felt drawn to the special energy emanating therefrom (the "dynamis"). At this time, the scientist also met Azuka Himemiya, the woman destined to become his hapless spouse and bearer of his progeny.

Dr. Madoka's choice of "Enkidu" as the appellation by which he comes to be known after the attack explicitly harks back to the *Epic of Gilgamesh*— reputedly, humanity's most ancient textual creation. The time-honored myth tells the story of the demigod Gilgamesh, his rejection of the goddess Ishtar when she expresses the wish to become his bride, his adventures in the company of the trusted friend Enkidu, his inconsolable grief at the latter's destruction by the irate Ishtar and, most crucially, his vain search for immortality.

In its utilization of the ancient legend, the anime performs an ironical mnemonic inversion. In the epic, the titular hero is portrayed as a ruthless oppressor who learns the value of mercy by opening up to the influence of Enkidu — at first his prime enemy and subsequently a soul so dear to his heart that an erotic attraction is hinted at. In Murata's show, Dr. Madoka toys with the pseudonym "Enkidu" from an early stage in his career but does not officially adopt it as his preferred designation until he has turned into a mass murderer and embraced an alternative career as the despotic leader of an army of clones.

The original Enkidu's ethically redeeming faculties are thus irreverently eschewed. It is also noteworthy, however, that Enkidu first enters the original saga in the guise of a wild man sent by the gods to plague Uruk's countryside in order to face the implacable Gilgamesh with a threat that would absorb his energy and thus prevent him from terrorizing his subjects any further. It is only when Enkidu himself has been captured and tamed that he is able to temper the despot's furor. Thus, it could be argued that Dr. Madoka's destructive proclivities echo the initial configuration of Enkidu as portrayed in the legend. Significantly, in his account of the *Epic of Gilgamesh*, Dr. Madoka only makes reference to Enkidu's positive influence on the tyrant of old.

Gilgamesh does not simply select mythological figures as plot threads to romanticize its revisionist archaeology of memory, nor does it merely revamp bygone tales for the sake of antiquarianism. In fact, it creates a whole alternate history — and correlative body of both personal and communal memories — through a dexterous connective treatment of traditional and novel motifs, sustained throughout by impeccably choreographed mise-en-scène and thoughtful dialogue. Right from the start, the script characterizes *Gilgamesh* as an archaeological exploration concerned with origins and their memory traces rather than a teleologically driven adventure. The use of monochrome stills to document relevant moments in the history of Uruk and its archaeological excavations elegantly contributes to the archaeological mood of the program.

The chief objective pursued by the scientists associated with Dr. Madoka echoes Gilgamesh's epic quest. Their aim was indeed to ascertain what kind of genetic organization had made the Mesopotamian hero a man-deity hybrid and, ideally, to move from that knowledge to the secret of eternal life. As part of this plan, the scientists replicated themselves as embryos to give themselves a "backup" and hence perpetuate their mission beyond their lifetime. The replicas were dubbed "Orga."

Heaven's Gate was extremely powerful and sponsored by numerous international forces, thriving unhindered until the destruction of "all experimental subjects," cessation of all research activities and concomitant closure within a year were unexpectedly enforced. The reason for this draconian decision was that a mysterious life form referred to as "Tear" had been found to be contaminating the embryos, and that this might lead to a disaster "unparalleled in human history." It was at this point that Dr. Madoka resolved to enter the seemingly immeasurable pit of "Delphys" wherein Tear had manifested itself, thus triggering the momentous explosion that would cause the whole planet to change almost beyond recognition. Paradoxically, Dr. Madoka himself had been the first to recognize that the experiments carried out at Heaven's Gate were potentially nefarious and had accordingly urged his colleagues to cease tampering with cosmic forces beyond their ken. His warnings, however, had been hubristically left unheeded. Having taken place on 10 October, the Heaven's Gate disaster is referred to as "Twin X" ("X" representing the Roman numeral for the crucial date).

The plot revolves around a brother and sister, Tatsuya and Kiyoko Madoka, namely the children of the aforementioned scientist and terrorist. Kiyoko, aged seventeen, is an ordinary girl born prior to the mirror era without recourse to bioengineering, whereas Tatsuya, three years her junior, came into this world in the aftermath of the catastrophe as Dr.

Madoka's clone. For Tatsuya, the very concept of a "blue sky" is of the order of an archaeological memory, since his whole life has unfolded under a flickering mercurial canopy of electromagnetic energy.

When we first encounter the two protagonists, they are living on the streets in a beleaguered society struggling to rebuild its former glory but failing with often dismal consequences. Rain, for example, is sufficient to cause its jerry-built skyscrapers to collapse as though they were no more substantial than puny sandcastles. Pursued by thuggish debt collectors demanding fulfillment of a contract signed by the two teenagers' mother prior to her demise, who are only too keen on obtaining repayment in the form of Kiyoko's body and at least one of Tatsuya's organs, the protagonists do not yet know that much more powerful factions are after them as well. Admittedly, their mother warned them about the day when dangerous people aware of their connection with Enkidu would seek them out. Yet, neither Kiyoko nor Tatsuya has thus far had any inkling as to where exactly the threat might originate. Tatsuya, for obvious reasons, has no recollection of his notorious father, whereas his sister merely remembers isolated snapshots (such as the image of her dad teaching her how to play the piano on a toy instrument), or else she is unwilling to disclose any more comprehensive memories of Dr. Madoka as a defense mechanism.

It soon transpires that two warring organizations vie for supremacy in the enlisting of Tatsuya's and Kiyoko's cooperation. On one side stands the superpowered cadre of "Gilgamesh": four women and six men ruled by Enkidu, eager to complete the task undertaken fifteen years earlier which they see as a salutary redefinition of the human species. The Gilgamesh are named Uno, Duo, Tria, Quattuor, Cinque, Sex, Septem, Octo, Novem and Decem on the basis of the numbers assigned to the experiments leading to their genesis. Among other skills, the Gilgamesh possess portentous psychokinetic powers (the aforementioned dynamis), and are able to morph into winged, multiclawed and befanged creatures which, when subjected to scientific analysis, prove composed of "antimatter" alien to the Earth's habitat. They would seem to come from a parallel universe. (At one point, Gilgamesh's tomb is said to have been built precisely to contain the cavern of Delphys—which means "womb of the Gods"—and that this constitutes a passage to an alternate reality.) The ten Gilgamesh are the adult forms of ten test subjects, infiltrated by Tear, taken by Dr. Madoka upon his flight from Heaven's Gate on Twin X.

In mortal opposition to the Gilgamesh stands a trio of mutants known as "Orga-Superior," who are themselves equipped with dynamis and are led by the Countess of Werdenberg, one of Dr. Madoka's ex-colleagues from Heaven's Gate. The Orga-Superior, named Isamu, Fuko and Tohru, are clones of three scientists formerly employed at the base that have developed special powers—like the Gilgamesh themselves—by coming into contact with Tear. Several cloned embryos apparently survived the disaster thanks to the reinforced test tubes in which they were housed, and made it into the outside world once the debris had been cleared. Before long, they came to be regarded as highly desirable commodities, capable of fetching handsome sums of cash on the black market as veritable "designer children"—after all, they contained the genes of some of the world's most brilliant minds.

The most fortunate of the embryos went to actual women, but for the majority, and indeed for the Countess's children, the hosting wombs were porcine. When Isamu, Fuko and Tohru eventually discover their true origins, they thus have to cope not only with their synthetic status but also, and more humiliatingly still, with the knowledge that they have been carried by lowly animals. Ironically, Fuko carries a stuffed toy in the shape of a mega-cute piglet and at one point, she even gives a sensational display of gluttony that temporarily gains the nickname "Miss Piggy."

The Orga-Superior's predicament is rendered all the more touching by frequent reminders that they are really just kids after all. The scenes where Fuko and Tohru chase each other in the hotel's grounds, playing blind-man's bluff or bouncing a baseball, neatly encapsulate this idea. The sequence where all three Orga-Superior children and Tatsuya play in the snow to practice their deployment of dynamis and, in particular, to refine the newcomer's burgeoning powers are most tantalizing. On the one hand, they could be seen as displays of martial prowess underpinned by a serious motivation: the development of skills meant to render the players stronger in their war against Enkidu. On the other, they never lose sight of the purely ludic fervor with which the kids approach the tasks at hand. A sense of innocence therefore imbues even the most portentous moments in the performance.

A mood of childlike candor is likewise conveyed by the scene in which Tatsuya and the Orga-Superior walk around the dense urban conglomerate chanting "We are hanging about town" to the tune of "Shall We Gather at the River?" The jocular displacement of the religious song adds a touch of iconoclastic humor to the scene. Another felicitous note that serves to remind us that the Countess's surrogate family consists, at base, of normal kids struggling with emotional issues pertinent to their age consists of Fuko's growing affection for Tatsuya. While the psychosomatic symptoms she exhibits — namely, uncontrollable sneezing and nasal leakage — provide scope for downright comedic glee, the intensity of her feelings is perfectly consonant with an ordinary teenager's sexuality and helps us relate to the character as a fully rounded human personality.

The cloning motif is ushered in at an early stage in the narrative by the sequence in which Kiyoko and Tatsuya enter a seemingly uninhabited mansion to hide from their enemies and discover a spooky gallery housing rows of large test tubes containing salamanders and other related creatures. Novem, one of the Gilgamesh who have already taken up residence in the edifice with the intention of intercepting the runaway teenagers, informs them that these specimens are clones produced in the days preceding Twin X. The entities are akin to archaeological relics from a bygone age, encapsulating dark scientific memories. Tatsuya is taken by surprise by Novem's disclosure, which suggests that cloning is an alien concept to him and touchingly reveals his total obliviousness to his own true nature.

Dr. Madoka, whom his followers refer to as "the Professor," needs his two children in order to complete his grand self-appointed task and sends three Gilgamesh fighters to rescue them from their *yakuza* pursuers to invite them to join their ranks. The Countess, however, has quite different plans in mind for the destitute pair. At first, Kiyoko and Tatsuya have no inclination to bind themselves to either of the parties at their heels but their freedom of choice is seriously curtailed when the Countess buys them off by repaying the fatal loan, and houses them in the palatial Hotel Providence to examine and then deploy their own powers in the fight against Enkidu.

The Countess, it is suggested from the very first episode, was not only professionally connected with Dr. Madoka but also harbored unrequited romantic feelings towards the brilliantly deranged researcher. At the end, it is disclosed that Tear was a pure life form that had acquired its destructive proclivities by fusing with the Countess's heart, poisoned by jealousy and resentment towards Dr. Madoka's wife. Just as Tear had merged with the Countess unbeknownst to the lady herself, it had later possessed Dr. Madoka and turned him into a criminal without his being able to put up effective resistance.

A third organization beside those run by the Countess and by Enkidu seeks to alter the current state of affairs: the Mitleid Corporation. (Please note that the spelling for the Corporation's name adopted in the shots displaying its grand front entrance is actually "Mittlight."). A key member of the group is Eriko Enuma, another former member of Dr. Madoka's team, whose goal is to return the sky to its original form. The cause of science is not Dr. Enuma's sole or main priority, however: in fact, it is disclosed that she lost an unborn child when the specular sky replaced its azure predecessor, and thus seeks revenge for largely personal reasons. The Corporation is situated in a vertiginously high edifice — the "Spire Tower"— that combines architectural features of various aspects of Mesopotamian civilization uncovered by archaeological research. From certain angles, it vividly brings to mind an elongated and slimmed-down version of the Tower of Babel. Archaeological memory therefore asserts itself with explicit iconic vigor in the representation of this particular setting.

The Countess refers to the Tower as an object merely "constructed in the guise of a new office building" but actually holding a special and inscrutable power. Dr. Enuma indeed regards it as the "magic wand" intended to return the world to its original state and calls it "Turangalîla." This term, as Paul Schiavo explains, "is a composite of two Sanskrit words and is rich in meanings. 'Turanga' refers to time — or, more precisely, to the movement of time, 'time that slips like sand through an hourglass or time that runs like a galloping horse,' in [Olivier] Messiaen's poetic explanation. 'Lîla' signifies love, life, movement, and the cosmic game of creation and destruction. Thus 'Turangalîla' implies the temporal occurrence or rhythm of life, love, and death" (Schiavo).

It is worth noting, in this regard, that the Tower of Babel and cognate aspects of Babylonian architecture are recurring motifs in cyberpunk and retrofuturistic cinema. Notable examples include Ridley Scott's *Blade Runner* (1982), Mamoru Oshii's *Patlabor 1: The Mobile Police* (1989) and Rintaro's *Metropolis* (2001). (William Gibson's *Neuromancer*, the seminal cyberpunk novel published in 1984, makes explicit reference to the Hanging Gardens of Babylon.) While sharing the Babel image, those films and *Gilgamesh* are simultaneously brought together by a common preoccupation with the workings of memory. *Blade Runner* offers an audacious treatment of this topos by portraying memories as prosthetic adjuncts emplaced in the psyche by recourse to photographs designed to furnish the individual with a coherent sense of personal identity. (Oshii's *Ghost in the Shell* [1995] adopts this same trope to remarkable effect in its depiction of brain-hacking.) *Patlabor*'s diegesis is sustained by the traces scattered by a deranged scientist across the city in the form of intertextual memories intended to supply cryptic clues to his nefarious agenda. Pivotal to *Metropolis*, finally, is the central villain's determination to have his memories of a lost daughter reincarnated in the form of an exceptionally sophisticated android.

The memory theme gains special resonance vis-à-vis Tatsuya's and the Orga-Superior's gradual discovery of their nature as clones when Dr. Enuma states that their physiognomies bring back many memories. This assertion is corroborated by the photograph of a group of Heaven's Gate scientists placed in her office. As the children wonder what she could possibly have meant by those words, Tohru suddenly recalls spotting the image of someone very much like Tatsuya standing next to a young version of the Countess in that picture. It is at this point that the young Madoka realizes that his father and the enigmatic lady are bound by a shared past.

Dr. Enuma's dream comes briefly to fruition but is conclusively shattered when the Gilgamesh boycott the experiment from within the Mitleid HQ and cause an explosion that replicates Twin X, albeit on a more modest scale, returning the sky to its specular configuration. The attack destroys a substantial portion of the city, leaving countless fatalities and casualties in its wake. The scenes in which Tatsuya and the Orga-Superior kids endeavor to help the survivors amidst the smoldering and smoke-saturated rubble throws into relief the show's sensitive take on ruins as material vestiges of human folly. The tangible sense of suffering that exudes from these scenes, punctuated by the victims' hellish wailing, demonstrates Murata's determination never to mellow down the story's apocalyptic connotations, even as he integrates the more sensational aspects of the drama with a melancholy mood redolent of the Japanese attraction to the aesthetic appeal of evanescence and fragmentation. This atmosphere is retained by the mournful sequences in which the Hotel Providence itself is transformed from a grand mansion into a temporary shelter for the victims, as a result of all regular hospitals having filled up to maximum capacity.

The Mitleid Corporation is helmed by the enigmatic Toranosuke Yuki, the original founder of the Heaven's Gate base. The Chairman's closest associates are his adopted child Reiko and his son Hayato Kazmatsuri. Reiko is a quiet girl garbed in a formal kimono who is revealed to have surrendered her own eyes to the old man and to be equipped with a greater amount of dynamis than any other character. Eventually, Reiko turns out to be the Chairman's own clone and hence a "he": this discovery unsettles deeply the naive Tohru, who has developed strong feelings towards the taciturn "girl." (The astounding success of the ocular transplant is thus fully explained.)

Kazmatsuri, born out of an affair between the Chairman and one of his countless concubines, is devoted to the construction of increasingly sophisticated anti–Gilgamesh troops—the most powerful of which is the "Blattaria" army (the "Order of the Insects")—that turn out to be alternate configurations of the Orga referred to as "transgenic" beings and to have been manufactured prior to Twin X, in much the same way as the salamanders seen through the series as a visual refrain. Combining various motifs drawn from Japan's traditional performance arts and, most notably, grotesque masks, the Blattaria constitute the show's apotheosis in the area of spine-chilling iconography. The scene in which they transfix a Gilgamesh member by means of multiple lance-like beams carries baleful ceremonial connotations redolent of both a sacrificial immolation and a witch-burning ritual, tinged with traces of vampire lore.

Both the Countess and the Gilgamesh insistently lay claims to the protagonists' abilities for their conflicting causes. Faced with the Countess's proposition that destroying the Gilgamesh is the only way of preventing the world's annihilation, on the one hand, and the Gilgamesh's plan to renew the Earth, on the other, Kiyoko and Tatsuya have no solid grounds on which to decide what to believe—let alone which cause to embrace or why. Deciding which party should be regarded as the villain of the piece and which as the hero is made difficult, not only for the protagonists but also for the audience, by Murata's eschewal of binary oppositions in favor of deliberately ambiguous characterization. Thus, the Countess exhibits genuinely caring maternal proclivities that render her endearing at times, yet there is little doubt as to her possession by a malevolent demon hell-bent on revenge. This condition results in unscrupulous actions that routinely include blackmail, enslavement, child abuse and both physical and mental torture. Beneath the patina of politesse typical of her every movement and the elegance of her costumes and surroundings, courses a torrent of contempt and hatred.

The Gilgamesh, for their part, are capable of switching from suave manners to undiluted brutality, and vice versa, at a moment's notice. Exterminating the innocent to achieve their goals is an option they embrace with bloodcurdling casualness, yet they are not totally devoid of human affects, including compassion and love. The scene in which a Gilgamesh member is so disturbed by the destruction of the black-tailed gulls he has been feeding that he loses concentration and is himself killed in the process is an especially felicitous touch. The Gilgamesh's capacity for eminently human emotions is most forcefully demonstrated by the relationship between Kiyoko and Novem. Despite the sadness and hopelessness pervading this desperate liaison, the sense of warmth it exudes is unique in the whole of *Gilgamesh*. (In the show's climax, Novem tells Tatsuya that he truly loved Kiyoko just before he draws his last breath, thus adding a quietly moving note to the sequence's frantic momentum and alarmingly escalating body count.)

The Gilgamesh are driven by a dogmatic and blinding faith in their cause that precludes the possibility of autonomous thought. Novem, for example, zealously maintains that the psychedelic sky is a "cocoon for giving birth to a new human race"—which Kiyoko, the disillusioned champion of unsavory truths, dismisses as vapid rhetoric and "hypocrisy." Yet, in spite of their unquestioning subjugation to their leader's gospel, the Gilgamesh are nonetheless capable of exposing truths that are very hard to refute. This is borne out by the scene in which Novem tells Tatsuya that people endowed with dynamis only exist *because* of the cataclysmic change triggered by Twin X and that there is no way to "turn back this clock." Hence, Tatsuya himself is what he is as a result of Twin X and denying the event would be tantamount to calling his own existence into question. At one point, we are even invited to feel sorry for Enkidu's troops as the Mitleid Corporation's Chairman states: "Gilgamesh, the beasts who are his [i.e., the mythical figure's] revived form. If you think about it, they should be pitied. Coaxed by a great fool, reduced to tools for terrorism."

It would seem that just as the world's natural contours and chromatic contrasts have been attenuated by the electromagnetic sky's blanketing effect, conventional ethical criteria have been simultaneously suspended. The memories fuelling both the Countess's and the Gilgamesh's schemes likewise remain objects of ongoing speculation, shrouded in mystery in much the same way as the world itself is enfolded by a monochrome curtain. In reflecting the world, moreover, the sky inevitably distorts, fragments and destabilizes its images, thus mirroring the twisted, partial and unreliable nature of both the facts and the people confronting the protagonists in their dire odyssey. This stylistic flourish is felicitously complemented throughout by Saki Okuse's and Masahiro Sato's unorthodox character designs, with their starkly chiseled features, gazing eyes, frozen expressions, complexions so pallid as to verge on the corpselike and even the vampiric, and hair so thick and solid as to appear to have been sculpted rather than drawn. The gritty graphic style is further consolidated by chromatic schemes that characteristically oscillate between the washed-out and the tenebrous, with just a few minimalistic concessions to vibrant hues punctuating the dominant gloom.

Split between two sets of potential allegiances, Kiyoko and Tatsuya struggle to remain steadfastly loyal to each other, but rifts begin to manifest themselves as it is discovered that the boy is endowed with possibly unmatched reserves of dynamis and is quite willing to cooperate with the Countess's adopted "family" of Orga-Superior as a means of finally confronting his father, whereas his sister is just a regular girl who feels no kinship to the group. Kiyoko does offer a sensational display of dynamis when she resists the Blattaria troops hellbent on destroying the fetus she bears. At that juncture, however, the power comes from the genes of the Gilgamesh Novem, who has won her heart and fathered the preternatural baby, not from herself.

Kiyoko's real talent is her almost intuitive understanding of music down to the subtlest nuances: she is even able to detect the individual notes emitted by each raindrop as it touches the ground. This skill is not, however, regarded as even vaguely comparable to dynamis and Kiyoko herself modestly admits to her limitations by expressing the desire to become a piano tuner instead of aspiring at a career as a performer. The Countess, for her part, unceremoniously dismisses Kiyoko's piano performance as "poor," although it is likely that what she truly objects to is the girl's execution of a piece that brings back painful memories of Dr. Madoka.

Gilgamesh's musical theme runs throughout the series at the levels of imagery, symbolism and terminology. (In this respect, it finds apt companions in both *Kanon* and *RahXephon*.) The prominence of the musical theme is attested to by several episode titles: most notably episode 1, "Les Préludes," episode 7, "Dissonance," episode 12, "Die Lustige Witwe," episode 16, "Nessun Dorma," and episode 17, "Hammerklavier." Where the soundtrack is specifically concerned, recurring pieces include Beethoven's Piano Concerto #5 in E-flat major, commonly known as the "Emperor Concerto," the "Merry Widow" Waltz by Franz Lehar, and the aforementioned Robert Lowry hymn "Shall We Gather at the River?"

Music also plays a key part as a theme, particularly in the scene where the Countess decides to use it as a means of intercepting the Gilgamesh should they seek to penetrate the hotel. The plan is to create a "sound field to surround the entire hotel" and to deploy "devices that search for changes in frequency." The assumption underlying this strategy is that if the Gilgamesh — as scientific research has indicated — have a radically different "physical composition" rooted in a preternatural genetic memory, "their absorption and dispersal of various frequencies will differ as well." By spotting such changes, it ought to be possible to "detect intrusions." In this sequence, the Countess also confirms her aversion to the concerto she associates with Dr. Madoka (and hence her unrequited love) by tersely telling the hotel manager that he is at liberty to pick any piece he fancies as long as he steers clear of that composition.

The tension between Kiyoko and Tatsuya escalates when the girl is kidnapped by the Gilgamesh, while her brother remains at the Hotel Providence. Kiyoko is released by her captors and returned to the mansion but flees it in order to resume a life on the run rather than endure within a cage of the Countess's making. Caught and thrown into a dungeon worthy of the spookiest Gothic setting, Kiyoko is conclusively separated from Tatsuya when the Countess forces her to sign a contract decreeing that she will have to refund the full amount paid out to buy her from the debt collectors earlier in the story — which will feasibly take her a lifetime — and releases her into the outside world.

This segment of the story yields some of the most moving memory-related images, as

Kiyoko recalls the days when she and Tatsuya were living in total neglect with a perennially intoxicated mother, and protecting her younger sibling was her primary concern. The close bond between brother and sister is poignantly communicated by the retrospective sequence in which the two children play in the snow and Kiyoko presents Tatsuya with a snow bunny to which they then apply eyes by means of red beads. This memory is revived in the scene where Kiyoko beholds an identical snow bunny placed by her brother on a railing outside the hotel as a farewell token. The same childhood memories are reiterated in the sequence where Kiyoko's lifeless body lies in the Hotel Providence's infirmary while the preternatural fetus inside her continues to grow and attempts to merge with her spirit. When Tatsuya rests his ear on the hybrid shape that was once his beloved sister's body in a desperate effort to capture her lingering voice, those scenes unfold in his mind's eye. It is at this point that the boy also receives a warning concerning the "Cleansing Flood," the world-regenerating event planned by Enkidu all along. Even though *Gilgamesh* deals with the memory topos on a predominantly epic scale, scenes such as these reveal that it is concurrently capable of gentle reflections on the power of intimate remembrances in its flashbacks. The balance between the two modalities is indeed remarkable.

The show's passion for dexterously orchestrated flashbacks manifests itself from its inceptive stages. A magnificent deployment of the technique is offered in the early part of the adventure by the sequence where Kiyoko and Tatsuya, having found shelter in an old house from the loan sharks at their heels, having met the trio of Goth-clad youths who turn out to be Gilgamesh, and having been rescued from the enemy by the latter's astounding martial skills, enter something of a time warp. When the three Gilgamesh engage in a further confrontation with the Orga-Superior, conveyed by the Countess to kidnap the Madoka children, Kiyoko and Tatsuya witness the fight's most puzzling moments, which include a Gilgamesh member's portentous metamorphosis into a full-fledged giant monster. They then escape into a nearby wood and are stalled by the creature. When we next see the protagonists, they are aboard a moving limo in the company of the Orga-Superior kids, who take them to a grand concert hall where the Countess has been awaiting them. The events linking the two segments of the action remain implied until an impeccably timed flashback later displays the climax of the intense fight resulting in the Orga-Superior's temporary neutralization of their antagonists' powers and in the capture of the Madoka siblings.

A recurrent flashback is the scene where the Countess converses with Dr. Madoka for the last time at Heaven's Gate while he listens to his favorite piece. This occurs again at several poignant junctures in the drama. Another important scene, the segment of the adventure in which Kiyoko and Tatsuya hide from the *yakuza* under a broken piano and the girl finds the tuning fork destined to accompany her throughout the adventure as a keepsake, is reproposed as a flashback later in the action — notably, in the sequence where Tatsuya meets Kiyoko in an amusement park having been allowed by the Countess to see his sister again. It is at this juncture that the gulf separating the two siblings becomes painfully obvious despite Kiyoko's efforts to protect Tatsuya from the bleak reality of her current situation by claiming that she works for a piano refurbishment firm when she has, in fact, been forced by events to become a prostitute.

We see the same old piano again in the sequence where Kiyoko (who has been revisiting the venue for about a month to tend to the instrument) attempts to tune it. The piano is mute but she can hear the notes in her own head and when Novem follows her to the derelict spot, he tells her that she has brought the instrument back to life and that he, too, can hear the silent tunes she plays on the silent keyboard. The depth of the connection between the Gilgamesh and the human girl is fully demonstrated by this scene. The retrospective mode is maintained in the sequence that follows, where Kiyoko and Novem return to the eerie mansion where they first met and become fully aware of their mutual feelings.

Alongside flashbacks, another temporal device used by *Gilgamesh* to great dramatic effect is anticipation. A paradigmatic example can be found in the scene where Isamu cryptically alerts Tatsuya to his special nature and background. Asked by the young Madoka why he fights the Gilgamesh, Isamu ripostes that this may be simply because he has nothing better to do, whereas Tatsuya has "a reason to take them on — them, and the one who's behind them."

No less effective is the use of sequences imbued with an uncanny sense of déjà vu. One such sequence is offered in the dramatization of the Gilgamesh's infiltration of the Hotel Providence to reclaim Tatsuya and Kiyoko. As the siblings seek to flee their hunters along the building's dusky corridors, we are transposed back to the moments where they enter the Gothic mansion, see the cloned salamanders and are then greeted by Novem. The sequence is reiterated as a mnemonic trick meant to disorient the Madoka children and force them to reconsider their current association with the Countess and the Orga-Superior team. When Isamu intervenes, the spell is broken, though not before the intruders have managed to capture Kiyoko. The illusory character of the sequence is reinforced by the visual effects used to represent its dissolution: an amorphous mass of mercurial blobs redolent of a cybernetic virtual construct. Nevertheless, it soon transpires that the phenomenon did not consist of a simulation but of an actual physical event, engineered by the Gilgamesh through their knack of altering the molecular organization of a portion of the hotel. This disclosure intensifies the uncanniness of the occurrence by situating it in a decidedly alien perspective, thereby also rendering the memories associated with it phantasmatic and tangible at once.

The same location appears again in the course of a nightmare experienced by Tatsuya in which he floats in a large test tube to which he is anchored by tendril-like cables while helplessly watching Kiyoko's and Novem's amorous dalliance. The scene captures the boy's feelings of revulsion towards himself as an artificial human, and towards his sister and her lover as progenitors of no less ominous an abomination. At the same time, they encapsulate his latent jealousy, emanating from a fraternal attachment so intense as to verge on the romantic.

As it inexorably advances towards its harrowing climax, the action offers another memorable illustration of retrospective drama. Having refused to have her baby aborted despite the Countess's conviction that the fetus's part–Gilgamesh nature makes it an aberration, Kiyoko hangs suspended between life and death. At this point, a patchwork of the girl's memories from various stages of her life and disparate moments in the series flows across the screen in a kaleidoscopic fashion. The deep sense of nostalgia pervading both Kiyoko's and Tatsuya's recollections throughout the show is movingly and economically encapsulated by a single line addressed by the girl to her brother: "I wanted so much to make happy memories for you to have."

A further approach to the memory motif is exemplified by the sequences in which the events surrounding Twin X are recaptured by recourse to pseudodocumentary interviews, filmed so as to resemble aged archive materials, in which various Hotel Providence employees give their accounts of their personal reminiscences of that fatal day. These are juxtaposed, through agile intercutting, with snippets of what purports to be footage of the disaster, including harrowing shots of the victims and of the Countess herself (then known by the name of Hiroko Kageyama) as her injured body is being transported to medical facilities. At the same time, the special mnemonic faculties held by the Orga-Superior are also highlighted. When Tatsuya and the Countess's little army penetrate the Mitleid Corporation to explore its archives in an effort to fathom their origins — a secret which the Countess jealously protects — they instantly proceed to assimilate phenomenal amounts of information from legion hefty tomes by simply "scanning" their pages and thus retaining mental images of their contents. (Unfortunately, their quest is stunted by the appearance of a host of biomechanoids conceived by the warmongering megalomaniac Kazmatsuri as security guards.)

As *Gilgamesh* enters its climactic arc, fresh clues to the characters' backgrounds, secrets and memories rapidly accumulate. An especially interesting turning point is the discovery that a much deeper connection than mere physical resemblance ties Tatsuya to Enkidu. Kazumatsuri indeed reveals that the terrorist has been able to tap telepathically into his son's power: it was an energy wave unwittingly emitted by Tatsuya, it transpires, that enabled the Gilgamesh to access the Turangalîla and destroy it and its surroundings. To investigate the nature of the phenomenon and ascertain whether Tatsuya is a willing accomplice in Enkidu's scheme, Kazmatsuri takes him into custody with the Blattaria's assistance.

The boy is subjected to thorough scientific examination, as well as grueling interrogation practices. It is later also disclosed that in the process, the devious Kazmatsuri has appropriated Tatsuya's genetic information and deployed it in the perfection of his appalling weapons. Tatsuya's and Dr. Madoka's DNA patterns are shown to be identical, which leaves no doubt as to the boy's status as a clone. The roots of his very existence having been drastically called into question, Tatsuya heads for Kiyoko's apartment as the only place where he may find some comfort. What he does find, alas, is yet another ill-boding setting, inhabited not only by his dear sister but also by Novem, to whom Kiyoko has by now become sentimentally attached, and another Gilgamesh member intent on taking Novem back to Enkidu. The action gains unprecedented kinetic momentum as Kazmatsuri and his troops attack the location and a substantial number of Gilgamesh fighters not seen before in the series come to their associates' rescue. As Kiyoko's home is pulverized, she has no alternative but to return to the Hotel Providence and thus consent once more to the Countess's oppressive custody.

The Orga-Superior's turn to find about their true nature comes when they pay a nocturnal visit to the shifty Kazmatsuri in the hope of obtaining answers that the Countess stubbornly withholds from them. It is at this point that they are appraised with all the unpalatable details of their origins (as delineated earlier) and descend into so deep a state of abjection that the very survival of the Countess's synthetic family is drastically threatened. Shortly after, the Orga-Superior kids obtain incontrovertible confirmation not only of their cloned nature but also of their mothers' porcinity thanks to documents obtained on Isamu's behalf by his *yakuza* contacts.

While Fuko and Tohru are simply devastated, Isamu resolves to confront the Countess once and for all, forcing her to disclose all that she has kept from her "children." The lady gradually opens up to Isamu and recounts her experiences at Heaven's Gate, thus allowing her hitherto concealed human side and her inconsolable grief to surface at last. Isamu remains dissatisfied with the Countess's explanations in the conviction that she is still hiding some crucial truths, and leaves her after announcing defiantly that he can hardly believe he ever thought he could die just to advance her cause. The intense exchange is nimbly intercut with scenes dramatizing salient moments in Heaven's Gate's doomed history and memories of the Countess's personal role therein — or, at any rate, what she is consciously aware of at this stage. In the trail of these critical scenes, Isamu and Fuko leave the hotel and all the Countess can do is watch their departure in the cold light of dawn, beset by wordless and inexpressible sorrow.

These scenes clearly demonstrate that thoroughly crafted dialogue plays a crucial part in the articulation of *Gilgamesh*'s mysteries and thematic subtleties through a focus on character interaction. Many shows centered on teenagers endowed with unique abilities and exploited by callous adults in the pursuit of motives which they keep hidden from the young rely on strings of adrenaline-pumping battle sequences in order to advance their plots and develop their personae. The result is that the latter objective is frequently neglected in favor of the action as such. *Gilgamesh* resolutely avoids this standard formula, often resorting to brief utterances or wordless glances to communicate economically its characters' inner complexity, which is what ultimately makes it a memorable contribution to the realm of anime at large, well after specific plot twists have faded from the viewer's memories.

Isamu and Fuko eventually return to the hotel, having visited the families of their and Tohru's "originals," the three Heaven's Gate scientists from whom they were duplicated. The reassembled "family" gathers together as customary for dinner, joined by Reiko, who has been rehomed by the Countess following Yuki's demise, and the Countess's personal butler, who has insisted on remaining by her side even after her purchase of the Hotel Providence and consequent departure of all its staff and guests. The company are locked in an uncomfortable silence until the normally reticent Reiko puzzles over their "gloomy" mien, implicitly encouraging them to open up to one another. A warm sense of conviviality gradually replaces the sequence's ominous mood. This is appropriately punctuated by shots of famous paintings focusing on the sharing of meals that function as symbolic mementoes of gregariousness and harmony. (The value of eating together as a symbol of cohesion, is also foregrounded by *Kanon, Kurau Phantom Memory, Elfen Lied, 5 Centimeters Per Second* and *Tsubasa: RESERVoir CHRoNiCLE*.)

Fuko and Isamu now reveal that the families of the originals welcomed them unconditionally, offering not only precious information about their children complemented by amusing snapshots but also genuine affection and respect for the cloned kids themselves. The Countess's glacial façade concurrently melts, exposing her humanity even more explicitly than the earlier scenes revisiting her past, and she frankly recognizes that she is very fortunate to have gained a family after losing everything in Twin X. To commemorate this newly found peace, the characters proceed to take pictures of one another around the hotel, enjoying their last stab at fun in an overwhelmingly compassionless world. Kazmatsuri puts a brutal end to this brief reverie by requisitioning the Hotel Providence as his operational base, and the Blattaria accordingly invade the grounds. (The Gilgamesh, meanwhile, have been refining their own powers to annihilate the enemy and bring about the "Cleansing Flood.")

These sequences paradigmatically capture one of the show's most distinctive traits: namely, its predilection for a quiet, deliberately paced and meditative rhythm. This cadence appropriately pervades the action in order to underscore the story's preoccupation with the cautious unveiling of its secrets over and above stagy sensationalism. As Carlos Santos observes, this foundational aspect of the anime is overtly conveyed by its handling of motion, and particularly its preference for "static situations." Although the "action scenes that do come up are exciting ... this series looks cooler when the characters are just standing around looking creeped out, rather than rampaging in battle" (Santos). Yet, *Gilgamesh* never comes across as ponderous or oppressively deliberate since the affective currents coursing the narrative invest even the most stationary tableau with intense, albeit composed, energy. The overall tone is not, therefore, lethargic but sublimely languid and grim by turns.

The series climaxes with a pathos-laden showdown in which three parties are involved. Kazmatsuri and his Blattaria, now abetted by formidable machinery evocative of much warmongering of recent decades, are determined to put an end to Enkidu's apocalyptic vision. The Countess, surrounded by her Orga-Superior acolytes, seeks revenge on Dr. Madoka for her personal plight — which, we are now informed, has entailed not only unrequited love but also a coma lasting several years in the aftermath of Twin X. The Professor himself at last appears on the scene, backed up not only by all of the ever-loyal Gilgamesh clones — including regenerated versions of the ones previously destroyed by the Blattaria — but also by the Orga-Superior's adult configurations: namely, the three Heaven's Gate scientists whence Isamu, Fuko and Tohru issued in the first place. The young clones' confrontation of their grown-up incarnations provides moments of distressing drama. Each member of the three blighted armies meets a more or less dismal end in a flurry of raw and unforgiving brutality.

The appearance of the Orga-Superior's prototypes in the show's climax mirrors in a symmetrically elegant fashion the early portion of the first installment. The two scientists from whom Fuko and Tohru have emanated there feature alongside a young version of the Countess in a scene located prior to the announcement of the base's imminent closure, while Isamu's original makes an appearance in the sequence where Dr. Madoka infiltrates Delphys to catastrophic effect. The series' structural sophistication is succinctly conveyed by this correspondence. Moreover, the "parent" bodies function as corporeal memories underlying the Orga-Superior kids as we have come to know them and relate to them throughout the adventure.

Finally, the Professor and the Countess resolve to join forces in triggering the "Cleansing Flood" intended to bring this bleak world to an end. The event itself is subtly alluded to instead of being explicitly dramatized on the screen, and this adds gravity — as well as a touch of classy cinematography — to a show that never indulges in spectacle as an end in itself and would therefore be doing itself an unpardonable disservice were it to do so in the closing frames.

By underscoring the archaeological dimension of memory, *Gilgamesh* draws attention to the eminently material inscription of a culture's mnemonic heritage. As noted, the image of the ruin with which archaeology is, by definition, imbricated at all times evokes the ethos of *sabi* as a respect for the old and the fading. At the same time, the show's engagement with the materiality of memories harks back to another important aspect of Japanese aesthetics. This pertains to the reverential attitude towards their materials typically evinced by

Japanese artists throughout the centuries. This disposition, it must be emphasized, does not only manifest itself in the treatment of objects and practices that can overtly be regarded as artistic in the Western sense of the word. In fact, it is also evident in activities that are deeply ingrained in people's everyday lives, such as garden design, flower arrangement, the tea ceremony and various culinary practices. In all of these cases, the material properties of objects and the cultural memories underpinning their creation and handling are of paramount significance.

The governing principle through which those properties are brought to the fore is that of design. This is not conceived of as a matrix imposed upon objects by humans in accordance with anthropocentric or anthropomorphic priorities but rather as a pattern determined by the innate attributes of the objects themselves. Quoting the *Book on Garden Making*, penned by an eleventh-century nobleman, Yuriko Saito offers the art of garden landscaping as an illustrative case in point. Its secret, the author avers, lies with the evocation of the distinctive "scenic effect of a landscape by observing one principle of design: 'obeying (or following) the request' of an object (*kowan ni shitagau*).... For example, the gardener 'should first install one main stone, and then place other stones, in necessary numbers, in such a way as to satisfy the request ... of the main stone'.... The whole art ... requires the artist to work closely with, rather than in spite of or irrespective of, the material's natural endowments" (Saito, p. 86). Respect for the material qualities of objects, as Jack Lenor Larsen stresses, applies to the creation of all sorts of artifacts within both traditional and contemporary Japanese culture: "Craftmakers working within Japan's ancient traditions respond to the generations of passed-on knowledge. This collective memory includes a deep respect for material and process, and respect too for the intended user" (Larsen, p. 12).

Japanese attitudes to packaging and food arrangement exemplify these tenets, insofar as numerous substances employed for those purposes are intended not merely to serve practical or commercial imperatives by accommodating particular products but also, and indeed more vitally, to bring out their intrinsic properties. The materials used are responsible for determining the design of the containers. For example, paper is amenable to a broad range of manual treatments (including folding, entwining, ribboning, and shredding) and is therefore capable of yielding a correspondingly rich variety of designs. In each case, the artisan's principal goal is to communicate his or her humble regard towards the material itself. An analogous attitude underpins Japanese cuisine, where ingredients are processed, flavored and arranged so that the most unique of their innate features can be revealed and allowed to flourish unhindered. As Kenji Ekuan maintains, this gastronomic sensitivity is encapsulated by the aesthetics of the indigenous lunchbox: "Our lunchbox ... gathers together normal, familiar, everyday things from nature, according to season, and enhances their inherent appeal.... The aim of preparation and arrangement revealed in the lunchbox is to include everything and bring each to full life" (Ekuan, p. 6). In other words, the prime objective of Japanese "culinary artifice" is "to render fish more fishlike and rice more ricelike" (p. 77).[4]

Gilgamesh upholds the principle of respect for material objects in its portrayal of the archaeological site on which Heaven's Gate thrives. As long as the regal tomb, the surrounding ruins, the cave of Delphys and the memories which these places harbor are honored, and the temptation to conquer their formidable powers is held at bay, they remain harmless. Once the scientists resolve to harness those forces to the pursuit of their hubristic goals, imposing a design upon the location that is inimical to its vestigial configuration, malign agencies begin to proliferate. Lack of respect for the *sabi*-saturated ruins, their essential design and their autonomous standing as life forms is the trigger of the nemesis wreaked by Gilgamesh on his latter-day emulators.

On a broader stylistic plane, the series foregrounds the concept of design as inseparable from regard for the innate features of materials through its pictorial terseness. Never allowing the fuzzier aspects of anime style to smudge or mollify the stark contours of its distinctive graphics, *Gilgamesh* prioritizes a notion of design based on the maximization of the defining properties of line and mass alike as corporeal entities. At the same time, the presentation of even the most minute accessory, item of interior decor and architectural ornament with studious care for the qualities of their materials echoes the aesthetic preferences of Japanese craftsmen and the collective memory perpetuated by their skills. Moreover, the painstaking constellation of food items on plates with a keen sensitivity to their formal and chromatic attributes, which characterizes each of the recurrent scenes devoted to the sharing of meals at the Hotel Providence, mirrors the traditional Japanese approach to the art of cooking as a specific cultural discourse.

While *Gilgamesh* foregrounds the importance of the material dimension with unmatched vigor, the other titles discussed in this chapter as ancillary illustrations also evince painstaking care for the tactile qualities of their narratives. In *Captain Harlock*, this is borne out by three intercomplementary facets of the anime. Its representation of disparate vestiges of pirate lore highlights their status as tangible objects grounded in a thoroughly designed, albeit fictionalized, milieu. The material heritage associated with the Mazone further contributes to the saga's palpable reality. Concurrently, the show's emphasis on the pathological addiction to worldly possessions responsible for human decline comments on the negative side of materiality as coterminous with brute materialism. In the titles inspired by eighteenth-century France, the passion for materials and the cultural practices associated with them is attested to by their attention to vestimentary, architectural and stylistic details, underpinned by a profound respect for design principles. It is largely from the shows' devotion to the physical matrices of their stories that their characters and actions gain affective density and textural richness.

In throwing into relief the material character of memory by recourse to archaeology, the anime here examined elliptically evoke Michel Foucault's writings, and specifically *The Order of Things: An Archaeology of the Human Sciences* (1973). Foucault uses the term "archaeology" to designate the investigation of the manifold processes through which human subjectivity is shaped within specific ideological and historical contexts with a focus on the material dimension of a culture rather than on abstract concepts. The anime discussed in this chapter do not explicitly engage in the study of actual societies since the worlds and epochs they depict are fundamentally fictional. However, those imaginary domains are traversed by traces of real historical moments (such as pre-revolutionary France) and therefore offer allegorical readings of real human experiences rooted in tangible realities. Thus, they do provide archaeological explorations of the kind theorized by Foucault himself.

The French philosopher's archaeology is underpinned by the concept of "episteme," namely the system of knowledge that regulates a certain historical period by establishing neat lines of demarcation between the legitimate and the illegitimate, the sane and the insane, the normal and the perverse. The anime here explored echo this perspective by dramatizing personal and communal conflicts that typically require the individual or the group to confront the dominant ideology within which they are situated and challenge its sanctioned mores. The clusters of memories accompanying this dramatic scenario play a crucial role in steering the characters towards a shared — but very possibly iniquitous — definition of morality or else towards an idiosyncratic — but feasibly fairer — redefinition of the so-called norm and its shackles.

Chapter 4

Memory as Quest

The Place Promised in Our Early Days
(feature film; dir. Makoto Shinkai, 2004)

> Footfalls echo in the memory
> Down the passage which we did not take
> Towards the door we never opened
> ...
> — T. S. Eliot, "Burnt Norton" (1935)

> I've been having the same dream over and over again ... In that dream all of me — fingers, cheeks, fingernails, heels, even the tips of my hair ache from such loneliness. The world filled with warmth ... the one where the three of us were together seems more like a dream than the dream I'm having now. But I feel that so long as I don't lose the memory from those days I may be able to stay connected to reality. If only by a fragile, fragile hold.
> — Sayuri, *The Place Promised in Our Early Days*

The OVA series *Spirit Warrior* (dir. Rintaro, 1988) offers a classic case of the quest topos as a struggle to reconcile seemingly incompatible opposites. Born under baleful auspices and endowed with prodigious supernatural powers, the protagonist Kujaku is brought up by priests who teach him how to harness his abilities to benefic causes and with no inkling of their darker hidden potential. Things change dramatically when Kujaku is enjoined to vanquish the Neo-Nazi Siegfried von Mittgard, a demonic force of reputedly unsurpassed strength eager to steal the hero's birthright and rule the planet as the Regent of Darkness. At this point, *Spirit Warrior* comes to be dominated by the schizoid tension between the hero's memories of the recent past, leading to his employment as a healer and a mystic, and his repressed memories of a more remote past tainted by dark omens. In its engagement with the ineffable, the OVA harks back to the concept of *yugen*.

Rintaro engages again with the interplay of memory and the quest motif in the feature film *X* (1996), a stylishly Gothic epic based on a hugely successful manga by CLAMP. *X* is an even more multifaceted exploration of the topos under scrutiny than the earlier production, and hence calls for closer analysis in this context. Like *Spirit Warrior*'s protagonist, the hero of *X* is endowed with supernatural powers. As a psychic of unmatched caliber, fifteen-year-old Kamui Shirou returns to Tokyo, having left when he was only a child, to honor the memory of his mother's dying wish. Determined to protect his childhood friends Fuuma and Kotori, Kamui soon discovers that the task laid before him is not merely a private quest but a mission of cosmic enormity. As Tokyo turns into the battle site of Armageddon, it is Kamui's destiny to decide the world's fate by choosing between the Seven Seals, a.k.a. Dragons of Heaven, and save humanity or the Seven Angels, a.k.a. Dragons of Earth, and cause the annihilation of all humans and the purging by fire of their abused planet.

The warring factions make it incontrovertibly clear that the protagonist is predestined to play a decisive role in the final battle whether he likes it or not. The most cruel aspect of Kamui's ordeal is that he is left with no choice but to engage in mortal combat with his childhood friend Fuuma, precisely one of the two people he has vowed to protect at all costs. The reason for this inexorable outcome is that Fuuma is Kamui's double, a creature that supposedly matches the hero in every respect and complements each aspect of its being in a specular fashion. This entails that when Kamui finally chooses to side with the Dragons of Heaven in an effort to save Kotori, who has been captured by the Dragons of Earth, Fuuma is fated to join the opposite camp. The tie between the two youths is graphically reinforced by the revelation that just as Kamui's mother hosted inside her very body the sword her son would be required to brandish in the climactic fight, and could only be extracted at the price of her life, so Kotori carries an analogous weapon for Fuuma to wield. While Kamui's mother willingly accepted her destiny and wrenched the sword from inside her with her own hand, Fuuma obtains the instrument by force, killing his once beloved sister in the process. This contrast invests Fuuma's actions with sadistic connotations that are quite alien to the protagonist's own disposition.

The only characters aware of the dismal fate awaiting the hero are the oracles for each faction, sisters Hinoto and Kanoe. As they vie for Kamui's loyalty, they both know that eventually, whichever cause the youth decides to embrace, *another* Kamui will automatically support the opposite side. In seeking to negotiate between his two potential roles as redeemer or destroyer, the hero is concurrently required to reconcile the legacy of the past and its memories with the baleful prospects of death and rebirth which the future ineluctably holds. The magnetic pull of the limitless unknown relates Kamui's quest to the poetics of *yugen*.[1] Although Kamui defeats Fuuma in the end, there is no joy in his victory — only the stark, inconsolable recognition that he has lost everything. If saving humanity in the process is supposed to be the consolation prize to be gained at the end of an unremittingly fraught quest, there is scarce evidence that the hero is in a mood to cherish it, let alone treasure it in memory.

Beautifully drawn and studiously detailed, *X* also delivers a great deal of explicit violence which some audiences might deem unsavory. Yet, even as severed limbs and gushing blood fill the screen, one does not sense any gratuitous indulgence in gory spectacle on Rintaro's part. This is because the horror is immersed in a surreal atmosphere sustained by a haunting soundtrack that lends it an almost oneiric quality. Repeatedly, the battle scenes literally give way to memory-infused dreamscapes and prophetic anticipations that reinforce that distinctive mood with symbolic potency. The very first sequence, in which Kamui's mother plunges a hand into her belly and withdraws the aforementioned sword, epitomizes Rintaro's stylistic approach to the world of *X*. While the sequence is unquestioningly disturbing in its graphic intensity, it is nonetheless rendered gorgeously dream-like by the deluge of *sakura* petals accompanying the act. No less graphic is the dream sequence in which Kamui wades through a sea of blood towards a crucified and wire-bound Kotori whom Fuuma, his alter ego, proceeds to dismember with casual glee.

Although the film capitalizes on rapidly paced action sequences, some of its more felicitous moments actually reside with slow-moving or even stationary frames devoted to the evocation of juvenile memories. These include the scene set in Fuuma and Kotori's garden in which their remembrances of the time they shared with Kamui as kids take the forms of evanescent phantom images of the three characters in their younger configurations. Also notable are the frames focusing on snapshots of the three friends at a traditional festival garbed in ceremonial attire. Additionally, the visuals include occasional flashbacks rendered intensely nostalgic by the use of overexposure and watered-down palettes.

Anime has a proverbial reputation for crossing the boundaries between the human and the divine, the sacred and the profane, the prosaic and the majestic. Both *Spirit Warrior* and *X* eloquently confirm this proposition in the articulation of their respective memory-informed quests. The TV series *Hell Girl* (a.k.a. *Jigoku Shoujo*) (dir. Takahiro Ohmori, 2005–2006) pushes this trend to daring extremes. In this show, people's memory threads are used to weave demonic tapestries of obsession, pursuit and vengeance that take on the stature of parallel histories. In the unfathomed vastness of the Internet, there lies a website where those eager to exact revenge on their oppressors may place a post at the exact stroke of midnight. It is then up to Ai (namely, "Hell Girl") to decide whether or not to come to the petitioners' assistance and thus fulfill their quest for retribution. Hell Girl's associates first attempt (at least ostensibly) to induce the wrongdoers to recognize their culpability but the outcome tends to be one and the same: the ferrying of the guilty parties to Hell.

Solemn and impassive, Ai undertakes her duty with stoical resignation, never appearing to derive any personal pleasure or gratification from the task at hand. Her measures are invariably effective in freeing the supplicants of their earthly troubles. This entails, however, that just as the victims of Hell Girl's revenge schemes are inexorably hell-bound, so are the humans whom she abets. What remains of their current lives might run smoothly but awaiting at the end of the tunnel is sempiternal torment. The revenge theme has pervaded Japanese art and popular culture for centuries. The live-action film *Ringu* (dir. Hideo Nakata, 1998), adapted by Hollywood four years later as *The Ring* (dir. Gore Verbinski), is a recent demonstration of the popularity of the topos. The treatment of revenge in Ohmori's series could therefore be regarded as a graphic memento of a treasured heritage. Furthermore, in terms of its background art, its rendition of interior design and decor and its costumes, *Hell Girl*'s pictorial style is often informed by vivid memories of Japan's traditional arts — especially in the presentation of the titular heroine's home and in the sequences offered in the opening and closing animations.

The story's traditional substratum is reinforced by its evocation of temporal repetition. As we move from one tale to the next, one social predator to the next, one helpless victim to the next, the same basic narrative pattern presents itself. Ai repeatedly metes out poetically apposite punishments to the villains and reminds her summoners with equal persistency of the eternal tribulations they themselves face. While *Hell Girl*'s content is brutally bleak, the anime's graphic style, stark and delicate by turns, is almost invariably elegant. This provides an ironical aesthetic mismatch that suitably parallels the two-pronged nature of Ai's interventions. Additionally, the visuals are punctuated throughout by the image of the *higanbana* ("spider lily"), a time-honored emblem for the Buddhist concepts of cyclicality and recurrence. Year after year, the *higanbana* blooms during the autumn equinox and dies during the spring equinox, vanishing completely until it blooms again the following autumn. Insofar as the equinoctial periods are ancestrally regarded as ideal times for communicating with the supernatural realm, the plant has come to be associated with that world and even acquired popular designations such as "hell flower" or "spirit flower." (Its possession of poisonous bulbs is likely to have contributed to its daunting reputation.)

It is in the uncanny transition from *this* world to *other*—varyingly menacing, somber or enticing—territories that *Hell Girl* engages most adventurously with the quest theme as a metaphor for psychic transposition. At the same time, the show's leaps from ordinary domestic circumstances to transtemporal dimensions of baffling complexity echoes the idea of *yugen*. More often than not, the quest for an alternate world is not a journey to a better realm but a vain attempt to flee what is ultimately inescapable. Thus, the story's parallel realities are never posited as redemptive promises of transcendence (of the kind expounded by the Western myth of "Felicitous Fall," or *felix culpa*) but as brutal careening plunges into everlasting chaos. The evil which the afflicted characters exorcise through Ai's intervention on their behalf only returns with obnoxious tenacity—just as memories of the injuries they have received and of the grudges they have harbored only ever repropose themselves as more distressing and more inevasible memories.

In *Hell Girl*, as in several other titles examined in this study, memory is brought into play at several levels. Ai's "clients," specifically, are haunted both by recollections of the time of their victimization and by projections of their fears onto the future. Even though the latter do not, strictly speaking, constitute memories insofar as they visualize moments that have not yet come to pass, they are endowed with a powerful sense of finality by the fact that the characters' damnation is ineluctable. In this respect, they acquire the tangibility of the already-happened despite their speculative import, which makes them perfectly solid instances of quest-based anime at its boldest. Past and future, in the process, become practically indistinguishable. This dimension of the show gains resonance from its sustained focus not so much on the grudge motif itself as on the afflicted characters' mixed motivations, hesitations, shame and even self-loathing.

Like *Hell Girl*, the TV series *Shigofumi: Letters from the Departed* (dir. Tatsuo Sato, 2008) boldly dismantles the boundary between the mundane and the preternatural by defying the very barrier between life and death and exploring the ongoing legacy of memories well beyond the grave in the material form of missives from the deceased addressed to the living. These are delivered by a solemn girl named Fumika and her talking staff Kanaka (which morphs into a pair of gleaming wings and a precious pendant when the courier necessitates transportation). Throughout the show, the collusion of memory and the quest topos provides the underpinning for a meeting of this life and the afterlife. A quest of sorts typically motivates the departed personae to pen their very last letters shortly after their demise—when the human body, in the logic of the series, is held not to have quite evaporated yet. It is at this juncture, *Shigofumi* opines, that people have a chance of expressing their feelings most truthfully and unreservedly, even if in life they have been mendacious or reticent. Alongside this quest, the living characters' memories unfold in the form of flashbacks.

In the arc centered on the character of Asuna Ayase and her would-be lover Shouta Machiya, for instance, the letter is written by Asuna's father and conveyed to the boy as a result of the man's yearning to reveal that his daughter is responsible for his death and his attendant thirst for revenge. Mr. Ayase's quest is interwoven with Shouta's memories of the girl he cherishes in the guise of flashbacks that highlight her seemingly innocent and trusting personality, on the one hand, and Asuna's own recollections of the dismal events leading to the murder, on the other. The latter show that Asuna has been the victim of severe parental abuse, her father having sold her body to unscrupulous agents for the purpose of pornographic photo shoots. Prepared to endure this torture to enable the callous parent to raise sufficient money to feed his family, Asuna finally resolved to turn against the oppressor when he threatened to exploit his younger daughter Miku, whom Asuna dotes upon, to analogously iniquitous ends.

Alongside the girl's own reminiscences of her calvary, *Shigofumi* deploys a recurrent shot intended to capture her experiences in a symbolic fashion. This consists of the stylized image of a nude female shape covered with typographic characters, which suggests that the memories surrounding Asuna's ordeal constitute corporeal entities that are literally inscribed on the body. This image is also deeply significant in terms of the overall diegesis insofar as it foreshadows the disclosure of the enigma surrounding the character of Fumika herself and her own traumatic recollections. Another example of the intermingling of the quest theme and memory comes with the story revolving around the high-school tennis champion Ran. The girl's mother's quest to have Ran recognize her undying affection even after abandoning the girl and her dad for another man clashes dramatically with the protagonist's determination to avoid the now deceased woman's epistle to exorcise painful memories of her departure.

In the segment devoted to the artist and videogame designer Takehiko Hibiya, the mnemonic dimension consists primarily of flashbacks recording the character's discovery of his vocation and his professional evolution, culminating with the decision to quit his job in the wake of the shocking discovery that he is terminally ill. This level of the story is economically complemented by a wholly visual *shigofumi* delivered by Fumika on his last day to the little girl whom Takehiko has looked after and saved from a car accident at the cost of his own life: a pencil sketch of the child and of a dog prominent in the artist's own juvenile memories capturing Takehiko's quest to express his gratitude to the sole human being who has not, ultimately, let him down.

Structurally, the series makes brilliant use of the enchainment strategy which enables each segment within a particular story — and, with it, a distinctive quest and related set of memories — to be satisfyingly integrated with its companions. Thus, in the Asuna/Shouta arc, the girl's father's accusatory letter leads to Shouta's own missive to Asuna after he, too, has incurred a violent death, and the latter, in turn, is conducive to Asuna's own communication to Miku following her likewise harrowing demise. At the same time, even though various segments may at first appear to constitute autonomous mini-narratives, they gradually turn out to be carefully constellated parts of a coherent ensemble wherein Fumika herself is the key actor. Fumika is supposed to be dead but the realization that she is not immune to ageing, voiced by her colleague Chiaki, calls that hypothesis into question. The girl is increasingly tracked down by former schoolmates who have believed her dead for the past three years, and it is eventually revealed that she never actually passed away but rather lies in a coma at a local hospital. The challenge posed to both Fumika's old friends and the viewer, at this point, is no longer to ascertain whether the protagonist belongs to the realm of the breathing or to that of the departed but rather how someone who looks exactly like the comatose girl could possibly be flying about delivering letters from the otherworld. (This situation closely recalls, through a deft directorial flourish of mnemonic cross-reference, the central mystery dramatized in the TV series *Kanon*, here examined in Chapter 6.)

Hints at the *shigofumi* carrier's double identity are dropped from an early stage in the show, as the character of Kaname Nojima recognizes her as a former classmate from middle school whom he vainly longed to date, reputed to have shot her father. No less important is the subsequent image of a girl lying in a hospital bed, ostensibly incongruous with the adventure centered on Fumika, Kanaka and the recipients of their peculiar messages. It would be practically impossible to realize that the unconscious patient is Fumika were it not for the presence by her side of a book bearing on its cover the name "Mikawa Kirameki"—a once popular writer mentioned by Fumika in conversation with her staff a few frames earlier, with the accompaniment of a telling citation from one of his works: "Death doesn't save humans. They just disappear." It will later be revealed that Kirameki is the heroine's own father. A further clue to Fumika's identity comes with the shot where the mail deliverer, chasing a *shigofumi* addressee that happens to be an elusive cat, catches a glimpse of the girl inside the hospital as she flies past her window.

The *shigofumi* courier and the hospitalized female turn out to be the two complementary halves of a single person, Fumika Mikawa, created as a reaction to paternal violation. Afflicted by a form of schizoid narcissism, Mr. Mikawa would act by turns as a loving father, bringing up his daughter single handedly in the wake of his divorce, and as a ruthless torturer when prey to hatred for his former spouse. Thus, the brilliant writer would routinely treat his daughter's body "as a rough draft" of his manuscript. This entailed writing on Fumika's flesh with a glass pen while showering her with a deluge of terrible accusations leveled at the filth and corruption which he deemed her to incarnate as the issue of a female traitor. Although the deranged author was supposedly just writing on Fumika's body, the violence of his actions makes his treatment of the girl's tender flesh more akin to carving or chiseling. The recurrent image from the Asuna-based story gains fresh resonance with these revelations.

Fumika's abuse gradually led her to perceive herself as a split personality, accommodating at once the "good" girl on whom her father would lavish his unconditional love and the "bad" girl on whom he would inflict unspeakable pain. The schism resulted in the genesis of a dyad comprising "Mika," the tough persona that eventually resolved to shoot (though not fatally) the opprobrious parent and then became the *shigofumi* carrier, and "Fumi," the longsuffering and timid creature that took it upon herself to pay for the crime by precipitating into a seemingly interminable coma. The mail deliverer is determined to wait for the sleeping girl to awaken but the twists and turns following this event—which finally occurs in the penultimate installment—are something neither Mika nor the audience could ever have anticipated. However, as they focus on the tension between Mika's desire to be destroyed by her counterpart to atone for her sins and her friends' endeavor to prevent this from happening, these developments effectively convey a vital lesson: the importance of coming to terms with one's memories as an inevitable stage in any genuine quest for self-understanding.

In sharp contrast with both *Spirit Warrior*'s and *X*'s epic scale and with *Hell Girl*'s and *Shigofumi*'s fantastical scenarios, *Only Yesterday* (feature film; dir. Isao Takahata, 1991) dramatizes a simple, though profoundly affecting, quest: a young woman's efforts to relieve herself of the burden of the past in the knowledge that she may only accomplish this goal by *reliving* the past, and hence reappropriating its legacy, through memory. Moreover, it is only by embarking upon this laborious process that Taeko Okajima might transcend both the past and her present humdrum existence in the city as a humble "office lady" and move towards a future life closer to Nature, where her heart has always secretly belonged. Past, present and future fluidly coalesce in Taeko's memory stream.

The quest portrayed in *Only Yesterday* may not appear overtly *yugen*-oriented. In fact, it is apparently prosaic and low-key. Nevertheless, the film dramatically reminds us that a person's endeavor to reshape her or his quotidian life is ultimately no less of a leap into the unfathomable than the most audacious expedition into the mysteries of either intergalactic vastness or esoteric mysticism. Furthermore, although *Only Yesterday* posits the personal dimension as paramount, it is vital to acknowledge that Takahata also enlists memory to the evocation of historical phenomena of greater resonance, commenting on aspects of feudal Japan and its iniquitous class system, on the impact of Western trends on traditional culture in the 1960s, and on environmental depletion and its effects on the country's economy, rural existence and customs.

As Patrick Drazen points out, Takahata's elaboration of multifarious memories of "the pop culture of 1966," namely the time when the protagonist was an innocent ten-year-old schoolgirl, is undoubtedly one of *Only Yesterday*'s most distinctive attributes: "Movies, commercials, pop songs, even bakeries from the period and a Takarazuka-style all-girl theater company [Takarazuka was a 1960 female troupe renowned for its musicals] are alluded to in this adaptation of a nostalgic manga by Yuko Tonai and Hotaru Okamoto" (Drazen, pp. 267–268). While the parent text engages exclusively in "an exercise in nostalgia" (p. 268) with limited plot development, Takahata's film offers a sophisticated narrative pattern based on the interpenetration of past and present through a "fascinating (if sometimes dizzying) series of memories" (p. 184) that binds the two dimensions indissolubly together.

The deliciously methodical pace at which Taeko's memories surface and become embodied is impeccably captured by the film's original title, which translates literally as "remembering drop by drop" or even "memories of falling teardrops." So vivid are the recollections experienced by the film's protagonist as to acquire a palpable life of their own alongside the empirical present. Especially memorable, in this respect, are the train sequences in which, as Taeko dreamily reminisces, incarnations of her childhood self and of her little school friends infiltrate the carriages as spectral yet uncannily tangible and sprightly presences. Daniel Thomas MacInnes' comments on Takahata's film are worthy of notice in this context: "*Omohide Poro Poro* is one of the great stories about a person's life, about a quietly disenchanted woman who begins to reexamine herself, her place in life ... relentlessly shadowed by the ghosts of her childhood. It is a story of the inner child that speaks to us.... No other picture captures so perfectly the idea of memories" (MacInnes). Amalgamating unmatched psychological complexity with almost reportorial realism and an array of alternately comic and tragic elements, couched in a distinctive visual style that favors poetically faded hues and delicate details, the action is especially convincing in communicating the idea — simple but disarmingly powerful — that memory is a bafflingly creative, indeed even manipulative, faculty. This is attested to by its knack of recording certain events as purely cursory flashes and others with searing clarity, quite irrespectively of their intrinsic significance or subsequent impact.

In inspecting *Only Yesterday*'s transitional sequences, it is worth noting that scenes involving trains and railway stations recur in anime as settings for moments of reflection, introspection and mnemonic association. This is borne out by other titles examined in this study — *Boogiepop Phantom* (TV series; dir. Takashi Watanabe, 2000), *Ocean Waves* (TV film; dir. Tomomi Mochizuki, 1993), *5 Centimeters Per Second* (movie; dir. Makoto Shinkai, 2007) — as well as titles beyond the remit of the present project — e.g., *Grave of the Fireflies* (movie; dir. Isao Takahata, 1988), *Neon Genesis Evangelion* (TV series; dir. Hideaki Anno, 1995–1996), *Perfect Blue* (movie; dir. Satoshi Kon, 1997), *Rumbling Hearts* (TV series; dir. Tetsuya Watanabe, 2003–2004), *Spirited Away* (movie; dir. Hayao Miyazaki, 2001), *Gunbuster 2* (OVA series; dir. Kazuya Tsurumaki, 2004–2006), *ef — a tale of memories* (TV series; dir. Shin Oonuma, 2007) and *Tetsuko no Tabi* (TV series; dir. Akinori Nagaoka, 2007).

Makoto Shinkai made a big impression with his first film, *Voices of a Distant Star*, a 24-minute production written, designed and crafted by the director himself single-handedly on his Macintosh G4/400 in his own home, and released in OVA format in 2002. The story explores the same main themes revisited by Shinkai in *The Place Promised in Our Early Days*, providing an apposite point of entry into the rising artist's output to date. Isolation, transience, relativity and temporal dilation are integral to *Voices* as they will later be to *Place Promised*, all the while supplying a magnetic backdrop for the exploration of memory's inextricability from a consuming emotional and psychological quest.

Widely acclaimed as a pioneering excursion into the territory of digital technology and the recipient of an array of coveted awards, *Voices* follows the long-distance relationship between Mikako Nagamine and Noboru Terao. The two have dreamt since childhood of a life together but are wrenched apart by war as Mikako, who flaunts exceptional test scores and physical stamina, is recruited by the UN Space Army as a Special Agent in a conflict against aliens while Noboru remains on Earth. As the girl must learn to negotiate between her martial obligations and her yearning for Noboru, the boy must face a less heroic but no less taxing quest: living through the loneliness which each new day brings waiting loyally, and perhaps futilely, for the time of his reunion with his beloved. What is most astonishing about *Voices*, given its minimal duration, is Shinkai's knack of drawing the viewer into the story immediately, allowing the whole of the available screen time to concentrate on the protagonists' development.

Voices engages with the theme of memory from its opening scenes. We first see Mikako in an empty city as she reminisces about the time when she was young and could still communicate by means of her cell phone, whereas now she seems incapable of reaching anyone and feels overwhelmed by loneliness. As she looks up, we discover that she is actually occupying the cockpit of a spacecraft, which intimates that the earlier frames captured a memory-laced reverie more than an actual location. The sense of temporal displacement is reinforced in the next sequence, a flashback depicting Mikako's school days and her relationship with Noboru. This flashback also offers an anticipation with the shot where Mikako and Noboru observe a UN ship taking off: a symbolic foreshadowing of the girl's impending fate. This nimble movement across disparate time levels, bolstered throughout by Shinkai's emphasis on the tenacious hold of memory, encapsulates economically the rhythm of the entire work.

Regardless of the amount of sci-fi hardware and software doled out by *Voices*, the film never indulges in the kind of techno-fetishism that plagues so much *mecha* anime. In fact, it is the intensely human quality of the protagonists' star-crossed love that ultimately makes it remarkable and capable of abiding in the viewer's memory well after more impressive pieces by the same director have made it to the big screen and gained legion accolades. The same rich and detailed graphic style to be later immortalized by the visual bounty of *Place Promised* and *5 Centimeters Per Second* is already in evidence in this early OVA. So is its director's dedication to the portrayal and animation of deep wells of emotion that accrue greater and greater resonance at each turn of the compact narrative thanks to a sustained focus on the characters' embroilment in tangled mnemonic skeins and endlessly deferred quests.

After Mikako's departure, the couple continues to communicate across the galaxies by email. However, as Mikako advances further and further into space, the missives take longer and longer to reach Noboru, to the point that the time-lag in the correspondence ends up spanning several years. In what is arguably the piece's most memorable scene, Mikako sits in her ship after her task force has left the solar system bound for a remote star, enfolded first in cold silence and then in the ominous whisper of a passing storm and, gazing at the fading sun, surrenders to tears. She next reaches for her cell phone and rapidly composes a message bearing the date 2047 addressed to "the twenty-four-year-old Noboru" by "the fifteen-year-old Mikako," which she consigns to a voyage of 8 years, 224 days and 18 hours.

The burdens of separation, loneliness and alienation, allied to the quest to reach out to loved ones across the vastness of time and space, are the motifs that bind *Voices* and *Place Promised* most potently on the thematic plane. The writing sustains these elements with unflinching dedication to character interplay and internal ruminations, underpinned throughout by a keen sensitivity to the power of memory. Technically, it is in the deployment of digitally supported artistry and animation that the two productions bear Shinkai's indelible stamp, especially in the rendition of breathtaking sunsets, gently rolling landscapes, studiously designed buildings and myriad accessories. Whether the focus is on a whistling kettle, a bracelet briefly gleaming beneath a sleeve, a falling raindrop, or else on mammoth machinery and towering edifices, the passion for accuracy is invariably the same. This imparts both films with almost photorealistic palpability without, however, failing to communicate an imaginative vision that photorealism of a purely documentary type could never presume to convey.

This aesthetic agenda is buttressed by the director's desire to bring out the affective connotations of his painterly tableaux, suggesting that his camera often shoots more for atmosphere than for narrative. The mood thereby conveyed is pervaded by simultaneously thought-provoking and moving allusions to lost memories. Both *Voices* and *Place Promised* could be cogently regarded as protracted flashbacks reflecting on how their respective characters feel about their current situations and about the people and things they have lost on the way to becoming what they are. The nature of the dialogue reinforces the two anime's reflective strain. Carefully chosen, terse and reserved, the words are never used as sheer auditory padding but flow in waves at apposite moments in the story to nourish the characters' ongoing development, as well as their retrospective journeys into the past.

While *Spirit Warrior* and *X* foreground the cosmic scale of the memory/quest dyad and *Only Yesterday* focuses instead on its more intimate connotations, *Voices* capitalizes on a deft commingling of intergalactic grandeur and unpretentious private drama. In *Place Promised*, Shinkai perfects this approach through the rendition of a memory-laced quest of simultaneously epic and personal significance. Commenting on his intentions concerning the execution of this project as a development of *Voices*, the director has noted that he "was trying to expand the scope in this movie." This led him to "to delve deeper into the characters" and to incorporate references to the "world events" unfolding around them. At the same time, he was eager "to show something truly pure" (Shinkai 2006).

Place Promised is set in an alternate-history Japan in which the country is said to have been partitioned, in the aftermath of a world conflict, into a southern section that is governed by the U.S. and a northern section, consisting of the island of Hokkaido (a.k.a. Ezu), that is occupied by the "Union." Coinciding with the "Separation" was the erection by the Union of a Tower of vertiginous height. At the time the story takes place, namely the late 1990s, the U.S. occupation of the southern area appears to have come to an end but the Union retains control of Hokkaido and contact between North and South is still prohibited, which often results in violent border clashes. The Uiltra Liberation Front, based in the South, meanwhile fights for reunification, carrying out frequent forays into the occupied territory.

These large-scale political events and the collective memories surrounding their development are interwoven with the personal memories of the three young protagonists: Hiroki Fujisawa, Takuya Shirakawa and Sayuri Sawatari. Through its synthesis of individual and communal narratives, *Place Promised* proposes that memory can never be automatically expected to yield a reliable record of past occurrences insofar as putatively objective facts are inextricable from skewed perceptions and interpretations of their import. The three protagonists' private recollections revolve around a promise made by the three characters in their school days that binds them indissolubly together. Its goal is to reach the Hokkaido Tower, which they can clearly see across the Tsugaru Strait from their southern location. Their means of transportation will hopefully be a reconditioned Maritime Self-Defense Force drone plane, whose wreckage Takuya and Hiroki have found and named "Bella Ciela," and upon which they lavish their amateur engineering skills in their spare time.

Before the promise has a chance to come to fruition, Sayuri inexplicably vanishes. Deeply affected by the loss of their female friend, the boys take divergent paths: Hiroki moves to Tokyo to attend high school and is unrelentingly beset by depression and haunting dreams of Sayuri, whereas Takuya joins a scientific research facility sponsored by the U.S. devoted to the study of parallel universes in accordance with the laws of quantum physics. The film's scientific premise finds a real-life correlative in the Large Hadron Collider, a gigantic particle accelerator designed to cause opposing beams of protons to collide and create a parallel dimension replicating the conditions concomitant with Big Bang. According to David Winn, chairman of the Physics Department at Fairfield University (Connecticut), the LHC "is in a sense a time machine to look back to the earliest moments of creation" (quoted in Waldman and Levin Becker).

The mysterious Tower goes on providing a narrative link between Hiroki and Takuya throughout the film, as Takuya and his colleagues discover that the edifice is capable of replacing matter around it with matter from other worlds, while Hiroki comes to the realization that the only way of bringing Sayuri back is to fly her to that "promised land." Hiroki's resolve to fulfill the old promise is sustained by his memories of Sayuri, as well as by a letter sent him by the girl just before her conclusive descent into a coma. Sayuri, it would seem, has herself entered an alternate universe. Although she appears to be the victim of a uniquely severe form of narcolepsy, the girl is actually adrift in a parallel dimension in which she is continually tormented by the apprehension of irrecoverable loss. Takuya's supervisor, Professor Tomizawa, is aware that Sayuri is somehow connected with the Hokkaido Tower and research into parallel universes but initially hides this knowledge from his young assistant. His primary concern is indeed Uiltra's struggle for reunification, which turns out to include a plan to bomb the Tower so as to trigger a conclusive war against the Union. To keep Sayuri safely out of the way lest she should indirectly interfere with the escalating crisis, the authorities lock her away in the high-security hospital ward at Aomori Army College. The Union, for its part, intends to use the Tower to replace the current world with an alternate one.

Among the interpersonal mnemonic baggages invoked by Shinkai, two are particularly notable. One of them hints at historical events surrounding the partitioning of North Korea and South Korea in the Cold War era. The other alludes to the operations of genetic memory, as the connection between Sayuri and the Tower would seem to have something to do with her and her grandfather's DNA, the old man having been both the Tower's designer and the first scientist to prove the existence of parallel worlds. The image of the building's skeleton in the shape of a double helix reinforces this idea. Echoes of quite a different area of the collective imaginary reverberate in the portrayal of Sayuri's ordeal as a modern-day interpretation of the Sleeping Beauty motif. (This topos is also elaborated in *RahXephon*— especially in its theatrical version— through the character of Quon).

The existence of a connection between Sayuri and the Tower is cryptically suggested from the start in the monologue where Hiroki states that these were the two presences for whom he and Takuya shared a deep admiration. Moreover, Hiroki's admitted "longing" for the awe-inspiring building can be interpreted as a self-censoring sublimation or displacement of his feelings towards the girl. The discovery that throughout her protracted coma Sayuri has been relentlessly dreaming, confirmed by recordings of her brain waves, leads to the revelation that her sleep is the "key" to restrain the Hokkaido Tower's activation and that to prevent the edifice from replacing the entire human world with matter from other universes, the authorities must "make sure Sayuri Sawatari keeps dreaming." (It is clearly no coincidence that whenever the girl comes close to waking up, the Tower's activity increases to alarming degrees.) Takuya's boss describes the girl's connection with the Tower as follows: "We're speculating that the reason why she keeps sleeping is because her brain cannot bear the information of the parallel worlds that flows in from the Tower. If her sleep is broken, I think the world would be swallowed up in an instant by the parallel worlds with the Tower at the centre of it all."

The formidable scale of the Tower's power becomes evident with the revelation that the structure is capable of affecting areas measuring no less than twenty square kilometers, while Takuya's colleagues must go through a lot of trouble merely to shift a portion of matter the size of a grain of sand from one dimension to another. This thrilling, yet sobering, discrepancy throws into relief the puniness of humanity and its resources in the face of the universe's inscrutable intricacy. The spirit of *yugen* comes resplendently to the fore in this aspect of the story. The use of related settings whose magnificence tends to dwarf the human actors — themselves endowed with an intentionally generic physical appearance — abets this mood. Moreover, while the characters' motion is kept to a minimum, the scenery is invested with a strong sense of dynamism. As a result, humans are portrayed as paltry presences not only in terms of size but also at the dynamic level.

Hiroki himself is haunted by oneiric events in which he appears to access the sphere of Sayuri's own dreams. In these, he repeatedly finds himself looking for the girl in a cold and deserted world very much akin to the setting of Sayuri's own recurrent vision, and by and large failing in his quest for reunion. Concurrently, dreams and reminiscences are inextricably intertwined. In this recurring dream, Sayuri tells Hiroki time and again that she cannot remember anything about her past except the old promise, and hence the quest which this implies. Moreover, even though Hiroki remains unable to find the lost friend in his haunting nightmare, he nonetheless senses her lingering "aura" as an almost palpable presence. This serves to invest the youth's memories of Sayuri with corporeal density. When Hiroki at last manages to meet the girl in the dream world, the mnemonic component becomes even more conspicuous. First making contact in a stark hospital room, the two characters are magically transposed to the old world of their teens, bathed in a magnificent sunset, where Hiroki renews the original promise and additionally vows to protect his former schoolmate forever.

This crucial sequence deploys the memory topos on two levels at once, making it both an instrument for revisiting and reviving the past, and a means of extending the past's legacy into an indefinite future. Uplifting as the images undeniably are, the sense of joy they could convey is held in check by a mounting sense of uncertainty regarding the meaning of reality itself. For Hiroki, the Sayuri-centered dream gradually becomes more "realistic" than the "reality" he inhabits in his waking life, while the girl observes that her chill and dusky vision disturbingly feels more real that the warm reality she shared with Hiroki and Takuya in the early days. All Sayuri is capable of retaining is a spectral and rapidly evanescing memory of that warmth and this is the key to her maintenance of an anchor to reality, albeit flimsy.

Hiroki is convinced that if he flies Sayuri to the Tower, she will wake up, and his personal quest is therefore to accomplish that goal. Takuya, conversely, has by now learned from his associates at the lab that Sayuri and the Tower are pivotal to a phenomenon of sweeping magnitude and that saving the girl and saving the human world are most probably incompatible objectives. Hence, he seeks to discourage Hiroki from his quest, at one point so brutally that he threatens to shoot his old schoolmate. Although Takuya does not carry out this extreme act, the two youths do come to severe blows in arguing for their conflicting causes. Yet, Takuya cannot ultimately fail to acknowledge that his own heart lies with Hiroki and Sayuri and is willing to lend his support in advancing Hiroki's quest. Thus, he removes the girl from the hospital and, as he does so, touchingly announces: "Sayuri, let's go to the promised place. This time for sure." Takuya is well aware that the promise is Sayuri's sole remaining "tie to reality."

Once Hiroki has added the final touches to the Bella Ciela, Takuya asks him to play the violin and he executes the very piece played by Sayuri earlier in the film, unleashing a chain of flashbacks that echo the three leads' early days. These scenes exude a pastoral feel that aptly encapsulates the innocence and hopefulness of that trio's experiences prior to the crisis enforcing their separation. The peaceful beauty of the memories captured in the flashbacks is drastically displaced in the following sequence, where Hiroki flies Sayuri to the Tower as war between the two zones is just breaking out. The Bella Ciela glides close to the ground while an intense aerial combat rages above it, offering the entire movie's most intensely kinetic moments. The pastelly hues employed in the depiction of the preceding flashbacks give way to baleful palettes ranging from the lurid to the tenebrous. The mood changes once more, and no less radically, when Hiroki's plane soars through the ominous clouds that hang over the fight like an oppressive dome and emerges into an azure sky punctuated by gentler banks of puffy cumulus oozing with *yugen*-inspiring sublimity. The pace of the action slackens nearly to slow motion and the earlier atmosphere of serenity is restored. The Bella Ciela's two pairs of wings begin to rotate in a four-leaf pattern of exquisitely minimalistic grace with a rhythm so calming as to verge on the hypnotic.

As mentioned, the film's engagement with parallel dimensions alludes to the findings of quantum physics. The aspects of this field most pertinent to Shinkai's movie are the concepts of indeterminism and probability. While in classical physics the state of a system is defined by determinable variables, in quantum physics the "Uncertainty Principle" (stated by Werner Heisenberg in 1927) stipulates that complete determinism is untenable and that the state of a system may therefore only be formulated in terms of probability. *Place Promised* imaginatively appropriates these ideas by eroding the feasibility of ever knowing a world with absolute confidence, and advocating the cognate proposition that anything one may perceive as *the* world is inevitably *one* of countless—and conceivably coexisting—worlds.

Although Shinkai is clearly not in the business of dishing out a quasi-theoretical tract, nor is he concerned with documentary accuracy per se, it is important to acknowledge that parallel worlds as dimensions that exist alongside our own have been an object of scientific research for some decades and do not, therefore, fall exclusively into the category of science fictional speculation. The unquantifiable totality of coexisting parallel worlds forms a "multiverse," or "meta-universe." The term multiverse, coined by William James in *The Will to Believe* (1895), designates a composite reality whose guiding laws are not fixed but rather vary according to the frame of reference within which its structure is hypothesized, which might be philosophical, cosmological, mythological or fictional.

As Fred Alan Wolf argues in his study of parallel universes, as long as human beings could ideate the cosmos as a "concrete solid reality," wherein "Light traveled at infinite or near infinite speed making every conscious event back here on terra firma always and forever eternally now throughout the infinite universe," both time and space were thought of as "infinite" and "unmeasurable." Since "the universe was imagined to be infinite in all directions," it was automatically assumed that "to try to think about infinite space was hopeless, a game for fools and poets." Reality was accordingly conceptualized primarily in relation to the matter that filled it and was held to abide by "exact rules of inertia and movement called equations of motion." As a result, "nothing in principle was undetermined or ... left for the imagination. All the universe was a giant machine ticking off throughout all eternity and occupying every corner of an infinite space." With the development of post–Newtonian science, and specifically of relativity theory and quantum physics, the classic worldview has been drastically unsettled. Contemporary science's endeavor to unify "a wide disparity of ideas and concepts ranging from the tiniest subatomic matter to the grandest galaxy" has exposed "great gaps. The science-fiction-like idea that our universe is not alone ... is the latest concept brought forward by the new physicists in their attempt to unify our knowledge" (Wolf, pp. 18–19).

Einstein's theories revolutionized the realm of physics by showing that there can be no absolute and universally applicable notion of reality. The Special (or Restricted) Theory of Relativity of 1905 advanced this view by revealing that time passes more slowly for a body moving at sub-light speed than it does for a body at rest. Einstein arrived at this proposition by investigating the ways in which the physical laws that govern the motion of a body are influenced by the motions of its observers. The Special Theory of Relativity focuses on frames of reference that move relatively to one another. The General Theory of Relativity of 1916 proceeds to study any number of viewpoints with mutual acceleration and reaches the conclusion that there cannot be an absolute space or an absolute time since the two dimensions are actually melded together in a space-time continuum.[2] The theory also entails that past, present and future are not unequivocally differentiable dimensions. As Wolf explains, a "pair of spatially separated simultaneous events for one observer" might be perceived as "past and future events for another observer" (p. 19). There will, consequently, always be disparities in the processes through which the memories of separate observers come into being.

No less relevant to the present discussion is the proposition, embedded in the mathematical formulae of quantum physics, that "the future enters our present," and that "our minds may be able to 'sense' the presence of parallel universes.... The laboratory of parallel universe experimentation may not lie in a mechanical time machine — à la Jules Verne — but could exist between our ears.... Modern neuroscience through the study of altered states of awareness, schizophrenia, and lucid dreaming" might feasibly glean "indications of the closeness of parallel worlds to our own." Parallel universes may turn out to constitute "worlds within our present senses" (p. 23). Sayuri's visionary experiences — and, to some extent, Hiroki's own participation therein — could be seen as fictional dramatizations of precisely the kind of scenario which Wolf depicts in his evaluation of the relationship between parallel universes and communication theory.

A further development in modern physics relevant to the topos of parallel worlds is String Theory. As J. D. Barrow explains, strings are "linear distributions of mass-energy" which "could arise during a particular type of change in the material state of the universe during the first moments of the universe's expansion from the Big Bang.... They would exist as a network of tubes of energy which gradually become stretched and straightened by the expansion of the universe." Strings supposedly "arise because underlying symmetries of nature break in disconnected ways in different parts of space and these linear or sheet-like structures form at the boundaries between regions of different symmetry" (Barrow 1990a, p. 820).

These propositions have been developed by the Superstring Theory promulgated by M. B. Green and J. H. Schwarz (Green). This proceeds from the premise that the basic elements of matter are not zero-dimensional points but rather linear strings, and that such strings unite, part, loop and twist in a space which contains more than just four dimensions: a "*shadow world*" (Barrow 1990b, p. 829). Jeanette Winterson describes the Superstring as a scientific model which adopts "no stable first principle" (Winterson 1997, p. 159). In this frame of reference, "any particle, sufficiently magnified, will be seen not as a fixed solid point but as a tiny vibrating string. Matter will be composed of these vibrations. The universe itself would be symphonic" (p. 98). The musical analogy, incidentally, sits well with the melody-saturated scenarios evoked throughout by Shinkai's film.

Mythology and religion all over the globe have been informed for time immemorial by the concept of parallel worlds. Within the specific context of Eastern tradition, Hindu mythology, and especially its *Puranas*, postulate the existence of a limitless number of worlds, each with its indigenous deities. Fantastic literature, drama and cinema have followed suit by assiduously adopting the theme in the shaping of narratives based on the presentation of different planes of existence allowing for the emergence of magical or otherwise preternatural phenomena, for the transposition of characters into an unknown realm wherein they can be tested, rewarded or punished, and for the creation of dark places in which baleful forces abide, threatening to leak into the characters' familiar world. In other tales, the concept of parallel realities is used to posit the possibility of alternate histories: the sequences of events that any one historical occurrence could have unleashed instead of the ones that have empirically come to pass.

Although it is by no means unusual for anime to deploy the theme of parallel realities as a pivotal diegetic motif (by either placing its action from the start in an alternate dimension or transposing its characters to such a realm as the action develops), the take on the idea proposed by *Place Promised* is quite unique. This is because the adventure suggests that *any* world — the domain inhabited by its personae, the potential worlds which their adventures might open up and, ultimately, our own extradiegetic reality — is just one organization of matter amongst countless others. All of the worlds are equally real and solid — or imaginary and ethereal, as the case may be. What we are made acutely aware of with each successive frame is the possibility of a multiverse in which things take place in parallel in infinitely forking and branching ways. Just as no text is meaningful independently of myriad other texts, and no memory self-sufficient independently of innumerable other mnemonic traces, so no reality stands autonomously either within the screen's boundaries or beyond.

The connection between parallel worlds and memory is thrown into relief by the character of Maki, a neuroscientist employed at the base where Takuya also works while pursuing his studies. Maki's objective is to investigate the influence of alternate dimensions on people's psyches, and particularly on memories and premonitions. In her research, a central role is played by the study of dreams — with which memories are intimately linked. Maki indeed proposes that the oneiric domain, and hence both the personal and the collective memories embedded therein, is key to the understanding of parallel realities: "You know how a person will have a dream at night? Well, the universe has 'dreams,' too. Our world hides all these different possibilities, things that could have been, inside dreams. We call these 'parallel worlds' or 'branch universes.'" Maki's hypothetical connection between oneiric and parallel worlds is corroborated by Sayuri's and Hiroki's interconnected dreams, the film's structural mainstay.

However, while it is vital to acknowledge that dreams and visions play an important part in *Place Promised*, it must also be noted that no situation ever signals a total descent into the vapidly oneiric. In fact, as Shannon Fay emphasizes, the degree of realism imparted to even the most marginal moments succeeds in conveying at all times a palpable atmosphere: "Even in inactive scenes, the animators will show the characters fidgeting or some background movement rather than using stills" (Fay). Furthermore, memories are materially enshrined in the physical objects associated with their origin and perpetuation — as evinced by the violins played by Sayuri and Hiroki at key points in the story, by the Hokkaido Tower itself, and by the meticulously designed Bella Ciela. Shinkai himself has commented thus on the design of the aircraft: "From the very beginning I wanted to depict a scene with a plane that takes off with the thunderous roar of a jet engine, and then switches over to engulfing silence during flight using a super-conducting motor. To realize this flying sequence, I created the design for a mechanism where the wings can be transformed to a propeller with a super-conducting motor mid-flight" (Shinkai 2005).

The director's own memories played a part in the ideation of *Place Promised*, and particularly in his uniquely punctilious approach to the execution of settings. Shinkai has indeed stated that his fascination with the environment and its translation into cinematic images (and, by implication, memories) is indissoluble from his recollections of puberty as a time fraught with uncertainties that could only be alleviated by loving attention to the world around him: "I feel that I was always saved by the beauty of the scenery. I clearly remember that I used to look outside from the train every day not to miss a thing because there was always something to note. So I'm constantly wanting to put such feelings into the movies" (Shinkai 2006). The painstaking care devoted by Shinkai not only to the environment but also to the interiors of the trains that punctuate *Place Promised* as a powerful visual refrain indicates that his eye for minutiae is no less acute when it comes to artificial constructs. Even the sparks of light flitting across the ceiling of a carriage as this emerges from a tunnel yield a vibrant sense of aliveness.

The character designs executed by Ushio Tazawa are no less remarkable, especially in their knack of registering subtle changes meant to denote the characters' ageing over a period of three years. This solicitous attention to convincing sceneries, props and expressions is most welcome in the context of a story that might otherwise have felt occasionally ponderous, given its emphasis on introspection and gently flowing interactions rather than snappy action sequences. As Joel Pearce emphasizes, "The world Shinkai has created comes to magnificent life through the animation, which blends cell animation with extremely slick CGI. The two elements have been perfectly blended, allowing for detailed and stylized characters on a colorful backdrop of gorgeous moving skies, richly painted backdrops, and subtle changes in light.... And the sound design is every bit as strong, full of detail and subtlety" (Pearce). The original title, *Kumo no Mukou, Yakusoku no Basho*, translates as "Beyond the Clouds, the Promised Place." This brings out its atmospheric quality more emphatically than its English counterpart. The soundtrack was executed by Shinkai's close friend Tenmon, and is made particularly remarkable by its integration of string-quartet and piano-based pieces, matched to the affective import of the scenes they accompany. The bittersweet violin melody employed on two key occasions (symmetrically situated within the film's diegetic structure) are noteworthy as melodic accomplishments of autonomous caliber.

The realism of the visuals is abetted by lighting effects on a par with live-action cinematography at its most proficient. Equally vital is the inclusion of minute accessories that truly seem to glow with an inner flame, pithily contributing to the film's emphasis on a ubiquitous sense of wistful loss. Indeed, while their flimsiness alludes to the transient nature of reality, their radiance invests that feeling of ephemerality with unmatched lyrical nostalgia. The poem "Haru to Asura" read by Sayuri at the beginning lucidly captures this very mood.

The intractably transitory nature of human endeavor is epitomized by recurring images of passing trains. Nuclear Buddha's observations on this topic are worthy of consideration: "Note that while the first half of the movie was set almost entirely on trains or in train stations (even if they are abandoned), this [i.e., the scene where Hiroki boards a train to find Sayuri] is the first time someone gets on a train after the '3 Years Later' mark. In fact, there are even scenes where the characters watch trains go by without them. Hiroki even goes to stations just to pretend he's waiting for someone there!" (Nuclear Buddha). Such sequences symbolize the characters' aching desire to move and progress, on the one hand, and the evanescence of the present moment, on the other. The melancholy mood of the views through which the trains pass by, a feature which *Place Promised* shares with both Shinkai's own *5 Centimeters Per Second* and Tsurumaki's *Gunbuster 2*, supplies a perfect visual correlative for the movie's opening line: "I always have a premonition of losing something." Nothing ever stays put in Shinkai's world, and goals are felt to have vanished even before they have been reached. The conclusion of any quest, therefore, ushers in not a conclusive sense of triumph but rather an apprehension of irretrievable privation.

The Hokkaido Tower epitomizes the collusion of memory and technology discussed in Chapter 1. This same motif, having already manifested itself in *Millennium Actress* in the depiction of the technology of cinema and in *Gilgamesh* by recourse to the theme of cloning, will again feature prominently in other productions here studied. *Kurau Phantom Memory*, for example, deploys it in the representation of pioneering research into alien life forms, while *RahXephon* harnesses it to the construction of an alternate history on the basis of hypothetical technologies. The motif will also make cameo appearances in *Boogiepop Phantom* (genetic mnemotechnology), *Memories* (military mnemotechnology), *Paprika* (psychotherapeutic mnemotechnology) and *The Melancholy of Haruhi Suzumiya* (evolutionary mnemotechnology).

Though motivated by personal goals, the central quest dramatized in *Place Promised* is couched in a cinematographical style that imparts it with a sense of metaphysical grandeur. In this respect, the film echoes the concept of *yugen* as a speculative foray into the limitless vistas conjured up in imagination alone beyond the workings of consciousness and common sense. Through its protagonists' journey into cosmic infinity, including the prospect of alternate universes, the film offers majestic portrayals of an awesome environment endowed with powers that defy reason and logic and exceed the safe boundaries of the merely beautiful. However, the film's cosmic dimension never dominates the screen conclusively. In fact, it is assiduously interwoven with a powerful sense of intimacy and modesty. Thus, *Place Promised* abides in memory as a lovingly crafted meditation on the impact of the passage of time upon its characters and their struggles to come to terms with the phantoms of loneliness and loss, as the drama oscillates between the present and the past, current perceptions and posterior reconfigurations of a youthful dream. Dispassionate in its rendition of the painful legacy of war and of the iniquity of political intrigue, yet lush and melancholy in the presentation of its memory-saturated landscapes, the film never allows either gritty realities or lyrical reveries to dominate the screen unequivocally. The two dimensions, in fact, permeate each other, continually filtered through the protagonists' variable perceptions of the temporal flow.

Although the film offers a resolution of sorts, Shinkai's decision to bring the action to an end immediately after the Hokkaido Tower has been destroyed, and Hiroki and Sayuri are still to make the journey back to their world amidst unforeseeable difficulties and dangers, makes it markedly open-ended. This choice is quite congruous with the director's aesthetic vision, central to which is the desire to invite the viewer to take a step "ahead of the screen" (Shinkai 2006), and hence speculate about potential developments stretching beyond the boundaries of the diegesis. The characterization of parallel dimensions as the dreams and memories of the cosmos, suggesting that the unconscious might have access to worlds and experiences outside an individual's timeline, is in itself a sufficiently tantalizing proposition to encourage the audience to ponder possibilities that the film deliberately leaves unexplored.

Chapter 5

Split Memories
Kurau Phantom Memory
(TV series; dir. Yasuhiro Irie, 2004)

> Every day is a journey, and the journey itself is home.
> — Matsuo Bashou (1644–1694)

> When sadness comes, just sit by the side and look at it and say,
> "I am the watcher, I am not sadness," and see the difference.
> Immediately you have cut the very root of sadness. It is
> no more nourished. It will die of starvation. We feed
> these emotions by being identified with them.
> — Bhagwan Shree Rajneesh (1931–1990)

When, in 2100, twelve-year-old Kurau Amami visits her father's laboratory to witness an experiment as a birthday treat, a refulgent bolt strikes her fortuitously and turns her into the vessel of a "Rynax": a binary entity. In light of the adventure that follows, it becomes clear that Rynax is not so much a kind of energy as an alien life form unto itself. Rynax, it further transpires, is a phenomenon capable of decomposing anything with which it comes into contact into its constituent atoms. By and large, humans touched by Rynax power have to endure agonizing deaths. This is not the case, however, if the binary life form radically reconstructs them, as is the case with Kurau. The show will incrementally demonstrate that what makes Kurau special, above all else, is her retention of humanity and of human memories even after becoming symbiotically tied to Rynax. Those who come into contact with the alien species and forgo their humanity, conversely, are doomed because Rynax will inevitably devour their bodies without any chances of mutual support between host and guest.

Its protagonist's catastrophic transformation supplies *Kurau Phantom Memory* with the starting point of a studious anatomy of the trials and tribulations of memory and its imbrication with split identities. The analysis that follows relies on a loose reconstruction of the most salient stages in the series' diegesis as a formal vehicle for the exploration of *Kurau*'s highly innovative—yet strangely familiar—mnemonic drama.

While one half of the creature housed by Kurau is a dynamic and sentient being in its own right, which retains the human girl's appearance and all her data and memories, the other half, as yet too weak to awaken, lies dormant within the same body. The Rynax trope succinctly captures the alliance of technology and memory, occupying at once the analytic realm of science and the affective dimension of personal experience. Dr. Amami is confronted with a bitter dilemma: namely, whether his daughter's human shape still accommodates Kurau's soul or is exclusively a container for the Rynax. This split in the scientist's perception of the heroine is axial to the narrative's psychological dimension and results in an attendant rift between latent memories of the innocent child and more recent memories of her altered, and potentially dangerous, state. The show deliberately refrains from meeting Dr. Amami's predicament with any conclusive answers.

The tension is brutally exacerbated by a relatively early scene in which Kurau, exhausted by the grueling experiments to which her dad's colleagues subject her round the clock as though she were a mere automaton, violently withdraws her cooperation, accidentally tearing out Dr. Amami's left arm in the process. Despite his pain, the scientist appears to be genuinely more aggrieved by his daughter's overwhelming feelings of guilt and shame than by the physical impairment. As the action progresses, Dr. Amami experiences a further psychological split as his determination to find a way of restoring Kurau's original identity — meanwhile keeping her safe from ruthless pursuers — clashes with the injunction to join forces with the enemy when he realizes that by working in their research facilities, he will stand a better chance of helping Kurau.

The active half of her being invests the heroine with amazing powers (including the abilities to levitate, to generate vast amounts of radiation, to penetrate physical barriers effortlessly, to combat large *mecha* without even getting scratched and, last but not least, to fly) and she ends up living an apparently emotionless and solitary existence, channeling those skills into a job as a top-notch crime-fighting agent. No assignment is too demanding or hazardous for the hard-as-nails Kurau, to the point that even the retrieval of stolen corporate data, a mission which her colleagues deem highly challenging, is something she can coolly dismiss as "a cinch." However, there are intimations that the heroine is dissatisfied with her situation and that her apparent toughness is just a façade, erected to conceal deep-seated turmoil. Kurau's troubled feelings in the early part of the series are economically captured by the scene from the opening installment where she tells a co-worker that she is eager to focus on her job without asking any questions because this way, "forgetting things becomes a lot easier."

Ten years after the fatal accident, Kurau's "Pair" — or symbiote — incandescently emerges from its slumber in the form of a candid and trusting girl reminiscent of the young Kurau. Having named her Christmas, the capable agent vows to protect her at all costs and the two embark on an emotionally complex relationship combining parental/filial, fraternal and romantic connotations. (As to Kurau's reason for choosing the name "Christmas," this will not be fully disclosed until the end.) The discrepancy between Kurau's and Christmas's experiences and related mnemonic baggages emplaces the themes of dissonance and rupture as fundamental to the entire narrative. A further split in Kurau's personality and underlying memories is signaled by the radical disparity between her cold and self-possessed mask prior to the Pair's advent, and her solicitous and affectionate attitude, at times reminiscent of that of a doting parent, in the aftermath of the awakening. From this point onwards, the narrative provides increasingly incisive clues to the current of warm and vulnerable humanity flowing beneath Kurau's grimly pragmatic exterior, seamlessly blending her all-too-human dimension with her alterity. This subtle synthesis of the human and the other is most effectively conveyed by the story's mounting evidence for the protagonist's possession of memories that do not literally belong to the alien Rynax, yet shape persistently her understanding of life and the world around her in both its animate and inanimate forms.[1]

Humans reconstituted by Rynax become "Ryna Sapiens" and are tirelessly hounded down by agents from the GPO ("Global Police Organization") if, like Kurau, they are not officially registered. What the authorities fear most is the prospect of Rynax flooding the entire world with utterly unpredictable consequences. As they flee their GPO pursuers, led by the implacable Captain Ayaka Steiger under the aegis of Inspector Wong, Kurau and Christmas are assisted by Doug, formerly a GPO member and Ayaka's boss now employed as an independent agent. He had no choice but to leave the force, we are told, because he simply did not like taking orders. Doug has been appointed via a broker to spy on Kurau by her father, ever keen on knowing her location and, if at all possible, on shielding her from her foes. As the story progresses, Doug increasingly develops protective tendencies towards the Rynax couple. The agent indeed ends up admitting that his being a father is one of the reasons for which he accepted the job of investigating Kurau in the first place. Subsequent developments indicate that this may have actually been the *principal* reason behind Doug's decision.

Ostensibly steeled and inviolable, the agent is actually an emotive and innerly scarred individual. The main cause of Doug's predicament is his separation from Ted, the preteen age son from whom he has been wrenched away by divorce and with whom he struggles to preserve an intimate connection, at times risking failure by behaving in ways Ted might consider "uncool" (e.g., calling him "Teddy"), and at others succeeding by appealing to the boy's fascination with the more adventurous side of his father's profession.

Having obtained incontrovertible evidence for Kurau's Ryna-Sapien makeup, Ayaka descends upon her and Christmas with a formidable army of "Attractor Rynax Units" (ARU). These are elite GPO agents trained to deploy a variety of sophisticated weapons designed to deal with Ryna Sapiens according to their classification. Those charged with apprehending Class-A Ryna Sapiens like Kurau, commanded by Inspector Wong, are strategically coordinated by Ayaka throughout the main body of the adventure. Kurau and Christmas narrowly escape capture by rising together into the night sky, shooting off into the distance like a comet and leaving a single sparkling star in their wake. This is undeniably one of the most dynamic, yet lyrically poignant, moments regaled by the show's early segments.

Aware that by deploying her powers "out in the open," Kurau has exposed both herself and her cherished Pair, and that this exponentially augments their vulnerability, she is now more than ever determined to leave the city. In an affecting exchange, she apologizes to Christmas for tearing her away from their home but the junior Pair reassures her, with characteristic cheerfulness, that nothing else truly matters as long as they can be together. The concept of togetherness will gather greater and greater resonance as the narrative advances, proving crucial to the welfare of Rynax and humans alike. This heart-warming feeling of mutual affection and concern is reinforced by the later scene in which the couple arrive at their new accommodation and Christmas instantly takes out a photo of the young human Kurau with her parents and proudly places it on the kitchen counter. Kurau was not even aware that Christmas had found either the will or the time to rescue the treasured memento in the course of the GPO attack.

The scenes focusing on Kurau and Christmas's mutual affection and concern, or simply dwelling on their enjoyment of each other's company, play a significant role throughout and communicate a profound feeling of warmth suffused with a magical aura of wonder, without ever degenerating into fuzzy sentimentalism or mawkish melodrama. In fact, Irie's show is firmly grounded in psychological realism and able to retain throughout just the right dose of emotional reserve. Most importantly, these moments foreground the idea that as the two halves of one single life form, Kurau and Christmas share not only thoughts and feelings but also the memories that sustain them, and that this binds them indissolubly together despite their physical separation as distinct human bodies. This point will be emphatically confirmed in the series' finale, where it becomes evident that the two Pairs' bond has been nourished all along by a "phantom memory" capable of transcending their corporeal partition.

The first mission undertaken by Kurau in her new setting proves especially arduous, leaving her feeling uncharacteristically "exhausted" and beset by a blustering fever. The cause of this unusual condition, it emerges, is Kurau's unintentional summoning of a Rynax into the human world. The entity, named Go, is now frantically looking for his missing Pair and rampaging the city in an armed pod with the GPO at its heels. Although Kurau can do nothing to help Go find what it seeks, she is capable of fully empathizing with the creature's predicament, remembering how she herself felt throughout the ten years of her existence as an unmatched Rynax, as well as the more recent anguish unleashed by the fear of having lost Christmas just minutes earlier. Go is attacked by the GPO by recourse to the newly developed "Attractor Rynax System" (ARS), a pair of weapons designed to either smother a rogue Rynax against a wall or else stun it with irradiation beams.

The damage inflicted on Go releases a portentous stream of Rynax light that seems to penetrate Kurau's body to its very core, whereupon she is able to return the alien entity to its universe while its host regains a human shape. The discovery that she has the power to send Rynax back to their place of origin carries momentous repercussions for both Kurau and her symbiote since it entails that she could, theoretically, free her body of the extraterrestrial presence and give it back to Dr. Amami as promised. What would become of either the Kurau she is now or of Christmas remains, at this point, a mystery.

These events foreshadow the show's dénouement, as well as the scenes where Kurau devotes her Rynax-unlocking powers to the cure of the victims of a large-scale industrial accident that has resulted in many unfortunate employees' contamination by Rynax. These powers manifest themselves when Dr. Amami takes Kurau and Christmas to the sanatorium where the victims are slowly and painfully dying, as larger and larger areas of their bodies are consumed by the alien life form. Kurau instantly senses the lingering presence of Rynax within the facility in the guise of a faint but unmistakable memory of that other unfathomed universe whence the alien force issues. Although she is aware that there are no full-fledged Rynax around, she nonetheless perceives the "marks they've left behind, like footprints"— or even, conceivably, like *phantom memories*. It is in this context that Kurau and Christmas realize that the energy they house may constitute a threat to humanity's very survival. As a result, they now feel torn between the prerogatives and interests of two seemingly incompatible species, no longer able to draw clear dividing lines between good and evil, friend and foe. As argued in some detail later in this analysis, the proposition that not all of the apparent villains unequivocally harbor malevolent motives is forcibly captured in the depiction of Ayaka's personal reasons for seeking out Kurau as the outcome of traumatic memories and inner conflicts.

Dr. Amami himself is revealed to have developed the ARS in order to suppress Rynax energy and thus neutralize its rampant hold on the patients' bodies, stabilizing their condition if not exactly eradicating it. He never suspected that the GPO could "pervert" the instrument to create horrific weapons to be deployed against Kurau herself. While Dr. Amami faces this grievous realization, Kurau is torn by an intractable conundrum. Having already obtained indications of her ability to return Rynax life to its inceptive locus, as intimated earlier, she now holds unequivocal evidence for her possession of this terrifying power. Hence, she could quite easily give the human Kurau's body back to her father, unbinding it from its alien guest. This would finally enable her to fulfill the promise by which she has been bound from the start. Sadly, the action would ineluctably leave Christmas entirely alone in the human world, as stranded and isolated as Kurau herself was throughout the first decade of her Rynax-dominated existence. In a deeply moving scene, Dr. Amami vows to find a way of saving both of the symbiotes, and assures Kurau that he is "proud" of her (her Rynax nature notwithstanding) and derives great comfort from seeing her behave as a strong and autonomous adult in the face of adversity.

One of the series' most dexterously choreographed elements is the gradual disclosure that Christmas harbors considerable Rynax powers despite her apparent helplessness. This is most obvious in the scene where a violent jet of incandescent light bolts out of Kurau's body (a symptom of her weakened state at that stage in the adventure), gravely endangering her being, and the junior Pair saves the day by absorbing it all into her own body. A balanced symmetrical reversal of this scene is offered by a later sequence where it will be Kurau's turn to incorporate the awesome flow of Rynax yielded by Christmas's body.

At a relatively early stage in the adventure, the protagonists are temporarily relocated to an island, where Doug relies on one of his numerous contacts to give the Rynax couple accommodation and employment as waitresses at his seaside restaurant. Christmas falls smoothly into her new role, rapidly gaining a crowd of fans besotted with her cheeriness and cuteness among the regulars. Kurau, conversely, seems only capable of looking "grumpy," breaking plates and flooding the sink with inordinate amounts of detergent. These frames provide some agreeable comic relief. At the same time, this particular segment of the story also capitalizes to memorable effect on the realistic portrayal of a touching domestic drama. This pivots on the character of Yuki, the restaurateur's son, and his consuming jealousy following the birth of a baby sister. Kurau's humanity is here thrown into relief by her ability to sympathize with the sulking kid and to reassure him about his ongoing importance within the family. This same mood pervades the scene in which the heroine holds the infant in her arms and her mind is momentarily flooded by visual memories of the human Kurau's deceased mother.

Yet, even in the midst of intimate domestic drama, the comedic mood characteristic of *Kurau*'s island segment is not forsaken altogether. This is clearly borne out by the scene where Christmas, who is utterly fascinated with the new-born baby, innocently declares that she wishes she knew how to get one such creature of her own, quite oblivious to the meaning of her words from a human point of view. Unsurprisingly, all of the male customers who hear her assertion (in their shocked embarrassment) simultaneously spew out the food and drink they have just ingested.

Kurau and Christmas's island life is not to last, however. Ichise, a top scientist researching Rynax on behalf of the GPO, has recognized Kurau in the pictures taken during an early battle. Dr. Amami claims to no avail that the person in those images is not Kurau in his unwavering determination to protect her. Unfortunately, Ichise is only too familiar with the girl's physiognomy, having been the chief culprit behind Kurau's enslavement to the excruciating experimental routine seen at the beginning. When the researcher hears about Christmas, he speculates that she might be Kurau's Pair and, in a frenzy of precipitous enthusiasm, proclaims that the opportunity to study a Rynax couple would give him and his associates "the key to unlocking the secret of the Rynax." Capturing the girls now becomes an even more pressing priority for the GPO.

While foregrounding Kurau's and Christmas's ordeal, Irie shows impressive narrative skills in his avoidance of a monolithic focus in favor of multiperspectivalism. Thus, even the seemingly emotionless Ayaka is incrementally emplaced as a character endowed with a rich and tormented inner life of her own rather than a formulaic villain of the piece. Memories play a key role in abetting this aspect of the story. Especially notable is the flashback to one of the Captain's visits to her derelict parental home that wordlessly captures her sorrow amidst the melancholy rural landscape. This scene is compounded by a subsequent flashback triggered in Ayaka's mind by the sight of a photograph of Kurau's Pair, which leads her to remark spitefully: "Christmas ... god awful name." The sequence that follows explains Ayaka's bitterness, leaping back to her childhood. We thus discover that fourteen years prior to the events dramatized in the main body of the anime, Ayaka's entire family was brutally murdered. Ayaka herself would have fallen prey to the assassins had she not been so enraptured by her first white Christmas as to venture outdoors to view the family home "shining in the dark" from a nearby hill, while her parents added the finishing touches to the lavish fare prepared in anticipation of a joyful party.

As the young Ayaka beholds the splendid view, all the lights within her home are suddenly extinguished and ominous flashes thereafter rupture the gloom. The girl rushes back to the abode, enters it tentatively and goes about exploring it in an excruciatingly suspenseful sequence that comes abruptly to an end as she slips and collapses into a pool of still warm blood. The visual style used for these frames contributes critically to their dramatic impact, especially in the adoption of a restrained monochrome in preference to the lurid palette one could expect of comparable moments in a stereotypical slasher. A grand ceremony is held in honor of Ayaka's father, the GPO Commissioner at the time of his assassination, and of his wife and son, at the end of which the orphan is mendaciously reassured that the people responsible for the tragedy have all been apprehended.

Ayaka does not seem to accept unquestioningly the veracity of this information, as though she could sense that the evil forces behind the massacre were still at large and indeed capable of yet more heinous crimes. Her suspicions are reinforced by the eerie sensations she experiences upon revisiting the deserted house. Legion voices echo inside her head, "laughing" at her and haunting the place as so many disembodied memories: "It's like a venom," she observes. "The venom that lingered in the house and refused to leave." A further flashback to the tragedy is offered in telescoped form in the scene where Wong inspects some documentary material concerning the atrocity, and then again as a rapid sequence playing in Ayaka's own mind. The festivity after which Kurau's symbiote is named is thus effectively used as a dramatic catalyst to bring together Kurau's and Ayaka's discordant recollections. While for Ayaka, as we have seen, Christmas is a time of tragedy coinciding with the loss of her family, for Kurau, it will prove synonymous with a panoply of cherished memories.

The sequences capturing Ayaka's traumatic past gain special pathos from their agile intercutting with some adrenaline-pumping and buoyantly comical action centered on Kurau's involvement in a "Pod Battle"—a hugely popular sport indigenous to the island that temporarily shelters the protagonists, attracting flocks of fans from outside as a major tourist attraction. The game entails the deployment of *mecha* suits in the shape of armored monowheels equipped with all manner of bizarre weapons, including giant drills. The scenes focusing on Kurau's fight as a temporary member of the "Skull Team" bear witness to Irie's penchant for instilling the drama with felicitously placed concessions to humor in spite of the story's pervasively somber mood.

Following their island-based exploits, Kurau and Christmas end up in California. Shortly after their arrival at this new provisional haven, Kurau senses a potent wave of Rynax coursing through her body which her Pair later senses, too, though on a smaller scale. By tracing it back to its source, she and Christmas discover a massive research facility, the "Rynax Energy Plant," devoted to the rapid extraction of Rynax power. Recognizing the magnitude of the plot into which she and Christmas have been inveigled, yet unaware of its ultimate objectives, Kurau concludes that much as she would like to go on traveling round the world with her treasured symbiote, she must confront her father and ascertain once and for all the true nature of Rynax.

Kurau is particularly distressed to realize that what she has perceived is an "extension" of the "will" of one of the myriad Rynax trapped within the facility, and that what the inmates desire is to be released into the vast world outside. Christmas fears that if the imprisoned Rynax were to make use of Kurau as their channel of escape, her Pair could be irremediably damaged. Yet, both girls are eager to find a way of helping the alien entities overcome their predicament. The GPO, however, capture them before they have a chance to formulate a viable plan. Kurau and Christmas are paralyzed by recourse to a formidable ARS and placed into insulated coffin-like vessels. Although Kurau regains consciousness and manages to escape her container, while Christmas remains comatose, the older Pair's own powers are left severely impaired by the GPO assault.

Kurau's distress escalates when, having been rescued by Doug, she must cope not only with the torment of having lost her Pair but also with the horror of the fate met by the caged Rynax within the plant. The creatures' telepathic response to Kurau's presence in their vicinity has apparently triggered an "abnormal surge of energy" in the facility's generator, and the activation of the safety system has resulted in the entities' total termination. Kurau's grief is exacerbated by her suspicions regarding Dr. Amami's possible implication in the development of Rynax energy, and hence in the activities carried out at the plant. In actual fact, as indicated, Kurau's father has indeed worked on Rynax energy and the GPO has contrived ways of using his research of which he sternly disapproves.

These events prove that despite her powers, Kurau does not belong with the magical superhero(in)es so common in sci-fi cinema. The latter are often so flamboyantly portrayed that any sense of their connection to a human bedrock is effaced, and any intimation that they may carry flaws as well as stupendous abilities is therefore avoided. Irie's protagonist, conversely, has limits that serve to remind us of her underlying vulnerability. The sensitivity to life's transience implicit in the ethos of *mono no aware* is tersely communicated by Irie's portrayal of his heroine. After her flight from the GPO, for example, Kurau comes across most explicitly not as a superpowered wonder but as a bloodied, battered and dispirited victim. Her habitually vigorous body is as limp as a mollusk's when Doug finds her and picks her up in his arms. Later, when her protracted battle against the twins and the Ryna-Sapien corps, combined with the struggle to return errant Rynax back to their world, finally takes its toll, the protagonist is visibly enfeebled and not even her Pair can unproblematically replenish her exhausted frame. Thus, while on the stylistic plane *Kurau* is far more colorful and friendly than comparable anime centered on hyperpowered heroines, such as Mamoru Oshii's movie *Ghost in the Shell* (1995), it nonetheless communicates a grave and, at times, even tragic mood in the depiction of the protagonist's intrinsically human weakness.

It is with Kurau's and Doug's concerted effort to remove both Christmas and Dr. Amami from the clutches of the GPO that the show most eloquently asserts its flair for spectacular visual effects abetted by technology at the levels of both onscreen imagery and behind-the-scenes animation procedures. Nevertheless, it is not through the hi-tech element that *Kurau* proclaims its distinctive artistic identity but through its evocation of a sense of the numinous suffused with human warmth that one might less readily associate with science fiction than with legend, mythology or the classic fairy tale. This is resplendently borne out by the climactic sequence in which Kurau and Christmas, mocking not just the GPO weaponry and orders but the laws of reason themselves, break through the formidable cages erected around them by means of anti–Rynax irradiation and defiantly soar above their enemies.

The adventure's multifaceted take on memory is unexpectedly complicated, at one stage, by the presentation of a lyrical flashback experienced by the otherwise impenetrable Inspector Wong. This features a young Kurau garbed in a long robe standing in a meadow covered with Alpine Roses. The meaning of this flashback will remain a mystery until Wong himself proffers explanation for the vision later in the show, while disclosing information that will prove of pivotal significance in the unraveling of *Kurau*'s secrets. Flashbacks become an incontestably dominant form of expression in the phase of the adventure where Kurau and Christmas's perilous odyssey takes them to Switzerland, where Kurau's aunt Kleine— her departed mother's sister — and her uncle Frank live. The tone is set by a flashback to Kurau's childhood recording the moment of her separation from her father. This discloses that Dr. Amami, having realized that the only way of preventing the girl's exploitation as an object of scientific analysis was to remove her from his laboratory, decided to entrust her to the care of his sole relatives, Frank and Kleine.

The portions of the adventure set in Switzerland undoubtedly constitute its most memory-laden component. Especially important, in this regard, are the sequences dramatizing Kurau's hiking expeditions with the endearingly plucky Uncle Frank, who plays a key part in helping the girl discover her goals and resolve to deploy her special abilities to help others. Frank's own professional background as a valiant agent would enable him to supply Kurau with memorable lessons, underpinned at all times by an emphasis on the incomparable value of the ultimate ethical pair: self-understanding and self-reliance. While these recollections benevolently sustain the present-day narrative, they also haunt it with intimations of lost innocence and fading hope: in other words, the mnemonic vestiges of an irrecuperable past. The spectral mood is corroborated by Kurau's realization that although there is nothing she would like more than to be able to contact her dad and Doug to tell them that she and Christmas are still alive, she cannot do so without making it possible for the GPO to locate the fugitives: this, she speculates, is what "it must feel like when you become a ghost."

The peaceful rural life provided by the Swiss location constitutes a welcome relief but the Alpine idyll is disrupted by the advent of Yvon Tardieu, another Ryna Sapien occupying the body of a young boy who is desperate to obtain a Pair and has his eyes on Christmas as an ideal candidate. Yvon's desperate pursuit of Christmas elicits sympathy for the unmatched Rynax (even though many viewers will feel instinctively inclined to side with the co-protagonist) because the memory of Kurau's own sorrowful loneliness prior to her symbiote's advent is still resonantly alive. What differentiates Yvon's struggle to put an end to his solitude from Kurau's own experience is that whereas the heroine endured her pain with stoical resignation, the boy's obstinacy appears to respect no limits. Thus, he does not hesitate to destroy human life with utter remorselessness when his scheme is hindered.

This indicates that not all Rynax are the same since individual specimens actually harbor distinct personalities. In Yvon's case, the potential for callous conduct results from the preponderance of "Rynax will" within his makeup. This is eventually explained as a corollary of the creature's origins: Yvon, it transpires, is one of several synthetic Rynax experimentally created by the GPO by infecting ordinary humans with the alien life form, and his dubious ethics are a direct outcome of his manufacturers' botching of the materials at their disposal. In contaminating the human boy with Rynax, they simply failed to preserve the element of humaneness that would keep him from following unquestioningly the commands of the Rynax within. This same curse, it is later revealed, afflicts other test subjects produced by the GPO — most notably, the twins Windt and Regel Delyus to be introduced in the adventure's climactic installments.

Kurau's adamant refusal to comply with Yvon's plan leads to violent ramifications. These include a tense fight in a forest that leads to a great deal of unplanned conifer-felling, as well as a subaqueous battle beneath the turquoise surface of a glacial lake. In this sequence, Kurau is able to enter her adversary's mind and hence witnesses, in the form of a flashback, the drama of Yvon's loss of a legitimate Pair at the very time of his conception as a hybrid species. These memories are deftly intercut with a flashback to the heroine's own entry into the human world — and especially the moment of her introjection of the strand of Rynax destined to become Christmas a decade later. Yvon's ordeal is rendered all the more tragic by his discovery and almost immediate loss of a substitute symbiote in the person of Jessica, a local girl who has lost her parents in the aforementioned industrial accident. Jessica herself was hit by Rynax at the time but was believed to have remained miraculously uncontaminated. In fact, the girl is a full-fledged Rynax with impressive abilities, unbeknownst to her as well as to the GPO (at least officially).

As she deploys her hitherto unsuspected powers to rescue Yvon from the GPO, Jessica is destroyed by their persecutors' brutal attack and dissolves into a gentle rain of preternaturally effulgent sparks. Yvon's grief is so overwhelming that he, too, appears to disintegrate into a nebula of Rynax energy. Kurau temporarily saves him and endeavors to protect him to the bitter end from both the GPO and his own suicidal derangement. Nonetheless, the bereft Rynax's thirst for revenge ineluctably leads to his annihilation, which triggers so intense a feeling of devastation in Christmas as to cause her body to release phenomenal hordes of Rynax. It is now Kurau's turn to counteract her Pair's unintentional but calamitous act by incorporating the entities and returning them to their world. These events demonstrate that even as *Kurau*'s action escalates to feverish levels, packed with breathtaking sequences and an ever-rising body count, it is not the dynamic element per se that infuses the series with memorable pathos so much as the genuine sense of the emotional and psychological schisms underpinning its kinesis. The tragic conclusion of Yvon's quest has much to contribute to *Kurau*'s emotive import and contrasts sharply with the serenity provided by the sequences concentrating on the protagonists' daily life and by the utopian hints at a regenerated habitat peppering the narrative.

This part of the narrative does not only yield memorable pathos in the orchestration of Yvon's vicissitudes; it also sows the seeds of the emotionally complex relationship between Kurau and Ayaka to be incrementally developed over the rest of the story. At this juncture, it is thanks to Kurau that Ayaka realizes that the GPO is keeping some crucial secrets from her. Kurau's revelation that Yvon was a manmade product is especially shocking, for it intimates that there might be many things which the Captain does not yet know about Rynax and how humans use them. Thus far, Ayaka has unquestioningly been hunting down Kurau in her hatred of Rynax life, which she holds responsible for the deaths of her loved ones. The heroine's eye-opening declaration induces her to reassess her position, delve deeper into her employers' agenda and eventually come to regard Kurau as an ally.

The turning point is the scene in which Ayaka realizes what exactly Kurau was doing in the wake of Yvon's disintegration by shielding the GPO vehicles from the storm of Rynax gushing out of Christmas's body: "She was trying to protect *us—us—* even after all we have done to her. And what did we do? We shot them." This time around, the leads' capture does not lead to long-term imprisonment; however. Wong has by now ascertained that the GPO's schemes are abominable and is therefore keen on holding Kurau and Christmas just long enough to share with them — and with Ayaka, at last — some unsavory truths. At this point, the Alpine flashback seen to be traversing the Inspector's mind earlier on is also explained. Wong saw Kurau in Switzerland when she was just a kid in the process of deploying her superpowers to soar over a lake but deliberately avoided reporting the occurrence to the authorities, even though he had just been appointed to locate such a creature, because he already had doubts about their goals and could not understand why they could possibly want to hunt her down. (The Alpine meadow in which the flashback is set is one of the show's most memorable settings, and Irie's desire to honor its symbolic significance is subtly conveyed by the use of that same location as the subject of a painting decorating the cabin where Kurau, Christmas and Yvon find temporary shelter.)

It is at this same stage in the adventure that Wong reveals that the GPO executives and scientists have been intent on producing artificial Ryna Sapiens out of humans, aiming to use them as combat drones "completely under their control" so as to keep the rest of humanity "under their heel forever." Promises are accorded a special role in *Kurau*'s diegesis, and this is succinctly corroborated by Wong's parting words to the heroine: "Since it's unlikely that we will meet again, please promise that you'll survive." Finally, just before he is unceremoniously removed from his post and officially "transferred" but most probably silenced, the Inspector reveals to Ayaka that the first germ of his suspicion concerning the GPO was planted the very day her family was massacred and that Commissioner Saito, the GPO's current head, was responsible for the crime. Additionally, Wong informs Ayaka that Saito, in cahoots with Ichise, is also the man responsible for initiating the production of synthetic Ryna Sapiens.[2]

It is in the aftermath of these harrowing disclosures that Ayaka leaves the GPO headquarters and seeks out Kurau, this time not for the purpose of apprehending her but to enlist her help. The scenes in which Ayaka visits Kurau in Switzerland at her aunt and uncle's home and gradually establishes a connection with her erstwhile enemy based on mutual trust, while the whole family readily accepts Kurau's judgment and treats the Captain as a welcome guest, exude a genuine sense of human warmth without ever indulging in cheap sentimentalism. This is largely due to Irie's ability never to lose sight of the domestic element that has made the narrative so disarmingly endearing from the start even when momentous political intrigues appear to dominate the action. That element is beautifully captured by the frames in which Christmas, eager to make Ayaka feel part of the family in preparation for dinner, thrusts a head of lettuce into her hands and prompts her to contribute a salad to the menu. The sight of the normally belligerent officer chopping vegetables in absorbed silence while Aunt Kleine and Christmas put the final touches to their near-legendary stew (another visual refrain of great mnemonic resonance) is one of the show's least sensational, and yet most enduring, dramatic gems.

These sequences bear incontrovertible witness both to *Kurau*'s emphasis on the adventure's human dimension and to Irie's avoidance of blunt binary oppositions in the apportioning of positive and negative character attributes. As argued, this is most persuasively demonstrated by the portrayal of Ayaka. However, even the dastardly Saito is spared stereotypical treatment as a cardboard villain by the revelation — through a blood-soaked flashback — that he has been led to his current course of action by devastating events, set about fifty years prior to the beginning of the series, in which he experienced firsthand the horrific consequences of civil unrest and hence conceived of the need for a system capable of guaranteeing unbreachable order. His determination to keep humanity under total control by recourse to artificial soldiers strikes its roots in those traumatic experiences and this makes it understandable if not exactly legitimate. In developing rich characters that typically walk the moral tightrope between good and evil within a meticulously layered plot, *Kurau* ensures throughout that its human and Rynax actors remain central to the narrative instead of being swamped by the potentially epic scope of its themes.

Kurau's and Ayaka's freshly established alliance results in the Rynax couple's decision to locate the twins Windt and Regel, former members of the GPO's "Special Missions Unit," on whom Ichise has performed dire experiments culminating in their metamorphosis into a Rynax dyad. Kurau's intention is to intercept the twins before the GPO tracks them down and they meet a dismal end analogous to Yvon's. As it happens, the protagonist's noble objective is quite beside the point, since Saito has actually instructed Windt and Regel to capture Kurau on his behalf. The twins, however, do not seem disposed to listen to anybody's orders, their sole governing drive being the Rynax they will host.

When Kurau and Christmas eventually pinpoint the twins in the picturesque town of Marseille, France, they do not come across as "victims" in the classic sense of the term.

Although we know, as the leads do, that the creatures are ill-fated casualties of Saito's diabolical machinations, Windt and Regel appear to feel in full control of their destiny at this stage. Their ultimate objective is to capture Kurau and cause Rynax life to pour out of her body so as to allow the species to inhabit the human world and hence experience to the full its vastness and beauty. As an interim strategy, they devote themselves to the feckless disruption of their environment and its human inhabitants. Turning a perfectly flat road surface into an undulating amusement ride, twisting lampposts into curlicues and creating surreal sculptures out of assorted junk are just a few of the flamboyant games played by the twins to throw the human world into disarray. Unfortunately, these relatively unharmful pursuits do not fully satisfy their expressive urge: the result is the perpetration of undilutedly nefarious actions — including the destruction of a bridge and a titanic train crash causing hundreds of fatalities — performed with the glee one might expect of a reticulated python entering a playground on a sunny afternoon.

Windt and Regel openly declare that they felt summoned by Kurau's voice and were drawn to the human world precisely as a result of her experiences therein. This places an unpalatable burden on the heroine's already fraught conscience. Up until now, Kurau has had good reason to believe that Rynax do not attack humans unless they are overtly threatened but the twins' actions force her to reassess her species' intrinsic nature since they are gratuitously destructive moves and not responses to provocation. The cause of Windt's and Regel's behavior is not so much the Rynax life form per se as its pernicious manipulation by Ichise, who has simply failed to perceive the importance of preserving a modicum of humanity in his test subjects. This partly condones the twins' performance, the brutality of which reaches its zenith in the context of a traditional ceremony in which large crowds float candles along a river at night to celebrate the forthcoming Yuletide. Finding the scene beautiful, yet convinced that they have the power to enhance its majesty, Windt and Regel flood it with monstrous waves of incandescent Rynax energy that cause thousands of lives to be "extinguished in a heartbeat." The tragic irony of the situation is that from a purely cinematographical perspective, the twins' deed indeed delivers sublime images despite its horror.

The protagonists' determination to track down the twins and put an end to their mindless rage engages them in a chain of fierce fights that take a dreadful toll on the older Pair. The action here witnesses the first overt deployment of the utterly inhumane Ryna-Sapien troops manufactured by Ichise at Saito's behest, providing some tantalizing spectacle. Yet, the human emotions coursing through the action are given priority over flashy displays of martial valor. Every hailstorm of deadly moves or fiery hits is counterbalanced by a tenderly poetic moment. This is most patently borne out by the scenes where Kurau and Christmas endeavor to help Windt and Regel reestablish a connection with their human substratum and recover the repressed traces of their lives as ordinary men. Especially powerful, in this regard, is the scene where Christmas, in the climax of a fight against Regel, silently communicates to him the memories she has accumulated in the human world to convey what she has experienced and why, in the process, humans of all kinds have become profoundly important to her. The twin instantly feels a forgotten sense of warmth radiating from his arm, touched by the girl while transmitting the images to his brain in the form of a rapid montage, and his own recollections of childhood and early youth suddenly resurface.

When Kurau is hounded down by the Ryna-Sapien forces and Regel rescues her, she immediately senses his drastic change and newly acquired warmth. This impression contrasts sharply with the sensation experienced by Kurau in her first physical contact with the twin, where her forearm goes bitingly cold the moment he touches it. Sadly, fate does not afford Regel the chance to enjoy his new state for long: the Ryna-Sapien army soon surrounds and destroys the reformed twin, causing his disintegration into myriad streaks of Rynax energy. However, his metamorphosis enables Windt to rediscover his buried humanity, as well. As with Regel, the recovery is ushered in by a stream of stirring juvenile memories.

As Kurau strives to send the invading Rynax back home, her already enfeebled powers receive an almost fatal blow. Nevertheless, she remains determined to see her mission through to completion though this may imperil her very life. She accordingly channels all her remaining strength into the pursuit of Windt, who is hell-bent on avenging his brother's death, to prevent his murderous ire from inadvertently inflicting further suffering on innocent humans. As Windt hunts Saito down through the GPO headquarters, Ayaka finds herself in the paradoxical role of the Commissioner's protector — a part she has spontaneously assumed in her commitment to the protection of life without pausing to ponder her personal feelings towards the infamous executive. Saito does meet a fitting fate at the hands of the implacable twin, while Windt himself unleashes a portentous swarm of Rynax which Kurau takes it upon herself to tame, in a climactic display of heroism and generosity.

Memory plays a particularly conspicuous role in the closing installment, where the climax of Kurau's confrontation with the myriad Rynax seeking to enter the human world is disclosed by means of flashbacks. The first plays out in Christmas's mind as she sits, utterly alone and disconsolate, on the plane taking her away from Kurau, while the latter lies unconscious in a hospital bed. The second issues from Dr. Amami's memories of the final moments of the heroine's momentous task. Taken in tandem, the two flashbacks reveal that Kurau has sent the Rynax invaders back to their universe, feeling responsible for their advent in the awareness that they were unwittingly summoned by her own voice. At the end, Kurau actually suggests to her dad that the Rynax life form possibly came into this world in the first place in response to her personal need to fill the void left in her heart by her mother's premature death. In transferring the Rynax to another dimension, the protagonist has concurrently caused the alien element within her to relinquish its human vessel. Kurau has thus regained her human identity, which leaves Christmas in the dire predicament endured by Kurau herself prior to the symbiote's arrival in the early part of the story.

Kurau's redemptive act endows her with godlike connotations. In this respect, she is comparable to other anime characters — such as the eponymous heroine in Hayao Miyazaki's *Nausicaä of the Valley of the Wind* (1984) and Shinji Ikari in Hideaki Anno's and Kazuya Tsurumaki's *The End of Evangelion* (1997)— who likewise embrace, both heroically and self-sacrificially, the role of savior. This idea is corroborated by an exchange where Wong informs Ayaka that the production of Rynax energy has been discontinued since its efficiency has dropped dramatically over the decade following Kurau's final mission. When he opines that the cause of this decline might be Kurau's removal of the Rynax to a remote cosmic location, Ayaka riposteS: "Kurau always did take it on herself to protect everyone else, regardless of the cost. That's just how she was."

In elliptically positing Kurau as a numinous entity, Irie's show echoes an indigenous tradition steeped in the teachings of the Shinto religion. While in the Judeo-Christian system, god is conceived of as external to both time and space, in Shinto the divine is a spiritual force filling the universe in its entirety — mountains, trees, rivers and rocks, as well as humans and other animals. Accordingly, in Judeo-Christian cultures, it is assumed that a more peaceful and harmonious world could only be brought about by god as a transcendental being. In Shinto, the idea that divinity flows through the entire cosmos entails that the world might be altered by *any* living presence — humans included. *Kurau* takes this proposition to daring extremes, suggesting that even a creature that is not wholly (or indeed primarily) human may feel so keen a sense of affection and responsibility towards the human world as to seek to rebalance it at the cost of its very survival.

Following her recovery, Kurau resumes a seemingly ordinary human existence in the old parental home but still remembers all of the things that happened when she was with the Rynax, and feels that "person" was happy to be where she was and deeply grateful to Dr. Amami for his kindness towards her. Yet, she also vividly recalls the creature's sadness at the realization that she would not have sufficient time left to bid goodbye to Dr. Amami. However, in using the very last "bit of energy" at her disposal to save the hosting body and thus give it back to the scientist, she was able to honor the promise made at the beginning of the adventure. The pivotal importance of promises in the entire series is thus conclusively confirmed by the finale.

The human Kurau's ability to remember intimately her experiences as a Rynax container also entails that Christmas is still effectively alive in her mind. As the heroine mulls over these emotions, the memory-saturated quality of the final episode is reinforced by a flashback to an especially happy Christmas celebration in her childhood: an event lovingly staged by her ailing mother in order to bequeath some happy reminiscences on her child in the knowledge that she has nothing else left to give. The symbolic significance of the occasion is also foreshadowed by the scene in which Dr. Amami declares that he could never bring himself to extirpate the Rynax from Kurau's body, since her decision to name her Pair "Christmas" tells him that she is still his child. The word indeed echoes the joyful festivity dreamed up by Mrs. Amami as her parting gift: it is the "phantom memory" transmitted by the human Kurau to the Rynax Kurau and then embodied by her precious Pair. (It is also noteworthy, in this regard, that Dr. Amami first feels with utter certainty that Kurau is still his daughter despite her invasion by Rynax just after she has experienced a flashback to the human Kurau's mother, destined to become pivotal to the story as a whole. It is as though the scientist could telepathically sense the child's fleeting memory.)

Kurau soon resolves to visit Christmas in Switzerland, where the girl has been relocated and leads a peaceful life as Aunt Kleine's and Uncle Frank's foster niece. At this point, the bittersweet mood pervading the closing segment asserts itself most poignantly — so much so that it is tempting to suggest that had the word "bittersweet" not existed, it would have been necessary to coin it just for the occasion. Most notable, in this respect, is the scene in which Kurau reassures Christmas that the bond between them has the power to endure thanks to the memories they both treasure. "I know that I'll never be able to take the place of your Kurau," the protagonist affectionately states. "But you're still very dear to me, Christmas. Because I was there, too, watching you all along ... watching you and your Kurau the entire time." Christmas, in turn, remembers the voice of the human Kurau's mother resounding through her soul every step of the way with the words "I promise I will always be with you." This voice, arguably, is the ultimate phantom memory planted by

Kurau's mother before her untimely departure alongside the memory of the happy festivity that inspired the choice of the word "Christmas" as the Pair's rightful designation. As a result, Christmas is now able to feel that the lost Kurau goes on living in her own heart. As Aunt Kleine intimates earlier in the show while talking with Christmas about Kurau's mother, "Sometimes it's your memories that make you what you are."

The resurfacing of the phantom memory has an illuminating effect on both girls, sharpening their understanding of both their past experiences and their future destinations. This is consonant with the etymology of the word "phantom" itself. Indeed, while the term is associated with notions of illusion and unreality, and — like the related term "phantasm" — with the idea of a spectral image, it is also linked, via the Greek words *phantazein* ("to make visible") and *phantasia* ("perception," "imagination") to the root *phos*, "light." Hence, though phantoms may at times be dismissed as whimsical figments divorced from reality, they also implicitly allude to epiphanic and enlightening possibilities likely to enhance our grasp of reality.

The phantom memory retained by the Rynax Kurau and passed onto Christmas is intangible, yet gradually acquires the quality of a palpable, solid presence. This makes it akin to a phantom limb: a body part that can still be felt after its amputation. The Phenomenologist philosopher Maurice Merleau-Ponty has speculated on this uncanny experience in ways that are profoundly relevant to Irie's series. Merleau-Ponty uses the image of the phantom limb to substantiate his belief in the corporeal character of human consciousness. He argues, specifically, that the mind-body dualism promulgated by René Descartes and Rationalism after him — which regards the body as a "machine" and the mind as the conscious spirit (the "ghost") that runs it — is specious. This is because it fails to acknowledge that consciousness is not a disembodied entity locked up inside the skull but rather a faculty that is experienced and enacted through the body. The phantom limb exemplifies this hypothesis: if the body were merely a machine and a part of it were removed, it would simply find a way of functioning without that part, as long as this was dispensable. The fact that people can feel a severed limb and even the call to use it suggests that consciousness does not go on exclusively within the head but actually inhabits the whole physical organism. The body is indeed the living entity through which we express our possibilities in the world. In the case of the phantom limb, hypothetical possibilities for its use remain even if the limb itself is missing and cannot therefore realize those possibilities. It still functions as a channel through which consciousness can express itself despite its physical absence (Merleau-Ponty).

Kurau communicates germane concepts in its articulation of the relationship between humans and Rynax. Witnessing the human girl's metamorphosis, we may at first be led to believe that her body has become purely a vessel for the alien life form, devoid of any connection with the human consciousness that inhabited it prior to the disastrous experiment. The ensuing action rectifies this initial impression by providing ample evidence for the survival of the girl's consciousness within that body in the form of enduring memories. The corporeal dimension of consciousness is thereby foregrounded. It is precisely because the shape of the human Kurau's body is salvaged that vestiges of her consciousness can be kept alive and communicated. The reconfigured Kurau may not be in a position to actualize the possibilities for expression available to the original Kurau. Nevertheless, her body goes on functioning as the vehicle through which those possibilities can continue asserting their validity — hence, her retention of a strong human component and eventual ability to return the human Kurau to her world. The phantom memory constitutes the sustaining force through which Kurau's human consciousness preserves its hold on the Rynax life form pervading her body. If the survival of the human girl's body had merely amounted to the survival of a machinelike receptacle devoid of consciousness, this could never have come to pass.

What is arguably most effective about *Kurau* is its sustained ability to foreground the concurrently physical and psychological nature of the split it dramatizes, never according either the body or the mind uncontested priority. Memory, relatedly, is seen to emanate from the main characters' material reality no less than from their spiritual essence. At the same time, the series employs the concept of *kire* as an axial narrative ploy, while also combining it with the germane principle of *kire tsuzuki*. Kurau's fatal accident constitutes an experience of corporeal and affective fracture so traumatic as to bear all the symptoms of an unhealable diremption. Nonetheless, synergetic forces connecting her fate not only with Christmas's but also with the destinies of several human personae usher in lines of continuity and hence the possibility of redemptive harmonization.

Although Christmas gains comfort from the realization that Kurau lives on inside her, her situation is far from ideal. Indeed, while all the surviving human characters (including Ayaka, Wong and a rehumanized Windt) move on, build families and consolidate their careers over the course of a decade, Christmas is left stranded in a world where she ultimately does not belong as long as she remains unpaired in a physical sense. She puts on a brave face, finds employment as a maid in a local restaurant and in time rises to the status of an acclaimed chef, maintaining close connections with Ayaka, Doug and Ted. Yet, Christmas feels grievously lonely and bereft and her situation does not improve as the years roll by. It is ironical that the habitually sunnier half of the Rynax couple we have come to know and love should stand out, at the end, as the more tragic figure. Ted, to whom Christmas at one point refers as her "boyfriend," is able to see through the girl's illusory cheerfulness, suggesting to his father that beneath each of her radiant smiles, there lies the shadow of unspeakable loneliness.

In a dreamlike sequence, Christmas eventually soars above the Alpine lake used as a visual refrain through a large part of the adventure and releases from her very body a young version of Kurau. Since approximately ten years have now elapsed since Christmas's own advent into the human world, it would seem that the girl has had to wait for her Pair to materialize for as long as Kurau herself had to wait in the first place. Although the Rynax corralled by Kurau in her final mission have seemingly migrated to a distant universe, Christmas's Pair has chosen to remain behind to be by her side and thus fulfill the old vow always to be with her. Promises remain crucial to the very end. As the new Kurau greets her Pair with the words "I'm home, Christmas," the human Kurau senses across space that the Rynax dyad has been reunited at last. Looking up at the Earth from her Moon-based location, she affectionately says, "Christmas — she's home, isn't she? Your Kurau."

Kurau undoubtedly offers some stunning visual effects. The most memorable coincide with the activation of Rynax powers in the course of various missions and battles. At times, Kurau becomes surrounded by an aureate halo that suddenly explodes into a tangle of lightning bolts and arcs. At others, the focus is on the luminous ripples that erupt in the gloom as each of Kurau's feet makes contact with the ground while she runs or leaps across roofs.

Especially remarkable is the Rynax-related visual effect portraying a powerful burst of light, bifurcating into the nocturnal city sky at a preternatural speed. This shot is vividly reminiscent of the frames from the very first episode devoted to the fatal accident from which the entire adventure emanates. This could be regarded as a stylistic and technical flashback, mirroring the show's assiduous use of thematic flashbacks through its unfolding. Yet, as argued, Irie's primary aim is to underscore the centrality of relationships and germane affects to the story's development, and he therefore intentionally refrains from glitzy or overblown spectacle of the kind so often dished out by futuristic anime. Relatedly, when violence erupts, which it regularly does, its import is dramatic rather than graphic. Moreover, an atmosphere of wistful longing pervades the series' most affecting moments, evoking the aesthetic legacy of *mono no aware*.

The psychological dichotomy explored in Irie's show is foreshadowed by the TV series *Noir* (dir. Kouichi Mashimo, 2001). This chronicles two women's intertwined attempts to reconcile their present activities as top-notch contract killers and their roots in a remote past steeped in myth. Indeed, as Mireille Bouquet seeks to fathom the mystery of her past and Kirika Yuumura struggles to recover her memories, the protagonists' lives reveal themselves to be inextricably linked to an ancient organization — "Les Soldats" — striving to realize a momentous event known simply as the "Grand Retour." "Noir," it transpires, is the name given by Les Soldats to a pair of young women, carefully selected according to time-honored ritual requiring numerous trials — hence, the repeated attempts on Mireille's and Kirika's lives punctuating the series as the two assassins carry out their increasingly challenging assignments. Critical to the story's dénouement is the discovery that when Mireille was little, Les Soldats were determined to train her within their ranks and that her family's refusal to comply resulted in their massacre. Kirika was sent to murder them and flawlessly accomplished her goal. Paradoxically, however, she also promised Mireille's dying mother to take care of the orphaned girl.

While Mireille and Kirika pursue their personal "pilgrimage to the past," the visuals themselves indulge in a glorious mnemonic journey through a plethora of European locations tinged with exotic connotations. (The notion of *akogare no Paris* mentioned in Chapter 3 is again relevant.) At the same time, the cryptic diegesis assiduously revisits bygone eras by recourse to elaborate symbolism and esoteric codes. Mashimo's attention to details is so punctilious as to evoke a credible sense of lived history even when the series indulges most candidly in the pleasures of fabulation. The boundary between historiography and fiction is thus irreverently eroded. *Noir* offers a classic dramatization of the notion of *kire* in its depiction of a schizoid scenario wherein the two heroines' memories are dissected and dispersed across their separate psyches. Yet, it summons the mechanism of *kire tsuzuki* no less pervasively, establishing a powerful bond between Mireille and Kirika that ultimately carries healing potentialities.

The themes of amnesia and mnemonic fracture anticipated by *Noir* and foregrounded by *Kurau* are also axial to *Elfen Lied* (TV series; dir. Mamoru Kanbe, 2004). The most sensational split is dramatized through the character of a "Diclonius," a mutant endowed with horn-like protrusions and unique telekinetic powers, that has escaped from a high-security lab leaving a hecatomb behind her. Having got shot in the head and fallen into the sea, the creature is rescued by a boy named Kouta and his cousin Yuka, who kindly offer her shelter. Dubbed "Lucy" by the scientists that held her captive, the creature is named "Nyu" by

Kouta and Yuka since this is the only word she is able to utter when they find her. The fall appears to have deprived the Diclonius not only of her memories but also of her fundamental personality, transforming the erstwhile ruthless Lucy into a meek and innocent *shoujo*. However, the persona of the gentle amnesiac salvaged by Kouta and Yuka is periodically displaced by a resurgent Lucy as bloodthirsty and compassionless as ever. Unlike Nyu, Lucy harbors very clear memories of her provenance and objective: namely, the extermination of the human race. The sequence in which she tears off the limbs of the Diclonius sent to apprehend her, Nana, while the latter begs for a peaceful negotiation is nothing short of harrowing. Subsequent shots of Nana's miserable body, enshrouded in heavy bandages like some grotesque, doll-like parody of a mummy and awaiting the fatal jab, further enhance the horror of Lucy's actions.

Kouta, too, labors under the bane of a mnemonic rift between the child self whose memories he latently hosts but has no conscious access to, having consigned them to oblivion in the aftermath of a major trauma, and the adolescent self trying to adapt to his new life in the town to which he has returned for the first time in eight years. Related to the split experienced by Kouta is the discrepancy between the boy's own haphazard grasp of the past, on the one hand, and his cousin's vivid remembrance of every minute detail of their shared childhood moments, on the other. Yuka, who has remained unwaveringly loyal to her cousin in all the long years of their separation in memory of their mutual devotion, feels betrayed by Kouta's utter inability to recall the images and promises she so deeply treasures. Although Yuka by and by accepts that Kouta is afflicted by amnesia and is therefore not to blame for his relative lack of warmth towards her, her emotional predicament is genuinely painful to behold—and by no means alleviated by Kouta's growing attachment to Nyu.

The two mnemonic strands involving Kouta and Nyu/Lucy are progressively woven together by suggestions that the two characters were at some point connected in a buried past: an event to which the show recurrently alludes through sudden flashbacks situated at especially poignant points. It eventually transpires that Kouta first met Nyu/Lucy when they were both children and that at the time, he was moved by her sadness and loneliness. Unfortunately, the Diclonius also turns out to have been responsible for the deaths of Kouta's dad and little sister. In an emotionally taxing dénouement, Nyu/Lucy tells Kouta that the only rays of sunshine in her otherwise unremittingly hellish existence were the days she got to spend with Kouta in infancy, and that the only thing that has kept her alive since has been the hope of meeting him again and apologizing for the immense trauma triggered by her violence. The first hint at a latent connection between Kouta's submerged memories and Nyu/Lucy's own past is dropped early in the series, when a casual reference to the Diclonius's "horns" evokes a blurred image of a creature with an outlandish cranial configuration in the boy's mind. Thus, an underlying sense of cohesion reminiscent of the aesthetics of *kire tsuzuki* gradually emerges in spite of the plot's *kire*-inflected emphasis on fragmentation and disjuncture. Morcellated and impervious to synthesis as the various characters' memories may seem, the diegesis draws them into a potent emotional continuum.

Dismemberments, decapitations, scenes of torture and explicit allusions to sadomasochism pepper the action, and blood accordingly flows, gushes and oozes by turns. Yet, although graphic violence and gore abound in *Elfen Lied*, these are not the factors that make it memorable. Far more important is the show's frank exposure of humanity's darkest side. It is through its unsentimental treatment of the themes of abuse, abandonment, pedophilia, discrimination and uncontrollable desire for power that *Elfen Lied* proclaims its caliber as an anime that transcends by far the limitations of the classic slasher or body count movie. This bleak outlook, moreover, does not entail that the show has no redeeming messages to offer. In fact, Kouta's and Yuka's "adoption" of Nyu/Lucy attests to the contrary. So does Kouta's later decision to house the runaway teenager Maya and the mutilated Diclonius Nana, when the latter is discarded by her "Papa" instead of being put to sleep — as would be expected, given her "uselessness" once she has lost her limbs.

Finally, it should be noted that *Elfen Lied* also engages with memory at a specifically iconic level, intertextually deploying images adapted from Gustav Klimt's most famous works in its opening. The employment of memorable gems of a well-known artist's opus in this context establishes a cross-temporal dialogue between the popular art of anime and the canonical art of painting with visual memory as its currency. "Lilium," the opening theme, is sung in Latin and its lyrics contain several references to the Psalms (as well as other biblical elements), which makes it sound just like a Gregorian chant. These additional intertextual echoes contribute significantly to the show's mnemonic tapestry.

The apportioning of related memories over distinct psyches is also at the core of the TV series *MoonPhase* (dir. Akiyuki Shinbo, 2004–2005). This proposes that memories elude classification as individual possessions and are indeed capable of soaring above personal boundaries, weaving subtle threads of connection among disparate beings. *MoonPhase* dramatizes this hypothesis by intertwining the lives of its protagonists — Hazuki (a cute vampire girl) and Kouhei Morioka (a photographer of supernatural phenomena) — around their respective memories of lost mothers. The bond is incrementally consolidated by the intimation that the two women's destinies are also connected. This diegetic strategy enables *MoonPhase* to cultivate an atmosphere of continuity-in-separation redolent of the principle of *kire tsuzuki*. Hazuki's and Kouhei's recollections thus transcend the limits of their individual experiences, establishing a potent bond between two otherwise extraneous life histories. This point will be returned to. The split-memory theme is further complicated by Hazuki's own division into her habitual self and an alter ego named Luna: an alternate personality forced upon her by her vampire relatives in order to keep her under control. The psychological schism experienced by the heroine as she oscillates between charm and viciousness, innocence and spite, coquettish cuteness and aggravating whimsicality, is reflected by the show's mood as clownish and brooding by turns.

When Kouhei visits the quintessentially Gothic German castle of Schwartz Quelle, where Hazuki is held prisoner, in the hope of photographing the compound and its ghoulish contents, the girl rapidly proceeds to suck the young man's blood in order to turn him into her slave. Yet, Kouhei has a reputation for being so unreceptive when it comes to paranormal phenomena (his grandfather, a mystic, describes him as "spiritually retarded") as to be immune to their power — hence, his ability to capture them on film as though they were utterly normal occurrences. Thus, Kouhei is left quite unscathed by Hazuki's onslaught and indeed sets her free, whereupon the girl resolves to go and live with Kouhei and his venerable ancestor in Japan. In the course of these events, the two main characters develop genuine feelings for each other, even though attempts to express them often result in arguments and rowdy slapstick. For one thing, Hazuki cannot quite accept that Kouhei has no intention of becoming her devout servant, and her reactions engender opportunities for hilarity even though the underlying darkness is never totally forgotten.

As mentioned, both Hazuki and Kouhei are haunted by the specter of parental absence. Indeed, Hazuki's principal reason for moving to Japan is her determination to locate her missing mother, who was forced to leave her at Schwartz Quelle when she was little. Kouhei at first accuses the girl of chasing useless fantasies, convinced that Hazuki's mother has deliberately abandoned her in the same way as he holds himself the casualty of intentional desertion on his own mother's part. Eventually, however, he agrees to help Hazuki in her quest, revealing mature respect for the autonomy of her memories. It is the enduring legacy of past experiences, albeit amorphous or occluded, that propels the protagonists into the future, thus underscoring the virtual interchangeability of disparate temporal levels. As the plot unfolds, it transpires that Hazuki is being hounded down by the mighty vampire Count Kinkel and by his most lethal assistant, the bespectacled babe Elfriede (once a human) so that she can be returned to the castle before their supremo finds out that she is missing. What Kinkel and Elfriede are actually seeking to advance, in this respect, is the perpetuation of illustrious memories enshrined in vampiric lore: a mission that requires the enlisting of Hazuki/Luna's powers to succeed. Once again, personal memories are shown to be inseparable from a sprawling heritage of encrusted recollections.

Emerging from a life in which every memory has been dominated by the schemes of her tyrannical family, Hazuki first experiences an authentic sense of freedom upon meeting Kouhei. This is because the young man, despite his apparent lack of paranormal abilities, is actually endowed with considerable psychic powers. As Elfriede reveals, the real reason for which no vampire can turn him into a servant is not that he is spiritualistically unreceptive but rather that he is a "Vampire Lover." Unaffected by the lethal bite, a creature of this ilk is also capable of neutralizing the servitude ties of any blood-drinker that feasts upon him. Having fed on Kouhei, Elfriede indeed resolves to destroy her own master, Kinkel. Kouhei's abeyant talent is akin to a repressed memory, and its gradual disclosure an allegory for a journey of self-discovery.[3]

As argued in the preceding analyses, all of the productions explored in this chapter engage with the aesthetic concepts of *kire* and *kire tsuzuki*. In so doing, they situate themselves within a distinctively Japanese world picture informed by the lessons of Zen. According to this philosophy, cutting oneself off from the constraints of contingent circumstances, and thus deliberately espousing a state of rootlessness, is the precondition of one's ability to grasp and adapt to the world's radical impermanence. All life forms and inanimate entities alike, Zen maintains, are essentially unanchored. To show things as they truly are, therefore, it is vital to present them as severed from any firm foundations. This idea is corroborated by the Japanese art of floral arrangement known as *ikebana*. Makoto Ueda maintains that the "ultimate aim" of this art is "to represent nature in its innermost essence" (Ueda, p. 86). "*Ikebana*" indeed means "make flowers alive" (*ikeru* = live, *hana* = flower). This may seem paradoxical, given that the art is predicated on the cutting of the living flower. In the logic of *kire*, however, it is precisely by detaching organic life from its roots in the earth that its true nature as a floating and transient phenomenon can be adequately revealed.

The works here examined dramatize the notion of *kire* by presenting their characters as adrift in a constantly mutating and unpredictable world, and hence as cut off from any prospects of stability. The severance manifests itself in two forms. On the one hand, the characters' identities are internally cut up. *Kurau*'s heroine is literally divided in half by the power of Rynax. In *Noir*, the female leads exhibit schizoid personalities produced by the conflict between a conscious self keenly responsive to its circumstances and a submerged self beset by amnesia. The partition of *Elfen Lied*'s protagonist into the lethal Lucy and the affable Nyu and the comparable splitting of *MoonPhase*'s heroine into Hazuki and Luna also point to inner cuts. On the other hand, experiences and memories are cut up within pairs of complementary personae: Kurau and Christmas, Mireille and Kirika, Lucy/Nyu and Kouta, Hazuki/Luna and Kouhei. Neither of the characters in each couple can function without its counterpart. This is brought home most overtly in the presentation of memories not as unified bundles unequivocally belonging to an individual but as slices of time carved up and apportioned to interdependent psyches. The anime thus emphasize the centrality of the concept of *kire* to their narratives. Yet, the cumulative effect of the cuttings they dramatize is to amplify the impalpable threads connecting the separate elements. This is borne out by the attribution of conflicting affects to distinct aspects of one single character's identity or else to complementary personae within a dyad. In both instances, the ethos of cut continuation encapsulated by *kire tsuzuki* is brought to the fore.

This trope connects the titles addressed in this chapter with Japan's traditional arts, thus making them heirs to a time-honored cultural memory. The notion of cut continuation is indeed typified by the traditional poetic form of the haiku, where the concept of division is foregrounded through the use of the so-called cut syllable as a means of simultaneously separating and connecting two consecutive images. The markedly stylized fashion in which performers move in classic Noh theatre likewise exemplifies the principle of *kire tsuzuki*. The player typically shifts the foot along the floor with the toes lifted and then abruptly interrupts the motion by dropping the toes to the floor. The instant the toes touch the stage, the other foot starts performing the very same movement in its turn. These lyrical and dramatic conventions serve to underscore the inherently discontinuous character of all life. Zen meditation, finally, enthrones the cut as the pivotal mechanism regulating its rhythm. A deliberate pause occurs between exhalation and inhalation, more protracted than the interval separating inhalation from exhalation, which intimates in symbolic form the idea that life could be rescinded at any point.

CHAPTER 6

Memory and the City

Kanon
(TV series; dir. Tatsuya Ishihara, 2006–2007)

> The life of our city is rich in poetic and marvelous subjects.
> We are enveloped and steeped as though in an atmosphere
> of the marvelous; but we do not know it.
> —Charles Baudelaire, "On the Heroism of Modern Life" (1846)

> All cities are mad: but the madness is gallant.
> All cities are beautiful: but the beauty is grim.
> —Christopher Morley, *Where the Blue Begins* (1922)

The feature film *Lum the Forever* (dir. Kazuo Yamazaki, 1986) focuses on the inextricability of the eponymous heroine from the town she inhabits, Tomobiki-cho. On the one hand, just as the town is destined to change over time to adapt to new trends and desires, so is the adolescent Lum as she moves into adulthood. On the other, while Tomobiki-cho seems to accept its fate — albeit, at times, with some reluctance — the heroine is not so willing to let go of the past. This leads to a conflict between the two wherein the town's memories, inscribed on its architecture, flora and fauna, clash with the character's own recollections and her concomitant yearning to keep those tangibly alive in the present. At the same time, the town's loss of its memories — symbolized by the felling of the giant cherry tree Tarouzakura intimately connected with its history — parallels the fading of Lum's image from the minds of her friends to the point that she becomes virtually invisible to them.

The once formidable alien princess clad in a tiger-skin bikini, crowned by emerald locks, and able to fly and electrocute her opponents, thus pales into a pathetic specter. It is for Lum and Lum alone, ultimately, to surmount this unsavory present by unsentimentally confronting her memories: a task upon which she embarks by entering Tomobiki-cho's depths in a journey metaphorically evocative of a return to the ancestral womb, and laying to rest the ghosts from the past in the guise of infantile versions of herself and her little playmates. Lum's mournful perception of change resonates throughout with the poetics of *mono no aware*.

Lum the Forever is a seminal title in the treatment of the collusion of memory and the urban environment. No less relevant to the present discussion by virtue of their psychological and philosophical undercurrents are *Boogiepop Phantom* and *When They Cry: Higurashi*. The former, a TV series directed by Takashi Watanabe and broadcast in 2000, deals with the themes of temporality, change and evolution by fusing a sci-fi yarn with legend as coacting vehicles for the exploration of the genesis of memories. These are consistently posited as autonomous forces that map themselves on individual destinies and intersubjective relationships alike, and manifest themselves physically through a relentlessly mutating urbanscape. It is indeed in the evolution of the body of the city that the passage of time and its mnemonic incrustations assert themselves most vigorously. The city allegorizes the processes through which memory continually defines and redefines people and their perceptions of both themselves and others as they grow older and learn to negotiate the tension between reality and illusion, while concurrently grappling with the burden of irretrievable loss. The architectonics of shared space thus asserts itself as a protean mnemotechnology of unmatched ascendancy.

The interrelation between personal experiences and the city is captured by the script at various junctures. On the one hand, "the look of the city changing" engenders a melancholy sense of irrescindable privation. The recognition of the city's relentless metamorphosis indeed conjures up a distinct mood of *mono no aware*. On the other hand, the drama stresses that "missing the old days" should not be tantamount to "being stuck in the past" because just as "the city must change over time, it's important that people move forward in their lives." Even when the ineluctability of change is stoically negotiated, however, the awareness that "the past will often attack the present with the pain of your memories" persists. Additionally, the hypothesis that "Time does not exist. Only the illusion of memories exists" is central to the anime throughout its tortuous unfolding.

The sci-fi narrative revolves around the idea that one in every million kids is an advanced specimen in evolution, and accordingly endowed with special powers. The worldwide organization Towa wants them destroyed and ruthlessly hunts them down by recourse to other special entities of its own making known as "composite humans." The lore-related dimension of the story, for its part, pivots on proliferating urban legends and on various mythical and fantastical creatures (including the titular character) of multicultural derivation. All of these play a role in either Towa's persecution of the special kids or in their protection.

An extensive cast of subtly interconnected characters fluidly moves in and out of the narrative from one episode to the next. Especially interesting, for the specific purpose of this study, is the character of Manaka Kisaragi, a girl whose special abilities are epitomized by a knack of magnetizing the town's memories and expressing them in the guise of shimmering butterflies. In the show's climax, Manaka herself turns into a glorious light composed of golden butterflies. Enwrapping the land, the radiance causes time to skip and enables people to perceive phantoms of themselves and long-forgotten events from the past. Before fading away for good, the girl restores her own mother's memory through the butterflies, healing the seemingly incurable amnesia that has afflicted the woman since Manaka's birth. Notably, Manaka's other defining attribute is a distressing echolalia — acquired upon being revived by the semi-mythical character of Echoes after her mother has tried to kill her in order to spare her from the shame of not having a father. As a psychosomatic condition, echolalia is deeply relevant to the present context in that it constitutes yet another type of performative memory.

Additionally, *Boogiepop Phantom* emphasizes that all memories play an important role in the shaping of human personalities and relationships. This is most explicitly foregrounded in the segment of the program focusing on Jonouchi Hisashi, a character able to sense painful memories and to extract them from their hosts in the guise of repulsive bugs. While the character may at first come across as a liberating force acting for the common good, his interventions are actually detrimental: for humans to learn from the past, they need to remember the chains of events that have led them to the present and propel them into the future. By excising sorrowful reminiscences from other people's psyches, Jonouchi is impairing their ability to grasp why they are what they are since a crucial piece of what previously shaped their being has now vanished.

Boogiepop Phantom's plot can only be reconstructed by means of repeat viewings due to its markedly nonlinear and multiperspectival orchestration, as a result of which the same events are reproposed several times in the course of the show, as seen from different angles and within different contexts. This strategy aptly emulates the eminently fragmentary and scrambled fashion in which recollections come into being. The multiperspectival format, moreover, enables the series to underscore the proposition that time is a flagrantly relative concept, contingent on the order in which various sequences of events are strung together and observed. Surreal visual effects, such as disorienting montages and uncanny juxtapositions of mirthful and forbidding images (e.g., an abandoned carousel steeped in gloom) contribute significantly to *Boogiepop Phantom*'s cumulative atmosphere, as does its brooding, somber and even ponderous pace. Vignette-style framing, allied to the pervasive use of fisheye lenses, desaturation and a washed-out sepia palette meant to foreground a ubiquitous sense of emotional debilitation, further define the show's distinctive style. Furthermore, *Boogiepop Phantom* engages with memory through a tapestry of varyingly explicit intertextual homages ranging from Japanese folklore and Persian mythology to Thomas Pynchon, and from Friedrich Nietzsche to Pink Floyd. Finally, *Boogiepop Phantom* echoes *Lum the Forever* in its symbolic capture of the past with the scenes where numerous characters are drawn to an eerie park where they find child versions of themselves.

A recent instance of anime's adventurous commingling of the phenomenon of memory and urban space is unquestionably *When They Cry: Higurashi* (TV series, dir. Chiaki Kon, 2006). The materiality of memory is here vividly underscored by the inscription of personal and collective recollections onto the body of the city. Based on a series of amateur murder-mystery games, the show stands out as one of the most frankly experimental anime of the past decade in both its visual style and its diegetic constellation. Creepy, sad, horror-laced and often downright gruesome, *Higurashi* never degenerates into violent spectacle as an end in itself, being in fact able to maintain a fine balance between action and thought, projection and retrospection.

The original games comprise several arcs, the original eight of which are divided into question arcs and answer arcs. The two sets are subtly interrelated, not merely by recourse to overt visual and verbal contents but also, more tantalizingly, by implied mnemonic echoes and cross-references. The question arcs present chains of invariably enigmatic events, which the answer arcs proceed to recapitulate from different perspectives, thereby supplying alternate endings and at least partial solutions to the mysteries in hand. The 2006 series covers the four question arcs and the first two answer arcs. (A sequel, helmed by the same director and released domestically in 2007, encompasses the closing two answer arcs. In addition, *Higurashi* games bound to add complexity and ramifications to the main yarn are still being released.)

The story pivots on transfer student Keiichi Maebara who, having lived his entire life in the big city, is suddenly transposed to the diminutive rural village of Hinamizawa. Being a well-adjusted urbane type, the boy has no trouble making new friends and soon joins a club consisting of the hypercute (and color-coded) girls Rena Ryugu, Mion Sonozaki, Rika Furude and Satoko Hojo. Also vital to the show are Mion's twin sister Shion, Satoko's brother Satoshi and the police investigators Oishi and Akasaka. While this initial setup may appear familiarly reminiscent of a standard "harem" comedy, the tone rapidly darkens as Keiichi discovers that the town labors under a horrible curse linked up with its legendary patron, the spirit Oyashiro-sama. Indeed, for the past four years, one person has been murdered and another has gone missing never to reappear in the aftermath of the Watanagashi ("Cotton-Drifting") Festival held to commemorate the local deity. Some believe that the crimes are caused by Oyashiro-sama, angered by an attempt to build a dam in Hinamizawa's vicinity.

It is worth noting, in this regard, that superstitions imbue Japanese lore no less pervasively than the traditional heritages of most Western cultures. While some of these may be easily dismissed as mumbo jumbo, others are firmly rooted in time-honored rites connected with key aspects of the societal fabric, such as obsequies and nuptials. As the entry for "Japanese Superstitions" in the online guide *Japan Zone* stresses, "The Japan of ... high-tech and high-speed trains may not seem like a superstitious place. But under the skin, Japan's is an ancient and originally animist or pagan culture.... The native religion of Shinto has had to give up a lot of mindshare to Buddhism, Christianity, new religions and cults, and of course modern consumerism. But it retains its strong but subtle hold on the national psyche" ("Japanese Superstitions"). As a result, most Japanese people are likely to respect at least one of the myriad superstitions embedded in indigenous tradition on a daily basis.

As *Higurashi*'s action progresses, it gradually transpires that the real causes of the grisly murders and inexplicable vanishings may lie with even darker schemes than those concocted by religiosity and myth. This is confirmed by the scandals and corruption brought to the surface by the clash between the promulgators of the construction plans for the dam and the local protest group determined to hinder them. The pernicious influence of the Sonozaki family plays a major part, in this context, with age-old privileges, on the one hand, and current interests, on the other, buttressing its authority. The twin sisters Mion and Shion act as the mnemonic conduits joining the past, the present and the future. More disturbingly still, Keiichi has reasons to suspect that his own friends may be hiding dire secrets and that he himself might be the next in line as a victim.

Reconstructing each arc in detail and retracing all of the steps leading to the possible solutions eventually disclosed by the series would be quite inapposite in the current context. However, a few examples of *Higurashi*'s multiperspectival approach can usefully illuminate its distinctive format. In the first arc, where Rena is the pivotal persona, the boy's rapidly escalating paranoia regarding the town's lurking horrors eventually drives him insane, inducing him to beat Rena and Mion to death and to tear out his own throat. In the second, where Mion is the center of attention, a surreptitious visit to a sealed local shrine culminates in two more violent deaths, while Keiichi again has good reason to fear for his life. With the third arc, the focus moves to Satoko, the victim of severe abuse at the hands of her uncle, and to Keiichi's bafflingly inconclusive execution of said offender. The fourth arc provides an even more radical shift of perspective, emplacing detective Mamoru Akasaka as the narrator and offering a reconstruction of the events surrounding the dam project and its boycott, based on his visit to Hinamizawa with the intention of obtaining information about the protest group. The locals unceremoniously warn him off the case — which is hardly surprising in view of the town's inhospitably self-insulating proclivities. This arc broadens the scope of the adventure by inviting reflection on the reliability (or even the availability) of officially recorded history.

Suspicion, fear and distrust take over Hinamizawa's ostensibly tranquil cocoon, spawning a miasma of noxious delusions. The plot is sustained throughout by a keen sense of the town's inextricability from both the body of memories underlying its rituals, legends and gods, and the more recent or even developing memories of its decidedly unholy inhabitants. In linking the city's present to a time-honored tradition steeped in myth, *Higurashi* seemingly keeps the past alive. Yet, in underscoring the inseparability of that legacy from a chain of destructive acts, the program also reflects on the inevitability of death and impermanence. In *Higurashi*, as indeed in all of the productions explored in this chapter, the fleeting nature of the urban environment is persistently entangled with the evanescence not only of places but also of people and hence of their memories.[1]

Aria the Animation (TV series; dir. Junichi Sato, 2005) offers a futuristic take on the coalescence of memory and the city with "Neo-Venezia." An imaginary ensemble imbued with collective memories of the real Venice, the city is one of the small settlements erected by humans on the oceanic planet "Aqua," a terraformed Mars, 90 percent of which is covered by water. The actual Italian city, in the logic of the series, is supposed to have sunk into its watery bed many years prior to the setting of the anime. *Aria* chronicles the day-to-day lives of its protagonist, the outwardly plucky but gentle and unflinchingly optimistic Akari, and of her two closest friends: the amusingly cynical Aika and the dreamy Alice. Each of the girls is an apprentice at one of the gondolier firms based on Aqua: Aria Co., Himeya Co. and Orange Planet, respectively. The president of each company is a blue-eyed cat endowed with fabulous intelligence, which makes the creatures highly revered throughout Neo-Venezia. This motif encapsulates a Shintoist world view according to which a fundamental spiritual force pervades the entire universe, and it is therefore not inconceivable for mental attributes found in humans to also manifest themselves in other life forms.

Focusing on unobtrusively portrayed interpersonal dynamics in preference to theatrical action, *Aria* is fundamentally a series about the importance of quotidian and even apparently trivial occurrences, urging the audience to recognize the value of what William Wordsworth once termed the "little, nameless, unremembered acts / Of kindness and of love" ("Lines Composed a Few Miles Above Tintern Abbey," 1798). Concurrently, *Aria* consolidates the value of such seemingly trivial acts by using simple gestures in order to connect the past and the future, thereby taking its heroine back in time to Aqua's early days, when the waters had not yet spread throughout the planet, let alone engulfed the whole of Neo-Venezia. No less vital to the show's emphasis on simple occurrences is its celebration of the here-and-now. As the protagonists stumble daily through their uncertainties and fears, we are invited to follow them moment by moment, recognizing the importance of the present instant regardless of where the action might take them tomorrow or the day after. As the *Neko's Thinkbox* review of the series points out, "The point of this anime clearly is Carpe Diem — enjoy every day to its fullest extent" ("Carpe Diem — an *Aria the Animation* review"). Originally used in Horace's *Odes* (23–13 B.C.), this Western concept is akin to the Japanese notion of *mono no aware*. It is this mood that bolsters at each turn the show's quietly beautiful slice-of-life atmosphere and endows it with an aura of intimacy capable of making viewers feel that they are a part of Akari's world rather than mere onlookers.

Aria evokes most potently the intrinsic aliveness not only of Neo-Venezia but also of the historical city behind it, thus underscoring the indelible charm of the semi-mythical memories embedded therein through its spellbinding visuals. These capitalize on a judicious integration of cel animation and CGI, as well as deftly nuanced palettes replete with lush greens, brilliant blues and soft pastelly hues. The alternation of stylized backgrounds, richly textured oceans and delicate bridges, aqueducts and gondola-strewn waterways is likewise stylistically pivotal to *Aria*'s visual impact. Where the show's visuals are specifically concerned, it should also be noted that these tangentially evoke a range of pictorial memories harking back to various artists who have assiduously engaged in the representation of Venice's unique architecture and setting, including masters such as Jacopo Tintoretto (1518–1594), Canaletto (1697–1768), Bernardo Bellotto (1720–1780) and J. M. W. Turner (1775–1851). Key to the effectiveness of the graphics is also their combination with a varied soundtrack harmonizing soft jazz, piano pieces and Italian folk music.

Like its Italian counterpart, the Martian city is a major tourist hub in which gondolas constitute a major attraction. In Neo-Venezia, a gondolier is known as an "Undine" and upon completing her apprenticeship, she gains the title of "Prima." It is also noteworthy, in this context, that *Aria* designates a number of its characters by recourse to "elementals," namely mystical creatures presumed to reside within the spirit realm of the elements. These entities are life forces responsible for governing the whole of nature. Undines, the spirits after whom Neo-Venezia's gondoliers are named, are Water spirits. Fire spirits are known as Salamanders and appear in *Aria* in the guise of people responsible for monitoring the planet's climate. Earth spirits, dubbed gnomes, feature as people charged with the task of regulating Aqua's gravity. Air Spirits, termed Sylphs, are the source of inspiration behind Neo-Venezia's airmail deliverers.

Gondoliers are highly regarded throughout Aqua as tour guides. This prosaic detail is worthy of notice because it acts as a reminder of the inherently commercialized nature of Venetian culture, healthily debunking the romantic inclination to visualize the city as a world of transcendent beauty. Mnemonic vestiges of the actual Venice proclaim themselves most sonorously in the show's evocation of the city's proverbially hybrid, prismatic and fragile fabric — a veritable paean to the spirit of *mono no aware*. Indeed, the visuals corroborate at virtually each turn in the narrative Jeanette Winterson's description of Venice as "a changeable city. It is not always the same size. Streets appear and disappear overnight, new waterways force themselves over dry land. There are days when you cannot walk from one end to the other, so far is the journey, and there are days when a stroll will take you round your kingdom like a tin-pot Prince" (Winterson 1988, p. 97).

As a metamorphic world built from literally fluid materials, Neo-Venezia — like its real-life model — regales the eye with an almost disorientingly airy and plastic architecture. The memories, both private and shared, it harbors are likewise resistant to definitive mapping, sprawling in unpredictable directions and, more often than not, in several discordant directions at once. Akari's and her friends' everyday adventures encapsulate this idea by positing the characters' wanderings as far more significant than their intended destinations. To date, *Aria* has spawned two additional seasons, *Aria the Natural* (dir. Junichi Sato, 2006) and *Aria the Origination* (dir. Junichi Sato, 2008), as well as the direct-to-video production *Aria the OVA-Arietta-* (dir. Junichi Sato, 2007). Since Akari aims at becoming not only an esteemed Prima but also, ideally, one of the three "Water Fairies," namely the very best gondoliers who are entrusted with the task of leading the aforementioned companies, it is not inconceivable that further series will be produced to chart subsequent stages in the heroine's professional development and psychological maturation.

It is with the TV series *Kanon* that anime enthrones most enthusiastically the coalescence of memory and the city as a topos of unmatched dramatic vigor. *Kanon* was first dramatized in 2002 as a 13-episode program directed by Naoyuki Ito. This largely met with disappointment among fans of the computer game on which the story is based due to limited breadth and, concomitantly, inadequate character development. The new show's director embarked on the remake with the wish to outshine not only Ito's antecedent but also his own earlier output.[2] Having established his reputation with *Air*, Ishihara aimed to "surpass [his] previous work." To achieve this objective, it was first of all paramount to impart *Kanon* with a distinctive look of its own. The strategy used to distinguish the show immediately from its predecessor was based on a disarmingly simple principle, highly effective in virtue of its very simplicity. This consisted of evoking a specific atmosphere at the levels of environment and climate from frame one. Thus, while *Air* revolves around the image of a "seashore in summer," *Kanon* capitalizes on the antipodal charm of a "pure white plain." This setting enabled the director to develop his narrative as, at base, "a love story set in snow country" (Ishihara). Tasha Robinson corroborates the importance of this motif within the overall diegesis: "Part of the series' conceit is that it's a winter story, that the town is always blanketed in snow and that Yuuichi and his friends often wind up walking around in beautiful, crystalline, snowy nights, representative of their frozen but slowly thawing mental states" (Robinson 2008).

In *Kanon*, it is a boy's return to a city he has not visited in seven years that rekindles not only submerged memories but also haunting secrets. The story chronicles Yuuichi Aizawa's arrival at the home of his aunt Akiko Minase and her daughter Nayuki in Northern Japan and ensuing encounters with several female characters bound to prove pivotal to the narrative: the sprightly Ayu Tsukimiya, the timid Shiori Misaka, the mischievous Makoto Sawatari and the solemn Mai Kawasumi. All of the key girls appear to have hidden agendas to which Yuuichi is somehow expected to contribute. The male lead's interactions with the various girls are dramatized in relatively discrete arcs, each of which is imparted with a distinctive atmosphere and tone intended to mirror both the personality of the character at its center and Yuuichi's own feelings towards that particular person.

The plot capitalizes on a multiperspectival approach, offering overlapping stories with the five primary girls as their leading threads. The various strands are elegantly orchestrated to guarantee overall balance with consistent reference to memory-related issues and imagery. *Kanon* invokes the theme of memory at various levels. Amnesia provides the foundational principle for its narrative constellation, the characters of Yuuichi, Ayu and Makoto all being afflicted by severe cases of memory loss. The arcs are also interwoven by recourse to more or less explicit leading threads — most importantly, in this context, by the tale's emphasis on the alternate evaporation and resurgence of mnemonic traces not only in the characters' psyches but also in the stone-and-brick fabric of their city. It is from these connectors, above all else, that *Kanon* derives not only structural coherence but also a driving sense of momentum that incrementally — and inexorably — leads to the climax of the story's cardinal relationship: the one between Yuuichi and Ayu.

Makoto is central to the anime's first arc. Having been introduced as inexplicably determined to vent her ire on Yuuichi, yet powerless to do so due to hunger and sheer exhaustion, Makoto soon finds herself installed as a member of the Minase household, where it becomes clear that she is a victim of serious amnesia. The only thing she seems capable of remembering is that she has a grudge against Yuuichi. Although Makoto features prominently in the show's opening segment, she does not unequivocally dominate the screen. In fact, other characters destined to play important roles in subsequent installments also feature repeatedly. One of them is Shiori, who makes a brief appearance in the second episode and is properly ushered into the story in the following one. Another is Mai, whom Yuuichi sees briefly on the school premises initially in daytime in the first three episodes and then at night in the fourth episode, mysteriously wielding a sword, in the fourth episode. Ayu herself makes several appearances prior to her incontrovertible emplacement as the series' heroine, her establishment in the Minase household marking an especially axial moment in *Kanon*'s cumulative diegesis.

Makoto, alas, is quite unsocialized: given money by Akiko to purchase groceries for the family, she only manages to squander it on manga volumes and meat buns. Yuuichi's decision to get Makoto a job in order to instill her with a modicum of common sense at first appears to yield salutary results. These are soon shattered as Makoto, walking home from the local nursery where she has obtained employment, once again indulges in reckless behavior — this time dropping a kitten off a bridge onto oncoming city traffic and then temporarily running away from home. Following Makoto reinstatement within Akiko's family, Yuuichi devotes more and more of his time to the strange girl, and memories of her identity buried in his childhood begin to emerge.

The resurgence of these abeyant psychic contents is largely triggered by the baleful warning concerning Makoto proffered by the supporting character of Mishio Amano. The impulsive girl, Mishio intimates, is not truly human but has only provisionally assumed her current form to meet Yuuichi. Although she is not aware of it, this brief miracle will cost Makoto not only her memory but also her very life. It is when Makoto's strength begins to falter and her health, accordingly, to deteriorate drastically, that Yuuichi conclusively remembers who she truly is — namely, a fox cub he found and nurtured as a kid. Having disclosed this disorienting truth, *Kanon* takes Makoto's story arc to a resolution in an exquisitely choreographed installment, where the protagonist finally comes to terms with the girl's inevitable fate and returns her to her place of origin. Here, he seals their bond by means of a deeply affecting private ceremony. A field outside the city's boundaries, Makoto's ancestral home accommodates its own distinctive treasurehouse of memories. The physical separation of the breeze-caressed hill from the urban conglomerate economically conveys the mnemonic gap between the two dimensions and, by implication, the ultimate incompatibility between the girl's true nature and her fleeting human configuration.

Mai's arc finds its inception in the immediate aftermath of Makoto's conclusion. Aware that her proverbial diffidence and aloofness have gained Mai rather a negative reputation, Yuuichi is no less keen on increasing her popularity among pupils and teachers alike than he was earlier in the show on enculturing the feral Makoto, and hence resolves to take her to the forthcoming dance festival. This portion of the series is especially notable as an instance of *Kanon*'s knack of interweaving ostensibly separate narrative threads. While revealing vital information about Yuuichi's past encounters with Ayu, the episode also intimates that one of Yuuichi's classmates, Kaori Misaka, is Shiori's sister but is hell-bent on concealing her connection with the timid first-year student. In the Mai-centered plot strand, nocturnal demon-hunting plays a key part. Although some of the show's most tantalizing action sequences emanate precisely from this ruse, *Kanon* does not employ the conventional anime formula simply as a means of regaling the eye with gratuitous spectacle but rather as a metaphor for Mai's troubled psyche. The demons indeed appear to be projections of the girl's emotions and memories: horrendous distortions of an otherwise benevolent disposition abetted by the possession of preternatural healing faculties.

The wistful mood that characterizes the culmination of both Makoto's and Mai's respective stories, intensely redolent of the aesthetic principle of *mono no aware*, asserts itself no less potently in the arc centered on Shiori. It indeed transpires that the girl is afflicted by a mysterious and terminal illness and that this is the cause of her prolonged absence from school. While Yuuichi is determined to do anything in his power to fill with happy memories what could well be Shiori's last days, and her doctor allows her to attend school for one week as though she were a regular pupil, Kaori remains reluctant to admit to her kinship with the sick girl. The most poignant portion of the Shiori arc focuses on the suspenseful buildup to her birthday, for which Yuuichi has organized a party to be held at a local café: a date beyond which, Kaori has ominously warned, her sister might not survive for much longer.

As *Kanon* advances towards its dénouement, Ayu is conclusively situated as the principal female character and retains this status right through to the end of the show. Her endeavor to find something for which she has long been searching without any clues as to its identity, except that it is very important to her, and Yuuichi's intention to assist the girl in her seemingly hopeless quest draw them closer and closer with practically each frame. While the protagonist tries to figure out the other characters' interconnections, repressed memories he has been trying to entomb gradually resurface. The culmination of Yuuichi's mnemonic recovery is the revelation that seven years prior to the beginning of the series, a terrible accident occurred and that he then chose to consign it to oblivion, at least until his return to the northern city. What complicates exponentially the magnitude of Yuuichi's struggle to piece together the nebulous patches of memory gradually resurfacing in the course of his sojourn is the fact that many of the flashbacks he experiences are interwoven with dreams or even couched as such. Even the climactic resurfacing of the traumatic events conducive to Yuuichi's amnesia occurs in the context of a dream.

Upon awakening from these chimeric visions, the youth does not generally appear to hold any real conscious awareness of the memories he might have regained while asleep. In thus foregrounding the eminently circuitous nature of memory retrieval, *Kanon* proposes that amnesia is not the sole affliction which its characters are enjoined to endure: recuperating the images (and attendant affects) they have lost would seem to constitute no less arduous a task. Moreover, by articulating Yuuichi's gradual reappropriation of his buried mnemonic baggage in oneiric form, the show sets up a subtle parallel between the male lead's experience and Ayu's own ordeal, since the heroine is portrayed consistently as being imprisoned in an ostensibly endless dream. Furthermore, there are frequent suggestions that lost memories cannot be recovered through revelations offered by others but must be retrieved by the bereft subject through an intensely personal and tortuous journey. This is demonstrated, for example, by the sequence where Nayuki tries in vain to jog Yuuichi's memory regarding past occurrences.

Kanon partakes of several formulae normally associated with romantic anime but transcends strict generic classification. For one thing, although the male lead interacts with no less than five females, none of the trappings of "harem" comedy imposes itself. Nor do the moving moments degenerate into maudlin melodrama as so often happens in stereotypical *shoujo* anime. The girls are invariably appealing, their attractiveness alternately deriving from *moe*-style cuteness, child-like charm or lofty beauty. Yet, these are only superficial adjuncts to the narrative articulated in the anime itself compared to the subtlety with which their inner personalities, individual histories and even gastronomic preferences are lovingly depicted throughout.

This last detail could be dismissed as a marginal element, yet it carries a distinctive value in sustaining *Kanon*'s overall narrative. For one thing, the food items cherished by each of the main personae are linked with specific memories, which their ingestion both keeps alive and reactivates at axial junctures in the story. Furthermore, as Yoshikatsu Nakagami argues, "It's when the characters are eating something really tasty that they seem most beautiful and alive ... having a favorite food makes the characters more realistic *and* more attractive to viewers" (Nakagami 2007, p. 63). Shiori, being unable to attend classes due to her protracted illness, is a melancholy character but glows with life whenever she is consuming vanilla ice cream — which tends to occur, ironically, in freezing surroundings. Sheer joy seems to enfold Ayu's whole being at the mere sight of *taiyaki* (a bream-shaped filled cake), whereas Nayuki harbors a passion for home-made jam and Makoto a craving for *nikuman* (meat buns), whereas Mai favors traditional cuisine, especially beef bowl. These elements are worthy of notice when assessing the show's commitment to psychological realism and fetching personalities. Furthermore, food operates as a cohesive force capable of bringing together disparate characters and experiences. This point is underscored by Yuko Minaguchi, the voice actress for Akiko: "Everyone in the [Minase] house sits down to delicious meals together. That's the important thing. Then, as everyone learns to care about each other, their bond as a family gets even stronger" (quoted in Nakagami 2008, p. 46).

The art book titled *Kanon Visual Memories* fully attests to the show's punctiliously nuanced character designs with its comprehensive galleries of individual physiognomies, costumes and accessories, as well as group portraits representing character interactions. The characters' personalities are consistently sustained and enriched by the scrupulous representation of the psychological fabric of the city itself as the repository of experiences, aspirations and, most crucially, memories. This fundamental aspect of the series is also exhaustively documented by the art book. In endowing the urbanscape with palpable life, location hunting was of critical significance. To immerse themselves into the type of world they sought to represent and enliven, the animators undertook fieldwork in relevant parts of Japan during the very same season in which the story is set. While a close focus on the habitat, its color schemes and formal properties was maintained, no less important was the observation of the "lifestyle of the townspeople" (Ishihara). (The director's and the scriptwriter Fumihiko Shimo's own origins in snowy regions also abetted the task.)

As for Yuuichi, he is by no means reducible to a conventional harem hero: an inveterately ineffectual nice guy/wimp. (The 2002 version of the character is much closer to that stereotypical modality.) In fact, he remains self-possessed even at times of heightened emotional turmoil, endeavoring to take full responsibility not only for his own actions but also for the people that surround him — even though, due to his amnesia, he is generally in the dark as to the causes of his current predicament. Occasionally, Yuuichi also departs from the classic harem lead by openly expressing his opinions, and not without a refreshing sprinkling of wit, sarcasm and playful cynicism. The combination of kindness and abrasiveness, sincerity and self-blinding tendencies, makes him a fully rounded, profoundly realistic actor.

Anyone even cursorily acquainted with the medium's narrative conventions will be aware that lost memories in anime typically allude to entombed tragedies. In *Kanon*, this convention gains special resonance through the meticulous accumulation of assorted morsels which it is up to the industrious spectator to piece together, albeit provisionally. So delicately reserved as to verge on the austere, *Kanon*'s opening installment betrays little about the tale's supernatural dimension. In fact, as Robinson contends, in the initial stages, the show "feels more like a low-key romance than a mystery" (Robinson 2008). Nevertheless, subsequent episodes are by no means remiss in seeding the visuals with riddles, all of which are invariably linked to memory issues and crises. This proclivity is already evident in the 2002 version of the show from the very first installment. When Yuiichi, having reluctantly agreed to return to the town of his infancy due to his parents' job-related move overseas, unpacks and wonders why he has no reminiscences of his time there as a kid, he finds a girl's hair band among his belongings. In a dream occurring in the wake of this odd discovery, he sees a little girl whom he promises to meet again the following day. When, the next morning, Ayu spectacularly clashes into him in the street, Yuuichi notes that she is wearing precisely the same hair band. The boy's next dream reveals that Ayu is the girl that appeared in the previous dream as well. The 2006 version scatters its clues with greater finesse.

The mnemonic motif is reinforced by the story's emphasis on the acts of promising and keeping promises through which past, present and future are intermeshed: Yuuichi makes binding promises to all of the five girls with whom he is, in varying degrees, involved, while concurrently fulfilling past promises made at the time when he used to visit the city as a child. The monster-related dimension of the story simultaneously abets the memory theme insofar as it illustrates contemporary anime's self-reflexive appropriation of established generic conventions traditionally cultivated by its predecessors. The series *The Melancholy of Haruhi Suzumiya*, also produced by Kyoto Animation and directed by Ishihara (and here discussed in the penultimate chapter), is tangentially referred to in a few scenes: in the second installment, for instance, through the allusion to spies and secret agencies and by the employment of first-person narration. Another TV show helmed by Ishihara prior to *Kanon*, the aforementioned *Air*, is also invoked in the first episode by means of an advert for the peach juice avidly consumed by Misuzu, that series' heroine. *Kanon*, too, is amenable to mnemonic citation by other titles, as evinced by the cameo appearance of Ayu, Nayuki and Makoto in a scene of *Air*'s second episode. (These characters would have already achieved popularity thanks to both the game and the earlier anime adaptation of *Kanon*.) Additionally, Ayu's insistent utterance of the nonsensical guttural sound "*uguu*" recalls Misuzu's recurring "*gao*" ejaculation. (Makoto, for her part, whimpers "*auuuuuu*" whenever she is cross or rebuked.)

Supernatural motifs, most notably miracles or apparent miracles, play a substantial role in *Kanon*'s plot — especially in the climax, where Akiko, Shiori, Mai and the latter's loyal friend Sayuri Kurata all recover from extremely serious injuries or illnesses. It is Ayu, however, who makes the most sensational recovery, awakening from a seven-year coma caused by a fatal fall from a massive tree. The seemingly miraculous event is largely inspired by Yuuichi's determination to remember the accident — which he has thus far resolutely repressed to protect his own ego — and keep the promise made to Ayu at the time that they would meet again. Miracles are not dished out like candy at a kids' party, however. In fact, they always come at a steep price, as the arc based on Makoto most painfully conveys. As noted in the *Minitokyo* review of the series, moreover, the characters are portrayed so convincingly that "even with the many twists of magic scattered throughout it seems natural that such magic should exist" (littlejonny100).

What prevents the resolution of Ayu and Yuuichi's ordeal from deteriorating into saccharine escapism, in particular, is the show's stylish cultivation of ambiguity. This is generated primarily by the incorporation of numerous scenes throughout the drama that feature Ayu roaming around the town in search of something immensely precious to her, yet unable to remember what it is, and interacting with both Yuuichi and his family and friends — to the point, as mentioned, that for a while she even takes residence at the Minase home. These scenes could be read as psychic projections of Yuuichi's inchoate memories. Yet, this interpretation is called into question by the fact that Ayu does not only relate to the boy in those scenes but also to other characters who know full well that Ayu is lying unconscious in a hospital bed. This suggests that the scenes involving Ayu actually emanate from the dream she herself has been experiencing day after day, as the sole means of hanging onto life, for seven long years. At one juncture, the drama intimates that the Ayu we see throughout the show is not quite real with the scene where she and Yuuichi discover a large clearing with a tree stump at its center in the woods — namely, a vestige of the once monumental tree linked with the heroine's accident — and Ayu, as though suddenly cognizant of everything she has thus far repressed, is so shocked as to vanish altogether.

The strand of the plot based on the revelation of Makoto's true identity as a fox demon temporarily endowed by love with human form is also open to interpretation. It could just as plausibly be read as an homage to indigenous mythology and mysticism; as a play-within-a-play encapsulating metaphorically *Kanon*'s supernatural strain; or as part of the Bildungsroman trajectory centered on Yuuichi, since the boy's gradual recollection of Makoto as a fox cub he found and nurtured seven years earlier and acceptance that her current incarnation is destined to disappear are important stages in his maturation. Interpretation is further problematized, at this level of the plot, by the fact that the preternatural girl appears to be modeled closely on the figure of a fully human Makoto Sawatari: an older girl whom Yuuichi deeply admired in childhood and meets again towards the end of the program. Not only does the human Makoto come across as the fox-Makoto's spitting image (albeit in more mature form): she also harbors the same passion for bells and meat buns. One of *Kanon*'s most tantalizing aspects, in this regard, is that it encourages the formation of mutable memories in the audience itself past its final scene by remaining open to different decodings.

Whenever Yuuichi wonders what he might be remembering about the past, as particular images or snippets of conversation jolt his psyche into recall mode, he is immediately drawn to think about the city. Walking along a bustling pavement, looking at the buildings, or purchasing food, the boy repeatedly considers what the place could conceivably have looked like seven years before in comparison with the present day. A powerful wave of *mono no aware* invariably surges over such scenes. Concurrently, the past appears to be the very fabric of the town, infusing each of its layers of brick and stone no less than the elusive messages and meanings mapped upon them by the drifting years. Since for Yuuichi, as for other *Kanon* characters affected by amnesia, that past is largely inaccessible, the town remains resistant to logical deciphering. Therefore, even when the protagonist might think he is moving straight ahead towards an answer, he repeatedly finds that he is in fact going round in circles. As also noted elsewhere in this study, memories are not wholly disembodied phenomena but actually assume tangible bodies in various ways. This is corroborated, in *Kanon*, by scenes where Yuuichi's vague sensation that things he is experiencing now remind him of events from the past smoothly translate into scenes showing younger versions of the protagonist and his friends as actual bodies performing actions akin, or indeed identical, to those dramatized in the present.

Kanon's musical infrastructure is of paramount importance to a comprehensive grasp of its unique rhythm as an elegant orchestration of recollections, reveries, fantasies and desires. The first episode succinctly foregrounds the centrality of the melodic element with the scene set in the café which Yuuichi and Ayu visit after their first collision, where the music playing in the background is, most felicitously, Johann Pachelbel's *Canon in D*. The same piece is again used in other poignant moments — for example, in the course of a conversation between Yuuichi and Sayuri central to the Mai arc. Like *RahXephon* and *Gilgamesh*, moreover, the series assiduously adopts musical symbolism and terminology. This is borne out by the titles of its installments, which include the terms introit, partita, caprice, serenade, divertimento, fugue, fantasia, berceuse, requiem, intermezzo, waltz, trio, concerto, sonatina, oratorio, Lieder ohne Worte, adagio, étude, nocturne, ronde, symphony, finale and, in a climactic position, kanon itself. It is highly appropriate, in this respect, for the ADV release of the show's first volume on DVD to describe it as "a poignant concerto of tears, laughter and pinky promises" (*Kanon* DVD, vol. 1 Cover).

With its emphasis on the supernatural, *Kanon* asserts itself as a deeply mystical drama. However, this aspect of the show never degenerates into vapid quasi-religious mumbo jumbo because the narrative tropes through which it is communicated, and particularly the incremental disclosure of the past by means of flashbacks, vividly recall the workings of memory in the everyday lives of very real people. In this regard, the series' engagement with the memory topos could be seen as instrumental to its evocation of an eminently credible world even when it may seem to seagull into ineffable fantasy. The review of *Kanon*'s first DVD offered on *Anime-Source.Com* tersely encapsulates the show's approach to memory: "this anime is guaranteed to make you look beyond the obvious and contemplate the surreal.... [It is] a series about never letting your past escape your memories" (xenocrisis0153).

The ever-present layer of snow covering the city contributes vitally to the enhancement of the hermetic atmosphere through which the narrative flows. With virtually every frame, memories — lost, repressed and resurfacing — are posited not as personal possessions but rather as attributes of the urbanscape that shapes them as it is, in turn, shaped by them.

The snow covering practically every inch of *Kanon*'s scenery, while realistically consonant with its location in the Northern region of Hokkaido, also provides a powerful metaphor for the accretional nature of memory. The accumulation of tiny flakes into large expanses, clinging together to create ever-changing shapes and perspectives, indeed mirrors the gradual accruing of flimsy mnemonic traces into dense and sprawling galleries of interconnected images. With the addition of even a single flake to the picture, the setting's entire configuration may appear to alter, develop into something new and unforeseen — in much the same way as even a single tidbit of memory is capable of redefining a vast cluster of reminiscences and related affects in a person's mind.

The image of incremental build-up finds a diegetic correlative as Yuuichi, aware that whole chunks of his memory are missing, gradually discovers that other people he meets also seem to suffer from partial amnesia. This perception gains momentum as the story progresses, leading the boy to wonder, "Is this town under some spell that makes everyone lose their memory?" Just as the image of a diminutive flake holds the potential for evolving into the broader picture of an extensive blanket of snow, so an individual character's private experience little by little grows into a pervasive scenario of mnemonic displacement. The cinematographical style used to capture the reflective moments disclosing these cumulative revelations often makes us feel that we are being allowed to capture glimpses of very personal thought processes, which adds a strong sense of intimacy to the viewing experience.

At the same time, the ephemerality of memory and the comparably transient spectacle of the urban environment witnessing the evaporation of both private and shared recollections evoke the aesthetic principle of *mono no aware*. *Kanon* captures the very essence of the phrase, officially introduced by the scholar Motoori Noringa (1730–1801) to designate compassionate sensitivity (*aware*) to the inexorable passing of all things (*mono*). However, the world view associated with *mono no aware* was already ripe in Japan prior to its academic theorization by Noringa, having found inception in the twelfth century with Zen Buddhism and its emphasis on the world's impermanence. In *Kanon*, the concept is methodically dramatized by recourse to intimations of the continually dissolving character of the city within which memories are fashioned and scrambled by turns, and of the disarming beauty of that space as a corollary of its very volatility. Furthermore, *Kanon*'s ubiquitous use of images of snow-coated streets, fields and forests encapsulates metaphorically the show's overall aesthetics, since the charm exuded by those frames is inextricable from the transitoriness of the element that dominates them.

Whereas in Western aesthetics beauty has been associated, at least since ancient Greece, with the timeless and the enduring, the type of beauty upheld by *Kanon* would be inconceivable independently of a Zen-oriented outlook that sees greater beauty in the melting snowflake than in the durable crystal, in a wilting flower than in one in full bloom. Everything is perceived as being always on the verge of dissolution into nothingness. Nothingness, in this contexts, does not constitute a state of absence or lack. In fact, it is a positive assertion of the invisible and intangible worlds extending in all directions beyond the boundaries of the limited reality available to the sensorium. *Kanon*'s take on memory affirms this view insofar as the facets of life which memory empirically discloses can never presume to equal the richness of the worlds that elude sensory experience and may only be approached by imaginatively embracing the mysteries of the inscrutable, the nameless, the inchoate, the unanchorable.

As the Zen thinker Dohgen (1200–1253) emphasizes, the prerequisite of a person's apprehension of the dynamically elusive richness of the universe and attendant openness to the unpredictable is the ability to relinquish egocentrism: "Acting on and witnessing myriad things with the burden of oneself is delusion. Acting on and witnessing oneself in the advent of myriad things is enlightenment.... Forgetting oneself is being enlightened by all things" (Dohgen, p. 32). The Zen Master Ekaku Hakuin (1686–1769) promulgates a germane approach in proposing that self-elision is the precondition of "seeing into one's own nature," which can only be realized if one has "cut off the root of life": "You must be prepared to let go your hold when hanging from a sheer precipice, to die and return again to life" (Hakuin, pp. 133–35).

Yielding a unique blend of drama, romance, fantasy and comedy, *Kanon* unobtrusively invites us to ponder at practically each turn in its diegesis the meaning of urban architecture and the importance of memory in the genesis of that meaning. The city is not something that simply happens to surround the characters but rather something that happens *to* them as they record it in their mnemonic storage. Generally, urban architecture is so pervasive and so much a part of day-to-day life that we do not see it. What we perceive is the life that spills over buildings — namely, activities such as playing, sleeping, drinking, eating and traveling associated with specific spaces — and not the spaces themselves. What *Kanon* dramatizes, conversely, is a situation where people perceive the places they interact with as such. Urban architecture is a dimension they can never take for granted because it defines them by alternately organizing and scrambling their memories. Memory, therefore, is the basis upon which meaning is erected, albeit haphazardly.

As argued not merely in the present chapter but in this book as a whole, memory establishes our connection to the world as every facet of experience becomes embroiled in the mnemonic process, even if only to be consigned to the limbo of amnesia. Promulgating this idea, *Kanon* emphasizes that memory both shapes our separate identities as discreet beings and holds individuals together to forge the identities of whole cultural ensembles. Moreover, the series suggests that memory supplies the connective tissue that links the present with both the past and the future: what its characters remember of their past — and, no less crucially, what they have forgotten — contributes to what they do now and influences what they will become. At the same time, the anime shows that as they go about trying to make sense of their lives, its personae produce meaning out of the memory of the city — the phrase alluding at one to their recollections of the city and to the city's own mnemonic heritage.

In the course of extracting meaning from the urban environment, a correspondence develops between an individual's reminiscences and the embodied memory of the city itself. On the one hand, people project their personal histories onto streets and edifices, thereby adding to the overall significance of the built environment in an eminently subjective fashion. This is borne out by Yuuichi's speculations regarding his perception of the city in the present by comparison with his submerged childhood recollections thereof. In this respect, the phrase "memory of the city" refers to a person's variable remembrances of the urban setting. On the other hand, a city's architecture can be said to have a memory insofar as each of its constituent parts holds a connection with time, which expresses itself through the patina acquired by buildings over the years, and to history, as evinced by specific styles tied to particular epochs. In *Kanon*, this dimension is illustrated by the town's capture of material traces of the passing of time which the characters gradually learn to detect and assemble into meaningful "texts." In this regard, the phrase "memory of the city" alludes to the built environment's own body of reminiscences.

In articulating these two aspects of urban memory as complementary facets of a singular phenomenon, *Kanon* persistently underscores the symbiotic interaction of individual and collective memories in the context of the city. In so doing, the show harks back to the very etymology of the word "context," the Latin *contextere*—i.e., "to weave together." The story arcs revolving around Makoto's metamorphosis, Mai's self-repression and Ayu's catastrophic trauma, among others, are precisely threads in a fabric that cumulatively represents both the characters' intersubjective connections and their relationship with the urban environment on which they map themselves as they are, in turn, charted by it. As various temporalities connecting private and communal memories merge and collide, specific sites are concurrently evoked. These do not deliver a uniform, let alone stable, sense of space but rather a space made multifaceted and fluid by its amalgamation of diverse time zones and its perpetuation of the past as a virtual archive of mnemonic fragments. Time is not simply superimposed on space but embedded in its landscapes and urbanscapes in the guise of a mnemonic galaxy.

From the foregoing remarks, it is not hard to see that one of *Kanon*'s most abiding lessons consists of its emphasis on the inextricability of space and time, situation and development, position and motion—in other words, city and memory. Urban settings are assiduously portrayed as dynamic scenarios that are ultimately no less involved with temporality than they are with spatiality, mainly due to their ongoing constructions and displacements of memory. Since memories appear to flow of their own accord rather than in response to voluntary retrieval, the individuals that experience them are repeatedly unsettled by swarms of images thought long-forgotten and are hence enjoined to face the limitations of both their consciousness and their will. In its elaboration of the city-memory dyad, *Kanon* also upholds most eloquently R. E. Park's suggestion that the city is "a state of mind," combining the characteristics of "an artificial construction" and those of "a product of nature" (Park, p. 1). Positing the concept of the city as inextricable from both private and collective memory traces, the anime concurrently echoes David Lowenthal's proposition that "every image and idea about the world is compounded of personal experience, learning, imagination, and memory. The places that we live in, those we visit and travel through, the worlds we read about and see in works of art, and the realms of imagination and fantasy each contribute to our images of nature and man" (Lowenthal, p. 260).

At the same time, in dramatizing its characters' yearning to fathom the enigmas of an elusive city, the show devises a novel version of the myth of the *terra incognita* as a fantasy of discovery and conquest that is also, inevitably, a tale about the ineradicability of the unfathomable. Even in an exhaustively explored and mapped-out world, where frontiers have been pushed to the limits of outer space, on the one hand, and the minutest particles, on the other, space retains obscurities and secrets. Discovery does not yield final knowledge but rather the desire, forever renewed and forever deferred, for further knowledge. As J. K. Wright observes, "If there is no *terra incognita* today in the absolute sense, so also no *terra* is absolutely *cognita*," since "the unknown stimulates the imagination to conjure up mental images of what to look for within it, and the more there is found, the more the imagination suggests for further search" (Wright J. K., p. 4).

Kanon forcefully proposes, with variable degrees of emphasis in different episodes, that the space of the city cannot be conclusively deciphered insofar as any revelations it offers always inaugurate as many opportunities for further speculation on the part of its inhabitants and visitors. When the characters presume to have solved the riddles at the heart of their town, they soon find that these solutions are precarious because there can be no incontrovertible evidence of their validity. At best, any provisional explanations work as clues to new questions. In the face of this abiding sense of the unknown, the characters' imaginations tend to formulate further puzzles nested within the original mysteries they aimed to confront, in the fashion of Russian dolls or Chinese boxes. Concurrently, the tangible urban settings which the actors occupy are traversed at all times by their fictional alternatives: the cities they might have been instead or might become either in reality or in visions. Jonathan Raban's reflections on the city's inherent duplicity are apposite: "The city as we might imagine it, the soft city of illusion, myth, aspiration, nightmare, is as real, maybe more real, than the hard city one can locate in maps and statistics, in monographs on urban sociology and demography and architecture" (Raban, p. 10). As noted earlier, *Kanon* removes the barrier between the subjective interiority of dreams and mirages and shared notions of objective reality by persistently interweaving the workings of consciousness with those of the unconscious. What may seem familiar one moment becomes uncanny the next. Accordingly, the buildings that go unheeded as characters go past them on their daily errands leap out terrifyingly when those same characters' hold on reality is enfeebled by anxiety or fear.

Higurashi communicates a cognate message by repeatedly transforming bucolic locations enfolded in hushed provincial calm into stages for the eruption of full-fledged horror. The soft-hued lanes along which the characters walk to their cozy rural school or to peaceful venues of relaxation and fun are capable of acquiring baleful connotations in the space of just a few frames. As the adventure progresses, the town's collective memory turns out to be the prime force triggering this uncanny transformation: the evil that is always on the verge of shattering Hinamizawa's apparent tranquility is enshrined in an age-old legacy of vengefulness and hatred. *Lum the Forever* also exposes the city's metamorphic powers in disquieting scenes that portray the heroine's mounting sense of alienation. As Lum moves through her environment to discover that not only her own grasp of reality but also other people's awareness of her very existence are rapidly vanishing, the once familiar streets, houses and shopping malls turn into ill-boding presences that seem to threaten the solidity of all she has ever known, trusted and treasured in her memories. When Lum eventually ventures into Tomobiki-cho's subterranean gloom and buried history, the town's defamiliarizing power reaches its apotheosis.

Boogiepop Phantom takes both its characters and its viewers on perilous journeys down the narrow alley in virtually all of its episodes, never allowing them to take refuge for long in reassuringly luminous locations. *Aria*, for its part, highlights the precariousness of people's perception of their environment by invoking Venice's legendary instability as a metaphor for sensory uncertainty and fluctuation. With *Kanon*, as intimated, the town's disorienting proclivities result primarily from the ubiquitous amnesia affecting its key personae. Any location is capable of assuming malefic connotations the moment a character senses that just beneath the veneer of the familiar lies an inscrutable tangle of repressed memories.

Henri Lefebvre's theorization of the city is also relevant in this context. Lefebvre emphasizes the multidimensionality of space by suggesting that it is crucial to differentiate between *spatial practice*, which is based on how the world is perceived; the *representation of space*, which proceeds from how the world is conceived or conceptualized; and *representational space*, which pivots on how the world is experienced by the human body. Lefebvre maintains that "the lived, conceived and perceived realms should be interconnected, so that the 'subject,' the individual member of a given social group, may move from one to another without confusion." However, he also concedes that the three domains only "constitute a coherent whole" in "favourable circumstances, when a common language, a consensus and a code can be established" (Lefebvre, p. 40). In the titles here examined, the fragmentation of reality—and attendant displacement of empirical facts by dreams, visions and hallucinations—point to worlds in which the harmonious scenario depicted by Lefebvre rarely obtains, if at all.

While it is tempting to ideate space as a dimension in which sensations, thoughts and experiences seamlessly coalesce, there is no guarantee that this will be the case. This is because the urban environment holds no built-in stability but only comes about as a contingent amalgamation of impressions, mental processes and actions that are neither organically integrated nor objective. D. C. D. Pocock argues that this fluidity results from that environment's openness to subjective and discordant readings: "Of the several kinds of meaning which may attach to a building or townscape—concrete, functional, emotional, symbolic—it is the symbolic interpretations, rather than intrinsic spatial attributes, which are important in city personality" (Pocock, p. 256). The preponderance of symbolic decodings over precise evaluations causes the space of the city to disintegrate, time and again, into a kaleidoscopic assortment of variable features.

Pursuing an analogous argument, Lefebvre points out that the current tendency to talk about urban space in terms of social practices does not automatically reduce it to a bundle of purely political or economic factors since all social space is also, inevitably, a geography of emotions, experiences and longings: "Representational space is alive: it speaks. It has an affective kernel or center: Ego, bed, bedroom, dwelling, house; or, square, church, graveyard. It embraces the loci of passion, of action and of lived situations" (Lefebvre, p. 42). This hypothesis is fully corroborated by the productions here explored. It would indeed be pointless to try to dissever locations such as the cherry-tree garden in *Lum the Forever*, the merry-go-round in *Boogiepop Phantom*, the shrine in *Higurashi*, *Aria*'s lagoon, and the hospital, domestic interiors, stores and school grounds in *Kanon* from their emotional significance, insofar as their effectiveness as animated worlds emanates precisely from that import, not from their documentary accuracy or statistical probability. The memories which disparate personae bring to bear on those spaces unrelentingly enhance both their affective richness and their aliveness.

Michel de Certeau's assessment of walking as a means of constantly remapping urban space by creating ever new routes through it supplies a relevant metaphor for the journeys undertaken by the anime's key characters. Voyaging through the city is tantamount to turning its space into a narrative. On the one hand, the critic maintains, this entails "conceiving and constructing space on the basis of a finite number of stable, isolatable, and interconnected properties" (de Certeau, p. 93), which invests it with an aura of permanence. On the other, as Steve Pile notes, de Certeau's argument draws attention to "the innumerable ways in which walking in the streets mobilizes other subtle, stubborn, embodied, resistant meanings. The streets become haunted by the ghosts of other stories.... The city becomes a ghost town of memories without a language to articulate them because walking is a transient and evanescent practice.... In this unmappable space, walkers ceaselessly move around in 'spaces of darkness and trickery'" (Pile, p. 226; subquotation: de Certeau, p. 18).

The anime's key characters are all portrayed as voyagers through urban settings that offer potentially limitless narrative webs. The routes they travel, no matter how regularly they do so, never disclose the same exact stories, since the signs they yield do not supply the characters with dependable meanings but only with baffling clues amenable to contrasting interpretations. As a prismatic ensemble, the works discussed in this chapter underscore the vital part played by memory in the apprehension of space, memory representing not so much a personal attribute or possession as the receptacle for a collective imaginary in which even the most intimate thoughts are endlessly translatable into public signs.

CHAPTER 7

Memory as Worldbuilding

RahXephon
(TV series; dir. Yutaka Izubuchi, 2002)
– and –
RahXephon: Pluralitas Concentio
(feature film; dirs. Tomomi Kyoda
and Yutaka Izubuchi, 2003)

> Ever drifting down the stream —
> Lingering in the golden gleam —
> Life, what is it but a dream?
> — Lewis Carroll, *Through the Looking-Glass,
> and What Alice Found There* (1871)

> Music is the art which is most nigh to tears and memory.
> — Oscar Wilde (1854–1900)

Anime's worldbuilding proclivities emanate from a venerable tradition within the history of the form that is intimately intertwined with the evolution of the intergalactic epic. In the OVA series *Record of Lodoss War* (dirs. Akinori Nagaoka *et al.*, 1990) and in the TV show *Vision of Escaflowne* (dirs. Kazuki Akane and Shouji Kawamori, 1996), for example, memory is employed as a crucial tool in the creation of entire universes, their histories, traditions, customs and moral codes. In blending disparate stylistic formulae, moreover, shows such as these deliver superb hybrids of science fiction and magic, and thus operate as dynamic memories of anime's evolution over the decades. *Record of Lodoss War* has also constructed a body of memories for subsequent anime to hark back to in the shape of parodies of its sword-and-sorcery discourse, as demonstrated by the *Elven Bride* OVA series (dir. Hiroshi Yamakawa, 1995) with its humorous infusion of *hentai* (risqué) elements into the format. The magical imagery, particularly in the representation of magnificent dragons and elfin physiology, has also paved the way to numerous imitations, thus emplacing itself as an influential mnemonic substratum for intertextual manipulation.

Vision of Escaflowne has likewise provided a rich tapestry of visual motifs and symbolism, memories of which can be sensed in myriad later titles. Through its interweaving of popular anime conventions, especially those associated with the *mecha* and sports-drama subgenres, esoteric practices informed by the ancestral art of Tarot reading, teenage romance, and jocular touches bolstered by impish characters such as cat-girls, the series engages in a sustained investigation of the meaning of destiny. In this regard, *Escaflowne* offers insights into the nature of memory as an extrapersonal legacy shaping human choices and actions beyond the empirically measurable. These titles, it must be stressed, are simply illustrative instances of worldbuilding proclivities so endemic in anime that any attempt to itemize their manifestations in detail in the present context would be not only overambitious but also quite inappropriate. Remarkable examples of worldbuilding sustained by mnemonic echoes of themes and imagery drawn from both anime itself and other forms abound and each deserves separate and attentive inspection. Both *Lodoss* and *Escaflowne*— as indeed several other works in the same tradition — capture the spirit of *yugen* in their epic sublimity. Quite a different interpretation of the idea is offered by the omnibus *Memories* (1994), where the engagement with the ineffable amounts to an effort to perceive latent connections among disparate genres. *Memories* indeed articulates the construction of alternate histories through memory by both individuals and communities by recourse to three apparently incongruous but actually intercomplementary generic scenarios: surrealistic romance; apocalyptic sci-fi; military dystopia.

The first piece, "Magnetic Rose" (dir. Kouji Morimoto), is overtly concerned with the interplay of memory and fantasy. The narrative follows a deep-space garbage crew as it responds to a distress call emanating from what is held to be an abandoned station. The source of the signal is traced to a "space graveyard" consisting of galactic detritus that emits a magnetic charm, poignantly underscored by a mélange of Puccini arias. When they reach their destination, the salvagers are faced with a palatial residence summoned from a barrage of holographic illusions and nanotechnological effects: a veritable Plato's Cave for the (post)digital age. Replete with graphic recollections of various architectural styles (e.g., Palladian, Gothic, Baroque) and of Surrealist paintings by artists as diverse as Frieda Kahlo, René Magritte and Giorgio de Chirico, this alternate world turns out to be a materialization of the memories of a defunct opera singer. The corporeal dimension of memory is thus graphically underlined. The obfuscation of the boundaries demarcating present events from recollections reaches its apogee as the crew members become totally absorbed in the former diva's virtual construct, unable ever to return to their original world.

"Stink Bomb" (dir. Tensai Okamura), the second segment, revolves around a hypochondriac employed at a government laboratory seemingly dedicated to the testing of new medicinals. Eager to combat the latest manifestation of its chronic malaise, the character ingests a pill that causes anyone in his proximity to plunge into a coma, while the entire environment is imbued with a noxious aroma. The pill, as it transpires, is not quite the kind of remedy the hero might have fancied, its effect actually resulting from secret research into chemical warfare. Of the three shorts included in the collection, "Stink Bomb" is the least explicitly involved with the memory trope. However, time is graphically brought into play in the sequences dramatizing the chemical's effect on the environment: the radical disruption of seasonal cycles in the space of just a few hours appears to have resulted in a temporal compression whereby climatic phenomena and expressions of vegetable and animal life associated with specific times of the year coexist in a kaleidoscopic glut of uncanny combinations. For example, cherry blossom and sunflowers are simultaneously in bloom. It is as though the planet's ecomemory had gone awry, and Nature's intrinsic temporal rhythms dissolved into an atemporal continuum akin to amnesia.

The final part of the triptych, "Cannon Fodder" (dir. Katsuhiro Otomo), offers a minimalistic vignette of a single day in the life of an average family through its numbing routine of cannon maintenance and shell production. Their entire city's resources are channeled into precisely the sorts of tasks they themselves quotidianly undertake, with no room left for any other activities or pursuits. The piece utilizes memory at two levels. On the one hand, its uncompromising representation of a totalitarian regime dominated by military imperatives and vapid patriotism is redolent of both actual historical moments, ranging from the Napoleonic Empire to World War I, and narrative sources as varied as George Orwell, Kurt Vonnegut and Margaret Atwood (to cite but a few). On the other hand, "Cannon Fodder" places considerable psychological emphasis on the idea that its characters, engrossed as they are in manufacturing huge explosives and lobbing them at an invisible and unnamed enemy, appear passively resigned to their fate, having quite forgotten — or perhaps repressed — with whom and why they are fighting.

It is in the interdimensional epic *RahXephon*, this chapter's focal case study, that anime's worldbuilding passion reaches its apotheosis, combining generic and symbolic ingredients partially shared by the other shows outlined in the preceding paragraphs.[1] *RahXephon* pivots on the character of seventeen-year-old student and artist Ayato Kamina as he is torn away from his uneventful existence in "Tokyo Jupiter" and enjoined to take charge of the RahXephon: a mighty biomechanoid capable of interconnecting flawlessly with its pilot both physically and psychologically. The saga's premise is that at the end of the year 2012, namely fifteen years prior to the story's beginning, the Earth was attacked by aliens known as "Mu" (short for "Mulians"), who deploy clay creatures dubbed "Dolem" as their principal weapons. Having appeared in the skies above Tokyo, the Mu were at first silent and inactive but a preemptive strike unleashed by mankind early in 2013 induced them to release their own weapons and proceed to decimate millions of people the world over. (The attack, it will eventually transpire, was actually ordered by an undercover Mu officer posing as the leader of the human forces, Masayoshi Kuki.)

By the year 2027, the invaders' threat still looms large even though they would seem to have limited their dominion to the enclosure of Tokyo Jupiter. This city's inhabitants believe they are the only survivors of the extraterrestrial onslaught, putatively thanks to the protective dome with a radius of approximately thirty miles raised for their protection by scientists — which, due to its resemblance to the planet Jupiter, gains the metropolis its current denomination. This, however, is only the official version of the truth, circulated around the city to keep its occupants stolidly quiet. It gradually emerges that the world around Tokyo Jupiter is, in fact, still operative, though severely depleted by the conflict in many areas. The city itself has been occupied by the Mu, who have erected the dome to prevent Earth's united forces, "Terra," from reclaiming it. To keep their captives in a state of oblivion and relative inertia, the Mu have thoroughly reconditioned their brains to make them forget practically everything they experienced prior to the capital's segregation. Moreover, they have warped their perception of the passage of time, as a result of which they lag behind the rest of the planet by twelve years. Thus, although Ayato is seventeen within his time zone, he would actually be twenty-nine in the outside world. The space-time curvature occurring inside Tokyo Jupiter is analogous to the phenomenon observed in the vicinity of black holes. This indicates that the Mulians have tampered with fundamental physical laws, yet made it possible for the humans trapped inside the domed enclosure to go on living quite normal lives, by generating a space that is capable of transforming time energy particles.

As in *The Place Promised in Our Early Days* (please see Chapter 4), so in *RahXephon*, the concept of multidimensional space postulated by quantum theory is accorded an important role.[2] Indeed, the space inside Tokyo Jupiter is essentially a pocket of a distinctive space-time that has managed to infiltrate the Earth's regular space-time after severing itself from another dimension or universe regulated by different spatio-temporal rhythms. The dome's surface constitutes an interdimensional layer separating not just two portions of the Earth, therefore, but two *worlds*. Hence, the series engages in what could be termed a bifocal worldbuilding enterprise, simultaneously constructing the human culture fostered by Terra beyond the boundaries of Tokyo Jupiter and the Mu-dominated culture within the dome.

In both worlds, the existence of space is inextricable from the flow of time and hence the formation and regimentation of memories. In the case of the alien civilization, the coalescence of spatial and temporal coordinates issues from its ability to cross interdimensional barriers by manipulating a large portion of space-time and insulating it within its own sinus of space-time. In Terra's case, the collusion is made possible by the development of interdimensional technology capable of piercing the dome's surface by recourse to preposterous amounts of energy (created with the help of quantum computers) that can form a sympathetic resonance between the penetrating vehicles and the space-time inside Tokyo Jupiter. A quantum computer is able to defy interdimensional partitions, at least in principle, due to its intrinsic modus operandi. While a classical computer abides by a binary logic whereby each of the bits of which its memory consists holds the value of either a 1 or a 0, a quantum computer works with "qubits." Each qubit can hold a 1, a 0 or a blend (*superimposition*) of both of those values. This property is a direct corollary of its adherence to the laws of quantum physics, according to which an object can be in several states at one and the same time—and also, by extension, inhabit several universes at once. These ideas are imaginatively invoked by both Shinkai's *Place Promised* and *RahXephon*'s use of quantum mechanics as a means of crossing dimensional barriers. As shown later in this chapter, the TV series *Zegapain* posits the quantum computer as a means of constructing alternate realities through simulation.

In expanding exponentially the properties of conventional digital memory, the quantum computer and the physical laws underpinning it concurrently inaugurate fresh mnemonic horizons for the entities they affect. Indeed, the hypothesis that the same entity may hold different states simultaneously carries as a concomitant the possibility of its participation in disparate clusters of memories. This is attested to by Ayato's experiences, where the boy's real childhood memories, the mnemonic baggage implanted in his psyche by the alien invaders, and the novel memories formed following his departure from the domed metropolis meet, merge and clash in variable constellations. Quantum theory is also invoked through the concept of "quantum condensation," a phenomenon seen in both the RahXephon and the Dolem that causes the mass of a portion of matter to increase and gravity in the surrounding space likewise to intensify. This is conducive to temporal deceleration. Moreover, the light rays emitted by a Dolem during a fight create a breach in space-time that draws matter from it into a "phase-space"— namely, an alternate reality that exists in parallel to the human world.

Terra, for its part, is controlled by the "Earth Federation" and has been established as a collaborative enterprise by all the countries disrupted by the Mu. Eager to ascertain the reasons behind the aliens' advent and to develop military resources capable of confronting adequately the indomitable Dolem, Terra consists primarily of Japanese personnel, Japan having been the country most severely damaged by the assault. The name "Terra" is an acronym of a phrase in Esperanto, the organization's official language: "Tereno Empireo Rapidmova Reakcii Armeo"—"Earth Federation Rapid-Moving Response Army." In their physical appearance, Mu are identical to humans. Yet, they harbor a genetic marker that causes their blood to turn blue as they reach maturity, at which point they also lose their memories. The memory topos is thus overtly articulated by the series as a key diegetic factor, the displacement of the aliens' mnemonic inheritance being essential to their psychosomatic constitution. As the Mu character of Maya at one point observes, "Forgetting is part of our fate."

Like *Gilgamesh*, *RahXephon* stretches back millennia to the dawn of human history, seeding enigmas in each epoch it touches. While the narrative plays fair with the audience and arguably provides all the important clues to the unraveling of its elaborate weave, unobtrusively scattered links easily go unheeded. The mnemonic exercise which viewers are drawn into is therefore quite exacting, though conducive to generous rewards. Clues to *RahXephon*'s ultimate mystery are disseminated so gradually — even surreptitiously — over its fabric as to be appreciable only through patient repeat viewings. A panoramic survey of the broad time scale against which the story unfolds — gratefully indebted to both Philip R. Banks' meticulous research and to the ADV Vision publication *RahXephon Bible*— eloquently attests to the grandiose scope of the show's worldbuilding venture and of the mnemotechnology thereby articulated by its diegesis. The events, relationships and plot twists outlined in the chronological reconstruction of the saga and its backdrop presented below as a study guide are disclosed in an emphatically non-chronological fashion by the series itself.

The Mu Empire is held to have found inception in approximately 10,000 B.C. on Earth, and to have excelled in all aspects of art and technology, as well as expanded steadily over the ensuing millennia through the foundation of colonies in Egypt, South America and Burma. This intriguing premise could be said to supply a mytho-historical memory underpinning the edifice of *RahXephon*'s worldbuilding venture. The apotheosis of the Mu's technological development is marked by the luminary Ernst von Bähbem's construction of the Xephon system (3,342 B.C.), an entity comparable to an artificial deity. Regrettably, a cataclysmic accident incurred in the course of the creature's assemblage results in the world splitting into two. The Mu find themselves stranded in a parallel-reality Earth, 95 percent of which is submerged, and resort to the erection of complex hovering cities to supply alternative inhabitable spaces. One such conglomerate is Hiranipra, the surreal citadel first seen floating above Tokyo in 2012 and then again in 2027.

At the time of the cosmic schism described above, the Xephon system itself is dimidiated, with the part referred to as the "Black Egg" residing with humans, and the portion dubbed the "White Egg" remaining in the Mulians' possession. By an act of nemesis, Bähbem is accidentally cut off from his people and left in the human realm. He does not, however, concede defeat. In a titanic display of hubris, a proclivity bound to be readily associated with his mindset as the adventure unfolds, the scientist invents a time-processing device that will eventually enable the Mu to return to Earth. Additionally, even though physical transfer across the two dimensions is as yet unattainable, he manages to establish channels of communication with the extraterrestrials and thus perpetuates the race's resolve to resurge as Earth's principal civilization. Aware that this operation could feasibly take centuries, Bähbem then proceeds to clone substitute bodies for himself wherein his mind can be hosted and hence ensures the endurance of his consciousness—and memories—over endless generations. Bähbem also believes that the Xephon's initial failure was due to the employment of an inappropriate "instrumentalist"—i.e., the person responsible for its activation—and that the perfection of this key agency is therefore of paramount importance. (Bähbem himself undertook the task in the first place.) Only the perfect instrumentalist has the potential to deploy the artificial god as a means of reuniting the Mulian and human domains before they regress to the state of primordial mud. The scientist gradually realizes that the person pivotal to the accomplishment of his grandiose goal must be seventeen years old and combine features of both Mulian blood and human blood.

In the late nineteenth century, the British occult writer, inventor, engineer and officer James Churchward (1851–1936) embarks on a punctilious study of Mulian culture after inspecting a set of stone tablets found in India said to have been written in an ancient language known by no more than three people in the entire country. Churchward later publishes his discoveries as *The Lost Continent of Mu* (1926) with the intention of proving the existence of the eponymous world in the Pacific Ocean. The Mu civilization, according to Churchward, flourished 50,000 years prior to his time, had 64 million inhabitants and housed the Garden of Eden. Its people were putatively named "Nacaals." Notably, the Nacaal Company, said to have been founded in 1576, is presented in *RahXephon* as the Bähbem Foundation's precursor. Churchward's book remains largely ignored, with rather infelicitous consequences in *RahXephon*'s fictive logic. Of particular interest, in the logic of Izubuchi's story, is Churchward's proposition that the Egyptian Sun deity Ra found inception with the Mu, "Rah" being the term used by the Nacaals to designate the sun, their divinities and their rulers. The RahXephon's godlike status is hinted at in various places, as is the supernatural function of its instrumentalist. This aspect is underscored in the finale of *RahXephon*'s theatrical adaptation. The virtual obliteration of Churchward's account in favor of orthodox versions of history pithily attests to the arbitrary fashion in which conventional historiography encodes and promulgates collective memories despite its insistent claims to objectivity. This macrocosmic distortion of historical truth finds a microcosmic correlative in the construction of Quon's personal life story. The girl is officially held to have been born in 2011, to have lost both of her parents in 2019 and to have moved to Nirai Town to live with her supposed brother Itsuki Kisaragi. In actual fact, as we shall see, she is a synthetic being conveyed to the human world by the Mu.

Having witnessed the First and Second World Wars, the Mu conclude that humans cannot be trusted with the handling of the Xephon. To deal with human unpredictability and lack of discipline, they create the Dolem: colossal entities operating as channels between the human and the Mu dimensions. Each Dolem is bound to a controlling Mulian. Some of the creatures are also connected to a specially prepared human being tagged a "sub–

Mulian" or "Dolem host" that binds the Dolem to the human dimension and thus enables the Mu to gain control of the human's body and consciousness with the assistance of an elaborate helmet-like contraption. When a Dolem is damaged or destroyed, both the Mu and the human to whom it is attached suffer the very same fate in their respective dimensions.

Satisfied with the creation of the clay giants, yet distrustful of the Mu's readiness to operate the Xephon system to its full capacity, Bähbem surreptitiously begins to train humans to do so instead should the necessity arise, gives them half of the Xephon system (the Black Egg) and eventually founds the Terra organization. Bähbem knows that the ideal instrumentalist is bound to recreate the world in accordance with the interests of his/her race and that the Mulian or human nature of the agency in question therefore carries momentous implications. However, he does not seem to harbor any real preference as to who is finally responsible for the tuning as long as he achieves his primary goal: to abide in memory as the ultimate designer. (In the saga's theatrical version, conversely, the character is hell-bent on seeing the Mu victorious.) Therefore, while not giving up altogether on his people, whom he continues to support and abet in their exploitation of human bodies and minds, Bähbem nonetheless associates himself with humans both in order to advance his personal agenda and in order to conceal from the Earth Federation his ongoing collaboration with the alien race. Thus, the arrogant inventor plays a potentially nefarious double game throughout the saga, concurrently committing atrocious crimes against humanity in both direct and circuitous ways. Ironically, Bähbem never witnesses the apotheosis of his grand schemes since he is shot dead on its very eve by Lieutenant Colonel Jumonji Takeshi, conveyed by the Earth Federation HQ to collect evidence of the scientist's crimes — a.k.a. Johji Futagami, the alias adopted by this character while he operates as an undercover agent pretending to be merely a nosy reporter. (In the film, the character of Jin Kunugi acts as Bähbem's executioner instead.)

In around 1980, Professor Shougo Rikudoh and his assistant Shirow Watari discover the Black Egg of Xephon in the Neriya Shrine, to which they have traveled with the Bähbem Foundation's financial backing. At the end of the same decade, the Mu convey to the human world two young women, Maya Kamina and Quon Al Padis, whom Shirow discovers. Quon, who is being raised to become an instrumentalist, is held at the Foundation in a dormant state until the time is ripe for her powers to reveal themselves. Maya, who has prematurely awakened only five years after her spiriting forth and cannot therefore aspire to the role, devotes herself to the conception of a human instrumentalist and is adopted by Shougo Rikudoh on Nirai Island. In the late 1990s, Maya and Shirow marry and go by the name of Kamina. In 1998, Ayato and Itsuki come into the world as twin brothers. These children are composed of genetic data drawn from Quon and Shirow, and it is hoped that at least one of them will turn into the perfect instrumentalist for the Xephon system. Itsuki is raised at the Foundation, whereas Ayato is given to Maya and Shirow to rear. Maya herself turns out to have been responsible for the erection of the dome as a means of insulating Ayato from the human world and ensuring that he would only come to know and love the Mulian culture and tune the world in accordance with its interests. Maya's plan is threatened by Ayato's childhood encounter with Haruka, which is why she has also endeavored to erase Ayato's memories of the human world. While Maya is referred to as Ayato's mother in the early part of the series, the youth's biological mother is actually Quon.[3]

Meanwhile, Bähbem and his associates are busy disseminating cloned instrumentalists throughout Tokyo, carefully blending them with the human population, to supply a conveniently primed pool of beings capable of synchronizing with the Dolem. In approximately 2009, Ayato Kamina meets Haruka Mishima for the first time while he is visiting his dad, who is still intent on the investigation of the Neriya remains, and the girl is holidaying with her uncle Shougo. It is on this occasion that the boy paints the picture of Haruka standing on a rock facing the sea which will haunt both his psyche and *RahXephon*'s whole diegesis. Ayato and Haruka meet again at school in Tokyo and become inseparable friends. At this time, Haruka also meets Maya but has no idea that Ayato's "mother" is her own uncle's adopted daughter. In 2012, as noted, the Mu make their first appearance over Japan and are preventively attacked by humans with catastrophic repercussions. Being outside the capital at the time with her pregnant mother, Haruka is wrenched apart from her beloved Ayato. When the Mu seal Tokyo off within the dome-shaped territory and modify the psyches of its citizens, Ayato is among the victims of the invaders' mnemonic reconditioning. Yet, the image of the girl on a rock facing the sea tenaciously lingers — and, with it, a phantasmic vestige of the flesh-and-blood Haruka herself. As a Mu, Maya is declared a traitor in the wake of the invasion, while her husband endeavors to protect his own repute by changing his family name to Watari.

Meanwhile, Haruka grows up in the outside world, thereby ageing at the normal rate. At one stage, she meets Itsuki at college and dates him — arguably because he reminds her of Ayato — until the young man discovers that she cannot forget someone caught within Tokyo Jupiter's impervious membrane. Haruka is eventually recruited by Terra alongside her sister Megumi, and both move in with their uncle Shougo. Upon their mother's remarriage, they gain the new family name of Shitow. In the year 2027, a massive military mission meant to guarantee Ayato's removal from Tokyo Jupiter at the hands of Haruka Shitow herself is launched. It is at this point that the action dramatized in the anime actually opens. The designation of the maneuver as "Operation Overlord" offers a mnemonic echo of actual historical events, being commonly used by the Allies in World War II to refer to D-Day.

At the beginning of the series, Ayato lives alone with his putative mother Maya, a high-ranking researcher whose demanding job allows her to devote precious little time to the boy. As he plods through yet another ordinary day, unfolding as customary at a sluggish pace, the protagonist is suddenly thrown into chaos by a momentous air strike launched by an unknown enemy. Amidst the rubble, Ayato chances upon a girl named Reika Mishima who uncannily recalls the female figure the boy is intent on painting when we first meet him: his former sweetheart Haruka Mishima. Beset by men with blue blood who claim to be security agents, Ayato is rescued by the athletically lethal Haruka Shitow. Although she urges him to trust and follow her, Ayato remains suspicious of her motives and ends up following Reika instead. Reika, it transpires, is actually "Ixtli": an incarnation of the RahXephon's very soul. (The word *ixtli* means "face" in Nahuatl, a language spoken by the Aztecs.) Ixtli/Reika proffers some intriguing designations for the RahXephon: e.g., "mirror of truth," "one who will tune the world" and "the forbidden song that will unify all things" (Hikawa, Kubo and Kaneko, p. 63). Her aspect indicates that the specific physical appearance she has assumed emanates from Ayato's own slumbering memories of the girl he so deeply loved prior to the Mulian occupation and has never conclusively eclipsed. A few cryptic scenes sprinkled across the show's early segments indicate that Ayato and Reika are bonded in a spiritual or even metaphysical way. The intimation that the girl is not human is first communicated by her lack of a reflection — unless, that is, she requires one.

In a particularly intriguing scene, the girl appears in Ayato's classroom and casually interacts with his friends Hiroko Asahina and Mamoru Torigai by tinkering with their memories and thus making it possible for them to remember someone they do not truly know and warmly interact with her. (Later in the show, Reika features as Commander Makoto Isshiki's assistant and seems able to modify the memories of the Terra personnel in an analogous manner. In this context, the girl actually calls herself "Haruka.") Reika's physical similarity to Haruka Mishima, whose empty desk within Ayato's classroom is the focus of some poignant shots, usefully contributes to the ruse. Also tantalizing is the scene in which Ayato speaks with Reika on the telephone. When Maya redials the number to find out whom her charge has been in contact with, she discovers that this is unassigned. This suggests that Ayato and Reika are somehow capable of using channels of communication that belong to a parallel reality — possibly of Reika's own making.

On the one hand, Reika could be said to have infiltrated Ayato's mnemonic storehouse by taking the shape of someone he has known and treasured, and further penetrated his quotidian existence by making him visualize her as a pupil and inducing his mates to do the same. In this respect, Ayato may seem to play a fundamentally passive part in the game. On the other hand, since Reika's countenance results from his own personal desires and memories, the male lead is simultaneously accorded an active role. Since the "contact" enabling the connection between an instrumentalist and a biomechanoid is supposed to be a person of great importance to the potential pilot, it is not surprising that Reika should assume Haruka Mishima's physiognomy. Strictly speaking, the figure of Reika is not really a person in its own right but the embodiment of an image ingrained in the youth's unconscious. (In the case of the RahXephon piloted by Quon, who is also an instrumentalist, the creature's soul takes the semblance of Ayato as the person presumably dearest to the Mu girl's own heart — which is not surprising when one considers that he is, after all, her son.)

As though by telepathy or incantation, Reika leads Ayato to the sanctuary where the RahXephon is just emerging from its egg. Synchronizing with the biomechanoid through powers Ayato never even vaguely suspected of possessing, the boy's consciousness enables the RahXephon to pulverize a Dolem quite effortlessly. Following the incident, order is restored and the epic confrontation consigned to consensual oblivion. Haruka again proffers help, promising that she will show Ayato the "truth." This time, he tries to flee Tokyo Jupiter with her but Reika once more steers him towards the RahXephon. Upon this second encounter with the creature, Ayato's hidden powers fully awaken. At this point, he also faces the shocking revelation that Maya's blood is blue. After defeating one more Dolem, the RahXephon produces a "corridor" that enables it and its pilot to fly out of Tokyo Jupiter's supposedly impenetrable canopy with Haruka in tow.

When Ayato eventually regains consciousness in the outside world, he learns the truth from his rescuer about Tokyo Jupiter, the Mu's occupation and the temporal and mnemonic warp to which he and his fellow citizens have been subjected. Due to time dilation and mnemonic reconfiguration, Ayato is obviously not aware that the Haruka Shitow he meets as a twenty-nine-year-old woman and the Haruka Mishima from his early teens are one and the same person. Haruka, conversely, is fully conscious of the temporal incongruity under which they labor. This disparity infuses many scenes in which Ayato and Haruka interact with a profound sense of emotional isolation that is, at times, genuinely painful to behold. Haruka is seemingly a woman with many faces, pulling off astounding martial feats one moment and exuberantly indulging in an alcoholic binge the next, handling her adversaries with sardonic nonchalance when the need arises yet melting into cutesy girlishness at the sight of a stray kitten. Nonetheless, her personality derives unsurpassed psychological coherence from a single and unwavering affect: her lifelong love for Ayato. (The climax of Haruka's and Ayato's mnemonic ordeal is undoubtedly the scene in which the woman finally reveals to the youth that they were a couple at the age of fourteen and that her feelings towards him have not changed even though she is aware Ayato cannot remember that time. In a moment of intense pathos, the youth ripostes: "I may not remember the past but I know the present. And the one I love is the current you. I'm sorry for making you suffer all this time.")

Taken aboard Terra's Special Duty Aerial Carrier "Lilia Litvyak," the protagonist encounters several people bound to play important roles in his subsequent exploits — among them, the enigmatic girl Quon Kisaragi. Originating from Tokyo Jupiter, and therefore regarded suspiciously, Ayato is imprisoned but when yet another Dolem surfaces from the ocean and the RahXephon responds to the boy's call, breaking free from its restraints and valiantly fighting it off, it is decided that Ayato should be officially accepted as a member of Terra and put to work on Nirai Kanai Island. Concurrently, he is assigned a new home by Dr. Itsuki Kisaragi (Quon's foster brother and Ayato's own twin brother), where Haruka and her sister Megumi also live. Baffled by his relocation to a world he thought had been annihilated, and reluctant to pilot the RahXephon against the wave of Dolem freshly unleashed by the Mu, Ayato cannot help feeling that he is being exploited as a mere pawn in a game governed by rules well beyond his ken. His stability is by no means sustained by the resurgence in his formerly numbed psyche of memories of the putatively lost Haruka Mishima, and possibly even of a reincarnation thereof in the outside world in the person of Reika. More disturbingly still, Ayato gradually realizes that the Mu's "reality" and human "reality" are not separated by a clear boundary, and that his own identity in relation to each of those realms is far from unequivocal. The discovery that he, too, harbors Mulian genes is most unsettling, in this respect.

Ayato's inner conflict is exacerbated by the other characters' contrasting responses to the revelation that he is partly a Mulian. Lieutenant Souichi Yagumo, whom the *RahXephon Bible* felicitously describes as a "friendly prince" (Hikawa, Kubo, and Kaneko, p. 54) by virtue of his amiable and loyal personality, believes that all people are "connected" in the cosmos and that it does not matter, therefore, where one comes from. This world view resonates with a quintessentially Eastern philosophical message that foreshadows the Shinto-inspired flavor of *RahXephon*'s finale. The formidable pilot Elvy Hadhiyat, conversely, is so embittered by her memories of the mates she has lost in the course of Operation Overlord, of which she is the sole survivor among the Terra troops deployed therein, that the discovery of Ayato's nature fills her with blinding hatred. Yet, she does not hesitate to abet Haruka's efforts to protect the youth when she finds out about her colleague's past connection with him, which makes Elvy's overall portrayal admirably multifaceted.

As familiar certainties remorselessly crumble, the protagonist must concomitantly face up to the flimsiness of the space-time fabric itself. Grievous as the Dolem's attacks undeniably are, what indents Ayato's grasp of reality even more severely is the soaring apprehension that the physical world as such is disintegrating beneath him. In facing this challenge, the protagonist cannot automatically rely on any support or guidance, as emissaries from both the Mu camp and the human ranks reveal themselves capable of turning into ruthless foes. This predicament gains special urgency in the installment where Ayato and Quon enter the "Shrine of Time," a gateway to the Mu dimension where time advances at the same pace as it does within Tokyo Jupiter. Another instance of temporal dislocation occurs when the Dolem Vivace restrains the RahXephon completely by modifying its own configuration and synchronizing with the creature's "waveform," which results in the formation of a "corridor" into "undetectable territory" and in the pilot's transposition to a parallel world that looks exactly like the domed city. An especially eerie sense of displacement is conveyed by the scene, ostensibly set in Tokyo Jupiter, where Ayato appears to be donning his ordinary civilian clothes but catches a glimpse of his reflection in a shop window suggesting he is garbed in the piloting gear he was wearing at the time of Vivace's onslaught. Thus, the concept of a split reality is aptly complemented by visual allusions to a split identity.

The labyrinthian quality of the urban district which Ayato aimlessly roams intensifies the incident's uncanny atmosphere, simultaneously recalling Walter Benjamin's reflections on the modern city as a labyrinth — namely, "the home of the hesitant" lacking any obvious sense of direction or destination (Benjamin, p. 40). The sequence's surreal mood reaches a grotesque climax with the image of a toy penguin acquiring a life of its own and then bursting. Inexplicably faced by an adult Haruka in a café in defiance of reason and logic, Ayato senses that the putatively familiar world in which he has been reinserted is no more solid than a dream. When he opines that the coffee he is drinking only looks and smells "real" because *he* thinks it does, Haruka ripostes that it does not matter if he is "the one who dreams the butterfly or if the butterfly is dreaming" him, thus echoing a famous anecdote associated with the father of Taoism, Lao Tzu. Haruka's proposition reaches its culmination with a tantalizing question: "If you believe that what you feel is real, doesn't that make it real in the end?" (As shown in the closing part of this chapter, analogous preoccupations pepper *Zegapain*'s dialogue and action.)

While the experiences thus far undergone by Ayato in the Tokyo Jupiter simulacrum have been disquieting enough to unsettle even the most confident of minds, the situation plummets into undiluted nightmare when the youth is brazenly encouraged by Haruka to indulge his deep-seated desires and have intercourse with her there and then. Ayato, terrified, looks at the picture of the Annunciation incongruously adorning a wall of the café and freaks out altogether as the Angel moves to face him and drops the symbolic lily to the ground. A traditional token of purity and innocence, the Annunciation is ironically at odds with Haruka's conduct. The destruction of those virtues emblematized by the Angel's iconoclastic gesture mirrors the shattering of Ayato's customary perception of the virginal Haruka in the face of her out-of-character behavior. At a later stage in the adventure, Ayato goes back to Tokyo Jupiter of his own accord to learn the truth about his place of origin and ascertain whether the enclosed capital is really his "home" or rather a prison designed to keep him and thousands of other people ignorant and oblivious. Although this time around the visit constitutes a real experience rather than a hallucination fed by phantom memories, it is no less dislocating, both physically and emotionally, than the experiences undergone in the shrine and the Dolem-generated territory. However, it succeeds in proving to

Ayato that his "home" is now the outside world, where he works for Terra and interacts quotidianly with other humans — and, above all, where Haruka belongs.

While the conflict mounts to a paroxysm of frenzy in an implacable crescendo, Ayato must by and by relinquish any extant trace of autonomy and even be prepared to sacrifice a close friend, Hiroko, to the cause he has been forcibly affiliated with. Once Ayato has removed her from Tokyo Jupiter, the girl is beset by baleful visions of herself as a Mulian connected to a Dolem. It gradually emerges that she has indeed been selected as a human host for Vibrato and is thus condemned to endure an agonizing death at Ayato's own hand. These tensions contribute vitally to *RahXephon*'s dispassionate anatomy of human psychology and thereby enables it, as Zac Bertschy observes, to transcend established generic formulae. "The ads may show *RahXephon* in action," the critic points out, "shooting yellow beams of light through some stone-faced monster in the sky, but the show doesn't linger on these scenes. Instead, we are treated to some of the most elegant character development ever written for the anime form. Here we have subtlety, slow growth, maturation, and ruminations on the nature of the human heart that surpass anything else in this genre" (Bertschy 2003).

Unremittingly jolted by multilayered riddles, the audience's own mnemonic faculties are further challenged by changes in the characters' family names resulting from their own reinscription into different relationships and concomitant time zones, as well as attempts to redefine the memories of themselves they seek to leave behind for the sake of reputation or secrecy. Thus, Maya comes into this world as Kamina but then acquires the surname Rikudoh upon adoption and regains the initial denomination upon marriage. Shirow is introduced as Watari, shifts to Kamina when he weds Maya and reverts to Watari when his wife's disgrace threatens to taint his own name. Haruka Mishima, for her part, becomes Haruka Shitow when her mother remarries. Within this tangled web, a major link between Ayato's lineage and Haruka's own lies with their respective connections with Shougo Rikudoh, Maya being his foster child and Haruka his niece.

It is ultimately Ayato's fate, the boy having been conceived as an instrumentalist in the first place, to engineer cosmic harmonization by merging with the RahXephon into a spiritual force redolent of Shinto's *kami* (please note that his surname indeed means "of the gods"), engaging in a fierce duel with his female counterpart Quon, absorbing her powers and returning the world to a primeval state whence it revives as an immensely more beautiful and balanced place. Interestingly, peace and serenity are two of the symbolic attributes most often associated with the color blue, the very hue distinguishing the Mu's genetic makeup. By retuning the world, Ayato and his biomechanoid modify the flow of time in such a fashion that neither Tokyo Jupiter nor time dilation have ever come to pass, and Haruka and Ayato have grown up at the same pace without suffering separation. An image of an older Ayato reminiscent of Itsuki with his wife Haruka and their infant daughter Quon crowns the series.

Quon's raison d'être is predicated upon the role she is intended to play in the finale. Endowed with a mysterious aura, a tendency to express herself by means of cryptic and intensely lyrical whispers and an otherworldly musical talent, Quon seems detached from the main action. Yet, there are potent intimations from the very moment she is introduced into the series that she is the closest of all the characters to the heart of *RahXephon*'s spiraling enigmas. The early revelation that her life hangs on by a frail thread, her survival depending on a gilet-shaped support module she can rarely afford to shed, ought, logically speaking, to attenuate any sense of her power. By a twist of irony, however, it is precisely by emphasizing Quon's physical vulnerability that Izubuchi succeeds in investing the character with incomparable dramatic vigor as the spiritual force indispensable to the fulfillment of the hero's mission. Quon gains special prominence about half way through the series with the sequence where she seemingly transcends space and time by teleporting into the RahXephon's cockpit, and hence attempts to reach the Black Egg to which she feels instinctively drawn. Bähbem stops her in the belief that she has not yet fully awakened and should not, therefore, "tamper with the egg." The extent of the scientist's power is fully conveyed by the effects of his restraining move, as the egg releases a deluge of dark feathers and sprouts titanic wings redolent of monstrous claws, while Quon's own image multiplies ad infinitum. The shattering of her desire is thus graphically paralleled by a dispersal of her very being and the memories ingrained therein. (The sequence would seem to anticipate analogous moments in *Tsubasa: RESERVoir CHRoNiCLE*, here examined in chapters 8 and 9, where the scattering of the heroine's mnemonic baggage in the form of myriad feathers is pivotal to the saga's entire trajectory.)

In accepting his role as the world's tuner, Ayato is not simply abiding by a cosmic imperative dictated by forces beyond his control. In fact, he is also, finally, acting of his own accord and hence pursuing the possibility of a world in which he and Haruka could grow up and live together. This proposition is corroborated by the crucial scene in which the hero rejects Reika/Ixtli and the tuning she seeks to initiate, thus causing the biomechanoid to regress to its ovate configuration and Reika herself slowly to disappear. This rejection is triggered by Ayato's realization that thus far, he has not been acting according to his own choices and decisions but merely in conformity with external expectations. This discovery coincides with the epiphanic recognition that the painting of the girl on a rock looking at the sea which he has so far subliminally associated with his lifelong love does not truly belong to him for it has emanated from memories implanted in his psyche by others and not from his personal recollections. Ayato's suspicion is confirmed by the scene in which Itsuki is seen to have produced exactly the same painting: since Ayato and Itsuki are genetically engineered twins, it is feasible that their brains have been programmed to accommodate identical memories which do not, strictly speaking, belong to either of them. Ayato's own genuine work is the one seen in the series' "Coda": the image of the girl has not changed but since this painting occupies a world in which Ayato and Haruka have not been parted, there can be no question as to its origin and subject (even though Haruka, endearingly, enjoys being reminded time and again who the girl in the picture is).

While memories play a key role in the characterization of *RahXephon*'s principal personae, they also abet substantially the realistic portrayal of its supporting cast, providing a connective tissue for disparate life stories. The Terra Operator Kim Hotal, for example, is driven by a desire for revenge fuelled by traumatic memories of her parents' death in a Dolem attack when she was a child. Inspector (and later Commander) Makoto Isshiki from the Earth Federation is shaped by memories of his upbringing by the Bähbem Foundation as a "chosen one" alongside Itsuki and Bähbem's niece Helena, in the course of research into the construction of effective Dolem and the training of their potential activators. Dubbed "The White Snake" due to his albinism and spiteful personality, Makoto is so deeply tormented by his memories as to progressively sink into a state of mental derangement that leads to a paroxysm of murderous frenzy. The character's mental instability is a direct corollary of a rampant inferiority complex fuelled by his juvenile recollections — and, most pointedly, by the knowledge that he is a clone sharing Bähbem's DNA and that he has always been pushed into a subordinate position due to his rating as a "D-type" instrumentalist. He successfully stages "Operation Downfall" and destroys the dome enveloping Tokyo Jupiter, taking advantage of his temporary appointment as Terra's Commander, but this only serves to unleash a formidable Mulian counterattack marked by the appearance of floating cities all over the globe. Hence, Makoto is deposed and incarcerated as it transpires that he has ignored the Earth Federation's order not to trigger the operation. The Bähbem Foundation, additionally, claims not to know him. As the character of Takeshi/Futagami points out, after Makoto has been disgraced and rejected, the man's fate has always been to be "tossed aside with the dirty bathwater." At this point, his simmering lunacy boils over to nefarious effect.

Helena Bähbem is also poisoned by rankling memories of failure. Raised as a spoiled and haughty child inclined to take advantage of her privileged position as the boss's niece to prevail over Makoto and Itsuki during their shared education, Helena must face an unpalatable truth when her dream of becoming an instrumentalist is shattered as a result of growing too old before awakening as a full-fledged Mu. This fills her with a gnawing resentment against anyone capable of attaining to the hoped-for status, and especially Quon. Helena's haunting reminiscences of a promising but ultimately futile past grow to pathological proportions as she starts hallucinating a little girl that looks precisely like her infantile self by Bähbem's side. The illusion is a projection of subliminal emotions, reminding her that she has only ever been one of her uncle's countless puppets. This is graphically confirmed, at the close of the adventure, by the arrogant scientist's decisions to switch bodies with her, which leaves Helena in the lifeless husk of a Methuselah, while Bähbem himself parades around — albeit for a short while — in the shape of a beautiful young woman.

The aforementioned Jin Kunugi, Commander of Terra's Tactical Division, is haunted by memories of his departed daughter Michiru and hostile ex-wife Mariko. The memories besetting Kunugi transcend the boundaries of his personal life story and shed light on some crucial events at the heart of the "Great Mu War." It indeed emerges that Kunugi was once under the command of Masayoshi Kuki, an undercover Mu officer in the early days and the Mu Defense Director at the time the main body of the saga takes place. Kunugi was ordered by Kuki to attack the Mu even though the aliens were, at the time, totally inactive, threatening that he would be court-marshaled were he to fail to execute the assault. As seen, the humans' preventive strike yielded catastrophic consequences and Kunugi's own daughter was among the millions of fatalities. It was at the behest of Terra's Director, Shirow Watari, that Kunugi thereafter agreed to join the organization, for no better reason that by then he had nothing left to lose. The ghosts chasing the somber Commander in the shape of baleful memories therefore carry global — or even transdimensional — graveness. Watari himself is constantly collecting material memories by traveling all over the world and regaling his friends and colleagues with all manner of souvenirs. However, memories are not merely toys in this complex character's history. Indeed, he must also live with the recollection of his relationship with Maya, of his part in the conception of Ayato, and hence of his contribution to the grand plan plotted by Bähbem over the millennia. As a point of intersection between the world of the Mulians and the world of humans, between Haruka's story and Ayato's story, between past and present, it is ultimately in the archaeologist Shougo Rikudoh that many of *RahXephon*'s enigmatic memories come together and the key to the adventure's origins could be said to reside.

Ayato's schoolfriend Hiroko is distressed by the memory loss she suffers upon developing into a full-fledged Mu. Having blinded herself to the reality of her blood's non-human coloration, she has no choice but to face up to her alien constitution when Ayato reassures her that one day he will employ the RahXephon to get her parents out of Tokyo Jupiter and the girl realizes that she has no recollections of a family. Hiroko's mnemonic predicament also echoes Haruka's: various flashbacks reveal that prior to the erection of the barrier, she was in love with Ayato and has never completely relinquished her feelings. The theatrical version emphasizes this dimension at an early stage with a scene in which Hiroko surprises the teenage Ayato and Haruka in an empty classroom as they are just about to kiss. Hiroko's current boyfriend, Mamoru Torigai, is also persecuted by troubling reminiscences with which he cannot conclusively come to terms. Even though the youth is a pure and highly esteemed Mulian whose Dolem, Obbligato, is at one point capable of challenging the RahXephon to spectacular effect, he is enfeebled by resentment against Ayato, whom he cannot forgive due to both his undying value in Hiroko's heart and his part in the girl's horrific end.

The most pathetic case of mnemonic disturbance is embodied by Itsuki's research assistant, Sayoko Nanamori. Afflicted by unrequited love for her employer, she is most ungallantly handled as something of a guinea pig when Itsuki gives her a crystal taken from the remnants of the Dolem Forzando as a Christmas gift and the object quickly expands to morph into the Dolem itself and engulf Sayoko. In this instance, the mnemonic heritage of an ancient civilization grafts itself upon a human body and its own memories. Though rescued by Ayato and the RahXephon, Sayoko henceforth embarks on a self-destructive path, conducive to her disclosure of top-secret information to the Bähbem Foundation and her discovery that the memories she harbors are false data implanted in her psyche by the old scientist. Even her feelings for Itsuki have been programmed on her behalf. The hypothesis that a character's identity may ultimately amount to his or her mnemonic inheritance is cryptically hinted at by Quon with this introspective question: "Recollections — is this what I am?" Another comparably sibylline comment issuing from the same character tantalizingly alludes to the undying hold of memories in the quest for truth undertaken, after different fashions, by all of *RahXephon*'s personae: "Guiding words descend, seeking long lost memories."

As Bertschy notes, *RahXephon*'s finale promulgates a positive vision, compellingly emphasizing that humans are endowed with "free will, and the most powerful thing to do with that free will is to establish meaningful, loving relationships with the people around us.... Ayato discovers that human connection is the most powerful force imaginable and creates a world in which love reigns supreme. It's a surprisingly upbeat ending for a show that could have come crashing down as a parable about human selfishness" (Bertschy 2004). John Oppliger provides a complementary interpretation of *RahXephon*'s conclusion based on a symbolic reading of the show's trajectory as a coming-of-age narrative. "*RahXephon*," Oppliger maintains, "plays on both the internal, mental evolution of Ayato Kamina's own psychological world, and on the external level of Ayato physically altering the world around him." This two-threaded yarn reaches an apt culmination in the scene in which Ayato openly confronts his female counterpart: "When he says that either his or Quon's world must be destroyed and absorbed by the other, he symbolically means that he must determine his own future. He can either take his place in adult society ... or allow himself to be absorbed, marginalized and victimized by society and life itself, represented by Quon.... Quon may be considered ... the pressure to grow and mature" (Oppliger).

Memory, its occlusion and its gradual resurgence are instrumental to Izubuchi's approach to worldbuilding at both the personal and the communal levels. On the one hand, the elision of the protagonist's conscious recollections, allied to his oblivion to his teleologically preordained destiny, is central to the dynamic development of his personality and actions throughout the diegesis. On the other hand, the state of mental passivity in which Tokyo Jupiter's inhabitants are held is comparable to a phenomenon of communal amnesia predicated on the dislocation of actual historical events and their replacement by an alternate and utterly synthetic body of knowledge: a prosthetic memory. The Mu's success depends on the repression of Tokyo Jupiter's memories, whereas the aliens' own mnemonic baggage is said to fade over time. Ayato must learn to revive his submerged memories of Haruka, while Haruka herself must negotiate the discrepancy between Ayato's and her own sense of the passage of time. Reika, for her part, appears capable of editing humans' memories at will. These are just some of the most salient instances of *RahXephon*'s unique handling of the memory motif. Myriad satellite references to the same topos pepper the saga throughout. All in all, however, it seems safe to propose that the show delivers a prismatic world built primarily on the basis of the shaping and reshaping of memories as plastic masses. By couching this enterprise as a dauntless excursion beyond the boundaries of space and time alike, *RahXephon* stands out as an incomparable celebration of *yugen* at its most awesome.

As mentioned earlier, *RahXephon* poses considerable challenges to the audience's own mnemonic faculties. Its riddles and plot twists are so numerous and so deftly distributed across the saga as to engage the careful viewer in an ongoing interpretative exercise. Insofar as several of *RahXephon*'s most significant facets are encrypted in the show's more transparent moments, the secrets are not instantly detected. At times, it takes quite a while even to realize that a seemingly innocent utterance actually shields a mystery. *RahXephon*'s enigmas only come to light, thereby inviting retrospective decoding, when memories of the early portions of the series are retrieved and brought to bear on subsequent developments. The very first installment is replete with daunting elements whose full import cannot be grasped until much later. We are therefore incessantly kept on our toes and enjoined to store a plethora of contingent impressions for future recollection and reassessment. Endeavoring to absorb *RahXephon* in a single viewing is a pointless pursuit since the story can only be genuinely enjoyed by gradually building up a reservoir of memories and then evaluating one's discoveries against that background to confirm or dispute its validity.

A parallel is thus maintained between the protagonist's experience and the audience's. Initially, Ayato is faced with bizarre occurrences that make no sense to him because he has no conscious recollection of his life prior to the establishment of Tokyo Jupiter. The audience, likewise, does not at first have any pointers to how to decipher the show's intricate premises because it is not in possession of a body of memories that would enable it to situate the action within its broader context. As the adventure progresses and Ayato rediscovers some of his buried memories and forms fresh memories out of his day-to-day life, so the audience finds itself watching the anime in the light of accumulated recollections of its earlier portions, while also developing a larger and larger cache of memories with each successive episode.

A theatrical version of *RahXephon*, directed by Tomomi Kyoda and helmed by Izubuchi in the capacity of chief director, was released domestically in 2003. Titled *RahXephon: Pluralitas Concentio* (the Latin phrase translates literally as "the harmony of the many"), the film offers an alternate take on the saga where the love-story dimension centered on Ayato and Haruka is given priority. Accordingly, the overall tone is more intimate. This is encapsulated by the idea that Ayato eventually agrees to pilot the RahXephon specifically because he wants to protect the human world in the hope of finding Haruka Mishima again. Although Quon is still an important character, her depiction in the Sleeping-Beauty role for the best part of the movie contrasts sharply with the girl's portrayal in the series, where she is by and large melodiously and poetically audible, though not exactly loquacious. Although about half of the footage in the feature is taken from the show, Kyoda's work adopts a more linear approach, foregrounding several plot elements which the series discloses incrementally over individual episodes right from the start. Stylistically, the film and the parent show are brought together by the consistent deployment of solid animation techniques that eschew flashy spectacle for its own sake, distinctive camera angles and musical scores, executed by Ichiko Hashimoto, of abiding force and terseness.

The memory topos is enthroned as pivotal from the film's very first scene, where Ayato and Haruka talk about the demolition of their old school. The girl is saddened by the thought that thereafter, "the place where [their] memories were" will no longer exist, yet "a part of her likes the thought of a special place existing only in memory." Ayato, for his part, is haunted by a recurring dream in which he thinks he sees Haruka, runs after her and wakes up just as he is about to catch up with the elusive figure. An interesting tension is thus conveyed by Haruka's reflections on the past's inevitable evaporation, on the one hand, and Ayato's experience of the past as a dimension that grows more and more vivid with each successive dream. (At a later stage in the narrative, Haruka is seen to be visited repeatedly by an analogous vision with a reversal of roles, whereby she is the pursuer and Ayato the pursued.) The movie's epilogue arguably constitutes its most radical departure from the series and the principal events leading to it accordingly deserve special attention. Ayato awakens Quon, who then levitates into the air and vanishes. She will, however, presently return with a fake RahXephon meant to accelerate the human world's collapse. Ayato and his own (true) RahXephon, conversely, hold the potential for a restorative retuning of that world. Haruka is eager to stop Ayato from embracing his appointed task because she fears that in doing so, he would lose his own humanity. Ayato, for his part, knows that if he does not undertake the mission, he will become a full-fledged Mulian and hence lose his memories: an option he is determined to avoid at all costs since it would inevitably entail forgetting his love for Haruka.

The drama reaches its crowning moments with a flawlessly choreographed sequence in which the younger and older incarnations of Haruka coexist and the conclusion is reached that Haruka must accompany Ayato beyond the human world as she has known it all her life. Ayato thus espouses his role as harmonizer, becoming the "Observer of Time" that is "everywhere and anywhere" by living "in the space between moments." It is at this climactic juncture that the memory motif is conclusively enthroned as one of the entire *RahXephon* saga's most distinctive preoccupations: humans can only exist, we are told, "as long as the amalgamation of their numerous memories makes them real." Although the clock cannot be turned back, once Haruka and Ayato have been returned to a hypothetical past where they can be together, they can also be given memories to sustain them and hence exist *as if* they had truly aged in unison. The sequence where this miracle occurs is felicitously set in the old classroom seen at the start of the film. In the logic of the movie, memories are real if they are perceived and treasured as such regardless of their empirical validity. This message is potently conveyed by Haruka in the finale, set in 2072, where she comments thus on the trials undergone by Carroll's Alice in the realm beyond the mirror: "It doesn't matter what world was real because she was left with memories, wonderful memories of her experiences in the looking-glass world and those were real to her." The film's ending is, on the whole, more concerned with Haruka and her love for Ayato than with the hero's godlike powers. While the series' dénouement portrays Haruka as a new mother, the movie presents the character as an elderly lady in the company of a granddaughter who, intriguingly, is named Reika.

While *RahXephon*'s theatrical version would probably not be fully appreciated by spectators unfamiliar with the original show, it holds unquestionable value for those who come to it after watching the series as it throws into relief the story's affective dimension and thus enables a deeper understanding of the characters, their motivations and their goals. The worldbuilding element is less obvious in the feature, much of the action being telescoped in such a fashion that the mythical infrastructure is encapsulated in a few symbolic sequences rather than threaded through the entire action. This strategy occasionally has the jarring effect of communicating *RahXephon*'s puzzles in the form of clips or vignettes rather than as fluid narration. However, for those already acquainted with the show's worldbuilding vigor, the film serves to imbue *RahXephon*'s universe with an emphatically human ambience. The focus on character development plays a major part in abetting the effectiveness of this alternative take on the adventure. Additionally, new scenes presenting situations that remain off screen in the show throw light on the underlying connections between disparate incidents in the story that could only be guessed at upon first watching the original series.

RahXephon also relies on intertextual memory in the construction of its symbolic infrastructure. Indeed, the show harks back to myriad sources, ranging from Lewis Carroll's *Through the Looking-Glass* (most prominent in the film's opening and closing frames) to J. R. R. Tolkien's *The Silmarillion*, C. S. Lewis's *The Chronicles of Narnia* and Gabriel García Márquez's *One Hundred Years of Solitude*. A copy of Frank Baum's *The Wonderful Wizard of Oz* is introduced about half way through the series as the book which Bähbem reads with the little phantom girl at his side (i.e., Helena's hallucination of her own younger self). The pivotal images are the Cowardly Lion (possibly a parodic distortion of Bähbem himself) and the Tin Woodman—an apt metaphor for the many artificial creatures peopling the saga. In the climactic sequence where several characters meet more or less violent deaths through a chain of vengeful acts, the same book can be seen again, lying on the floor next to Bähbem's body. Baum's audacious experiment with the interpenetration of alternate realities indubitably constitutes a close correlative for *RahXephon*'s own universe. Another important point of reference is Robert F. Young's seminal time-travel short story "The Dandelion Girl" (1961), after which the TV program's "Coda" is explicitly titled. The show's intertextual matrix also encompasses more or less explicit hints at other anime, including the aforementioned epics *Record of Lodoss War* and *Vision of Escaflowne*. With the former, Izubuchi's show shares an appetite for highly convoluted fictional histories stretching over thousands of years and unrelentingly threatened by the phantoms of war and destruction. *Escaflowne*, for its part, is echoed by *RahXephon*'s transposition of its protagonist to an unfamiliar world wherein the character is enjoined to deploy hitherto unsuspected superpowers. Echoes of Hideaki Anno's OVA series *Gunbuster* (1988) can also be detected. However, the anime title to which *RahXephon* has been most assiduously compared, with widely contrasting verdicts, is Anno's TV series *Neon Genesis Evangelion* (1995–1996).[4]

Echoes from diverse areas of the visual arts can also be heard, as attested to by repeated references to the Surrealist artist René Magritte's *La Grande Famille*, where the sky is seen through the silhouette of a dove, and Salvador Dalí's so-called "soft-watch" pictures and their distinctive dreamscapes. Notably, many of *RahXephon*'s mysteries are disclosed in oneiric sequences, as well as in flashbacks providing insights into both the global history that surrounds its worldbuilding project and individual life stories punctuated by mnemonic disturbances. *RahXephon*'s taste for surreal visuals is ushered in, early in the series, by the dreamscape in which the titular creature makes its first appearance: a cloud-flecked chamber replete with classical columns that appear to float in the sky and ethereal waterfalls. Furthermore, this visual mood is ideally complemented throughout by Hashimoto's soundtrack, with its alternation of fractured jazz pieces, luscious orchestrations, plaintive melodies, operatic vocals and unusual arrangements. *RahXephon*'s unique feel is additionally abetted by an original handling of chromatic gradations. Where numerous sci-fi anime rely on intense hues, such as deep blues and greens, vibrant reds and oranges and solar yellows, *RahXephon* shows a preference for mellowed-out palettes replete with May and grass greens, salmon pink, strawberry red, kingfisher blue, dewey silver and ochre, redolent of watercolors. These tones evoke an atmosphere of restrained brightness that contrasts felicitously with the somber tenor of the show's themes. Moreover, they impact on the mechanical components no less than on backgrounds, character designs and costumes, endowing them with a fluid and near-organic elegance.

Moreover, allusions to various aspects of pre–Columbian culture (and most pointedly Aztec and Mayan mythology), interspersed with references to biblical lore and the Kabbalah, contribute further complexity to *RahXephon*'s mnemonic palimpsest. Both Ayato and Quon are referred to as *Ollin*, which means "movement" in Nahuatl and thus confirms the importance of music in the series. Moreover, in Aztec mythology, Ollin Tonatiuh is worshipped as the Sun deity believed to be the leader of all heavenly entities. An oblique reference to Mayan lore is supplied by the choice of date for the Mu's first appearance, 28 December 2012, which the character of Takeshi/Futagami defines as the "day when the Mayan calendar ends." A further reference to the Mayan calendar is the song titled "Fate of Katun," which is used as a symbolic bridge between the protagonists' past and present selves. The *katun* (also spelled "*kat'un*" or "*k'atun*") is a time measurement in that culture that corresponds to 7,200 days (approximately 20 years). Soundtrack composer Hashimoto has stated that the song "expresses the situation of people who were lovers in a different world, but who don't remember that in this world. It describes both breakdown and harmony. The idea is to evoke long-lost memories" (quoted in Hikawa, Kubo and Kaneko, p. 79).

Echoes of Mayan sculpture and architecture abound, as do hints at other Mesoamerican arts, including step pyramids and Nazca lines. It is barely coincidental, in this respect that Mayan civilization should be held to have derived from a Mu colony and that the Mu leader should be named Maya. Additionally, the citation from Octavio Paz's "The Obsidian Butterfly" offered in the closing installment — "The obsidian butterfly finds a last song in the deep blue forest"— is a direct allusion to the Aztec goddess Itzpapalotl, a fearsome warrior presiding over the paradise reserved for the victims of infant mortality. Furthermore, in Hindu philosophy, *Maya* is the term used to designate the illusory veil concealing the mysteries and complexities of the cosmos that prevents humans from perceiving the world as anything other than a dream. This trope is obviously relevant to *RahXephon*'s engagement with delusory realms. Where Hindu culture is concerned, it must also be noted that the show hints at Hindu art in the depiction of some of the Mulians in charge of the Dolem and particularly their postures — a case in point is the entity that takes control of Sayoko's body when her pendant morphs into Forzando. Buddhism is graphically referenced in the movie's finale in the guise of the *butsudan* (an indoor shrine) bearing Ayato's name. Christianity also makes a cameo appearance, thus complementing Izubuchi's religious cocktail, with the image of the church adorned by magnificent (and refreshingly secular) Art-Nouveau windows. It is also noteworthy, where the series' religious infrastructure is concerned, that the world-tuning trope pivotal to the show's culmination harks back to several creation myths, and most prominently to the mythological system upheld by the Hopi, a Native American culture.

RahXephon simultaneously alludes to various aspects of Japanese culture and mythology. One of Japan's best-known folktales, the story of Urashimatarou, is explicitly invoked by Ayato to describe his situation after leaving the domed metropolis. This revolves around a fisherman who rescues a turtle and is rewarded with a visit to the Sea Dragon's Palace, where he is treated most ceremoniously. Following a prolonged sojourn, the hero decides to return to his village, carrying as a parting present a casket he has been instructed never to open. Upon reaching the old world, the fisherman finds that decades have gone by during his absence and when he opens the casket for help, he instantly ages in accordance with the time zone he has reentered. In addition, Professor Rikudoh refers to the no less illustrious tale of the Bamboo Princess. In this story, a woodcutter finds and adopts a baby who grows over time into an exceptionally beautiful woman admired by scores of suitors. However, the girl cannot partake of earthly pleasures for she is not human and knows that the Moon people with whom she belongs will eventually reclaim her — which they indeed do despite her adoptive father's fierce opposition. Rikudoh refers to the tale in conjunction with Maya, who likewise leaves him when her Mulian nature is fully revealed.

The supernatural phenomenon of "spiriting away" (*kamikakushi*), veritably endemic to Japanese lore, is also brought into play, as is its reverse: the act of "spiriting forth." The island of Nirai Kanai (or Niraikanai), where the Terra base is situated, features as the place in the sea where deities live in the mythological system indigenous to the Ryukyu Islands, an animistic creed centered on ancestor worship and a firm belief in the interconnectedness of the living, the departed and all spiritual entities across the fabric of the universe. The architectural style used in the depiction of the Shrine of Time is itself overtly redolent of Ryukyu family tombs. Moreover, indigenous beliefs are consistently brought into play by means of intertextual reverberations of Shinto myths surrounding the world's creation and evolution. The egg from which the RahXephon emerges at the beginning of the series is itself an allusion to Shinto lore, where the world is said to have initially consisted of an amorphous mass akin to an ovular blob. The references to the Black and White Eggs associated with the splitting of the "Xephon" are likewise redolent of that mythological corpus. So is the allusion to the primordial mud to which the world is destined to return should the ultimate tuning fail. Shinto is also invoked through the visual reference to Mount Fuji, a location of great spiritual importance in that corpus, and by the scene in which the character of Yagumo performs a Shinto New Year rite garbed in traditional ceremonial attire.

The Shinto-inflected strand of the narrative is consistently bolstered by references to music as a mystical force whose supreme objective is "tuning the world": namely, transforming the chaotic Earth into a more harmonious and peaceful environment. The musical theme is also evident in the show's titles, where the term "Movement" is consistently employed, and in the names assigned to the Dolem: e.g., Allegretto, Fortissimo, Grave, Ritardando, Larghetto, Sforzando, Vivace, Alternate, Falsetto, Arpeggio, Metronome, Forzando, Obbligato, Brillante and Vibrato. Each Dolem is associated with a particular melody and different sound waves correspond to specific battle strategies. Both the Dolem's and the controlling Mulians' facial expressions, moreover, indicate that singing is instrumental to the interaction between the clay giants and their manipulators. Furthermore, music plays a key part by pervading not only *Rahxephon*'s indigenous vocabulary and symbolic repertoire but also the very fabric of its prismatic settings. At practically each turn in the action, these are filled alternately by melodious areas and portentous vibrations, soothing echoes and whirling chants, peaceful harmonies and sinister whispers prophesying discord. Music, no less importantly, provides the invisible thread connecting Haruka's achingly vivid memories of Ayato and Ayato's own submerged memories of Haruka. This is attested to by the sequence in which Haruka's singing voice brings Ayato back from his hallucinatory wanderings through the parallel reality he has inadvertently accessed by entering the enchanted shrine. The scene's importance is consolidated by a later sequence where Ayato suddenly recognizes the melody sung by Haruka at that crucial moment and although he has no clear recollection of when or how he heard it in the past, he instantly knows that it brings him warmth and a pervasive sense of well-being.[5]

RahXephon's graphic constellation captures the spirit of *yugen* as a reaching towards the impenetrable mysteries of the cosmos. Its aesthetic characteristically conveys a disquieting sense of unreality, often by recourse to figures fleeing through urban environments constructed according to an unorthodox grasp of perspective. *Yugen* celebrates the elusiveness of reality beyond the boundaries of the here-and-now and of pragmatic attitudes governed by common sense and consciousness. *RahXephon* echoes this ethos and endeavors to foreground the immeasurable vastness of the universe by eroding the validity of the contingent dimensions experienced by the senses. When those worlds are rendered especially suspect by their manipulation through mnemonic tricks, their unreality becomes blatant. Startling images of hallucinatory intensity dominate the screen time and again, as the characters vainly struggle to bridge the gap between empirical realms they can perceive but cannot trust and metaphysical planes of existence that might hold the truth but cannot be accessed. Imagery that irreverently exposes the limitations of consciousness by alluding to realms transcending cognition is ideally suited to the presentation of a world view that defies logical explanation.

An intriguing variation on the use of the memory topos as a means of spawning complex worlds is provided by the TV series *Zegapain* (dir. Masami Shimoda, 2006), where the trope is deployed to construct two coexisting domains: an actual world and a virtual one. Combining *mecha*-centered sci-fi action with an intense personal drama and philosophical speculations redolent of *The Matrix* and cyberpunk fiction, the show takes as its principal premise the idea that the protagonist, Kyo Sogoru, lives in a simulated world and must learn to recognize the illusion and protect the people therein while also endeavoring to save its authentic counterpart. Both the virtual and the real dimensions are carefully crafted in accordance with specific worldbuilding formulae and within each, memories have a key role to play. In a radical disruption of the chronological flow, *Zegapain* frequently forces its characters to move back and forth in time — and hence face unsettling déjà vus and premonitions — as their mnemonic faculties are concomitantly manipulated. Strictly speaking, neither of *Zegapain*'s realms is truly "natural," for reality and virtuality alike are products of sustained exercises in worldbuilding.

Memory features prominently in *Zegapain*'s dialogue and overall diegesis in the form of intertextual references to famous philosophers. At one point, the AI named Lemures tries to elucidate the illusory nature of putative reality by recourse to three quotations: "Cogito, ergo sum" (René Descartes); "To be is to be perceived" (George Berkeley); "Sorrow is knowledge: they who know the most / Must mourn the deepst o'er the fatal truth" (Lord Byron). Elsewhere, Kyo's school counselor mentions the aforementioned "dream of a butterfly" ("*koucho no yume*") associated with the Chinese sage Lao Tzu. In the related anecdote, the thinker notes that his dream of being a butterfly could actually have been the vision of a butterfly dreaming of being Lao Tzu.

The hero is initially introduced as an enthusiastic swimmer keen on keeping his high-school swimming club alive at any price, which is no mean feat given he is its sole member and his classmates resolutely refuse to join the venture. Kyo's ambition is complicated, much to his frustration, by his sightings of a girl, Shizuno Misaki, whom nobody else at first seems able to perceive — not even when her image has been supposedly captured on video. Kyo's frustration turns into downright bafflement when the hitherto invisible girl suddenly reappears as a transfer student at his school and although he has never heard of her before, she is reputed by his friends to be one of the most popular pupils around. The enigmatic creature acquires a pivotal role in the protagonist's existence as she ushers him into what would initially seem to be a game world. In this dimension, Kyo is required to pilot the Zegapain *mecha* named "Altair" in a war against robots known as "Gardsorm" amid a postapocalyptic urbanscape.

Although playing a game of this kind would, in principle, constitute a perfectly ordinary pursuit for a youth of his generation, Kyo is profoundly disquieted by the realization that piloting the Zegapain and harmonizing with it feels uncannily familiar. The supposedly ludic domain gains greater and greater palpability as the hero is progressively drawn into it. Before long, Shizuno reveals that the ordinary world Kyo comes from is actually an illusion and that the devastated land in which his *mecha* exploits are set is reality. The people Kyo has thus far taken for granted as incontestably genuine entities turn out to consist of data stored as "meta-bodies" on "quantum servers." The cities they inhabit are accordingly virtual.

The crucial disclosure occurs when Kyo struggles to get outside his town, Maihama, and Shizuno explains that this is impossible because there is no such thing as an "outside." In fact, as the girl herself puts it, "The human race was destroyed by the Gardsorm. There are no more living creatures on Earth.... We live in an illusory world inside a machine. We are memories of the downfall of mankind!" The data hosted by the servers represent human memories, personality traits and physical characteristics that capture a person's state at the time they were saved into the server. Hence, the meta-bodies which they produce do not age or develop and are, by and large, unable to leave the server in which they are stored. When a meta-body is required to engage in combat, the data can be transferred to a Zegapain *mecha* and enabled to interact with various holographic elements in its vicinity. While the virtual reality generated by quantum servers is quite convincing, it is constrained by technological limitations that prevent it from simulating infinite time. As a result, it operates within a fixed temporal frame and once its life span has been exhausted, all of the data—memories included—are reset to their inceptive condition. Thus, any memories formed by a meta-body in the course of one run of the program vanish when the reset mechanism is triggered.

As the preceding paragraphs have plausibly indicated, an important aspect of *Zegapain*'s worldbuilding enterprise lies with its indigenous vocabulary. The axial terms are "Celebrum," which designates an organization devoted to the protection of the quantum servers' inhabitants, and "Celebrant," which describes a person "awakening" from the simulated realm and thereby gaining admission to the Celebrum. Kyo's mission, following his awakening, consists of joining the Celebrum in the war against the Gardsorm to save the people that are still caught inside the quantum servers, the ultimate goal being the resurrection of humanity and the world's attendant regeneration. (As in *RahXephon*, this motif is neatly encapsulated by a climactic allusion to birth.) Kyo's present self is just one configuration of a character said to have undergone several changes over time. His past self appears to have had a relationship with Shizuno, brought to an end by the loss of his memory as a result of suffering severe "wet damage" upon sacrificially self-destructing in a battle and being then reborn. The concept of wet damage is a clear indicator of the importance attached to memory in *Zegapain*'s world construct. It indeed designates a radical impairment of a Celebrant's mnemonic baggage, as a corollary of which memories are lost beyond any hope of recovery. "Dry damage," namely an injury suffered by a Celebrant's body, is deemed far less serious since it can be repaired by recourse to average meta-body data. The show thus proposes that in its world, the only thing that makes people unequivocally unique is the faculty of memory. The idea that Kyo's past is far more complicated than he seems to understand is concurrently conveyed by snippets of the action in which his friends allude to occurrences of which he has no recollection whatever.

As the anime unfolds, the protagonist develops feelings for Ryoko Kaminagi, a cheerful and perceptive girl who awakens to the real world far more painlessly than Kyo himself does. Ryoko also displays impressive piloting skills when she joins the hero in the Altair but her talent is nipped in the bud as the *mecha* is attacked and her data are annihilated. This incident and its repercussions constitute one of the most poignant elements in *Zegapain*'s cumulative narrative. Although Shizuno manages to detect Ryoko's data, compressed in the *mecha*'s digital memory, and hence makes it possible for the girl's meta-body to be restored and reinserted into the Maihama server, her emotional data component remains trapped in the Altair. Therefore, her "apparition" in the server is gravely impaired—to the point that for quite some time, she merely lies in a hospital bed in a comatose state. Even when she regains consciousness, the new Ryoko proves robotically emotionless except when she is transferred to the Altair for martial purposes, at which point her pristine self resurfaces. This entails, most affectingly, that the budding couple can only interact satisfactorily on the battlefield.

CHAPTER 8

Submerged Memories

Tsubasa: RESERVoir CHRoNiCLE, TV Series: Season 1
(dir. Kouichi Mashimo, 2005)

> No matter how far apart we are,
> as the miracle repeats itself,
> we will come face to face again.
> — Maaya Sakamoto, "Loop"
> (*Tsubasa: RESERVoir CHRoNiCLE* Ending Theme #1)

> Right now I'm having amnesia and déjà vu at the same time.
> I think I've forgotten this before.
> — Steven Wright (1955–)

Tsubasa: RESERVoir CHRoNiCLE plunges straight into the fathomless waters of a multidimensional epic with its opening installment, where we are immediately introduced to the young protagonists: Princess Sakura of Clow and the young archaeologist Syaoran. Sakura, we soon discover, is endowed with an uncanny power of world-changing amplitude. Just as her hitherto unsuspected ability begins to awaken, ghostly wings sprout from her back as a physical manifestation of her memories. Concurrently, her body begins to merge with an emblem traced within the ruins which Syaoran is excavating. The unearthly phenomenon is observed by magical means by mysterious forces eager to appropriate the girl's gift in order to gain the power to defy spatial and temporal boundaries. Syaoran endeavors to rescue Sakura by tearing her body away from the magnetizing symbol but in the process, her wings are shattered, her heart and soul pulverized, and her memories sent adrift in the form of floating feathers, which effectively condemns her to certain death.[1] As the royal priest and soothsayer Yukito ominously announces, "A body with no heart is just an empty shell. Without those memories, the princess will die."

The depiction of Sakura's mnemonic attributes in eminently corporeal guises instantly communicates a potent sense of the materiality of memory. (The Japanese word for "wings," it is worth pointing out, is *tsubasa*. In the saga's title, the word can be taken to allude to both the princess's transformation and the shape of the ruins wherein this occurs.) Rescuing the dispersed feathers is the only way of saving Sakura herself. The task is made not merely arduous but downright monumental by the fact that the feathers have left not just the princess's body but also the very world which she and Syaoran have thus far inhabited. Yukito helps the couple by conveying them to Yuuko the Dimensional Witch, the formidable enchantress who holds the secret to transworld travel. Determined to track down the elusive fragments for the sake of his lifelong love, and prepared to risk everything in the process, Syaoran embarks on his heroic quest in the company not only of the hapless princess herself but also of Kurogane, an exiled warrior, and Fai, a cursed wizard.[2]

Where Kurogane is gritty, grave and robust, Fai is jovial and ethereally graceful. Both characters have made decisions that carry serious repercussions in the shaping of their destinies: Kurogane, by committing himself wholeheartedly to his beloved Princess Tomoyo, endeavoring to prove that he is the mightiest fighter in the world, and hence incurring Tomoyo's displeasure through an excess of martial zeal; Fai, by locking his own loved one — the masterful wizard King Ashura — into a preternatural slumber. Kurogane has been conveyed to Yuuko's haunt by Tomoyo in the hope that journeying across dimensions might heal him of his belligerence, even though she is well aware that the separation will cause her great sorrow. Fai, for his part, has sought out the sorceress of his own accord, wishing to travel to remote worlds where King Ashura, where he to regain consciousness, would be unable to descry him. The warrior wants nothing more than to return to his world and to Tomoyo, while Fai is driven by the diametrically opposite drive to keep as far away as possible from his home. However, both characters have chosen their paths knowingly and therefore have no choice but to negotiate the pain engendered by their decisions with stoical resignation.

The mage and the ninja are also brought together by their ability to empathize instinctively with Syaoran's plight, having both endured tormented emotional relationships. Fai is quite open in the expression of his feelings towards the star-crossed couple from Clow, and the grief he experiences on their behalf is explicitly communicated by the sorrowful shadow that falls over his normally cheerful mien at poignant junctures in the drama. Kurogane, conversely, shields his emotions behind stern and circumspect expressions, often accompanied by an unsentimental aversion to romance. Yet, the animation manages to convey the magnitude of his personal turmoil, and attendant recognition of the protagonists' predicament, in pathos-laden close-ups of the warrior's visage that are no less effective than the shots communicating Fai's overtly empathetic responses.

Syaoran's choice to hunt down Sakura's memories demonstrates not only his devotion and courage but also his sacrificial selflessness, since he knows that were he to recover the feathers, the girl would have no recollection of their time together and of her feelings towards him. Indeed, when they are granted by Yuuko the power to world-hop in search of the feathers, the protagonists also have to accept that in exchange for this gift, Sakura must be forever deprived of her memories of Syaoran. Syaoran's attitude to his mission is characteristically encapsulated by a line he speaks in the course of a particularly dangerous duel: "I made a promise and I am going to keep it. I'm not stopping for pain." Please note that the sorceress does not impose her seemingly ungenerous conditions because she seeks to enforce an arbitrary power but because she knows that the universe requires an underlying balance to be preserved at all times, and that any gain must therefore entail a loss of comparable proportions. Yuuko's philosophy is fully expounded in the parent manga, where she states that although "at first glance, the world seems to be chaotic," and "individual actions and events may seem like they're scattered and confused, the whole balances out to proceed on a certain course" (CLAMP 2008c, p. 24).

The situation is made all the more woeful to witness by the fact that even though Sakura and Syaoran's friendship has evolved into love over time, neither has dared declare the feeling to the other. Syaoran has been restrained by his awareness of the gap in status between a princess and a mere commoner like him, while Sakura has been held back by sheer modesty. The girl is on the verge of expressing her feelings in the course of her last exchange with Syaoran just prior to her fateful metamorphosis but settles for a demure "I'll tell you next time" with no inkling that there will simply not be a "next time." Ironically, however, Sakura does seem to harbor premonitions of some unforeseen turn to come: that statement is indeed accompanied by the words "Things are going to change. I can feel it." The central characters are not the only ones who are required to give up something extremely valuable to them in exchange for the ability to traverse dimensional barriers: Kurogane and Fai, too, have to pay high prices. The warrior must surrender his trusted sword, a weapon of mythological repute, and accept that he is doomed to become weaker every time he kills; the magician must lose the tattoo on his back that enables him to regulate the control of his magic — which practically amounts to giving up the art altogether since Fai is not willing to trifle with its potentially lethal strength.

To aid the protagonists in their interdimensional odyssey, Yuuko entrusts them with Mokona Modoki, a creature so reminiscent of a stereotypical cuddly plush toy as to seem scarcely capable of big-time magic. Yet, Mokona proves that looks can be very deceptive indeed by exhibiting a knack of sending several people across world boundaries a limitless number of times, as well as functioning as a dexterous feather detector. Moreover, Mokona also functions as something of a "translation device" allowing the travelers to understand each other even though they come from different cultures and feasibly speak disparate languages. This is revealed by the sequence where Mokona is temporarily kidnapped, and we hear Kurogane express himself in Japanese and Fai in French while Syaoran, utterly bewildered, is powerless to hear anything other than "gibberish." In the second season, Fai will confirm Mokona's interpreting powers: "if we stray too far from Mokona," he remarks upon his and Kurogane's temporary separation from their traveling companions, "we wouldn't be able to understand each other." Nevertheless, Mokona is only capable of taking the company from one world to another and has no control over the choice of destination. The characters' itinerary is therefore entirely at the mercy of fate. Yuuko's own philosophy advocates that "There's no such thing as coincidence. There is only inevitability." In a sense, the Dimensional Witch is not so much instructing the motley crew at this stage in the story as intimating that they will have to play along with destiny (and hence with one another) whether they like it or not. (Yuuko's world view will be returned to in the next chapter in the discussion of the double feature comprising *Tsubasa RESERVoir CHRoNiCLE The Movie: Princess of the Birdcage Kingdom* and *XXXHOLiC the Movie: A Midsummer Night's Dream*.)

Yuuko's prepping provides a tantalizing point of entry into *Tsubasa*'s multilayered adventure and its many mysteries and deserves special notice, in this context, since her assertions will carry momentous resonance over the entire story: "You'll travel together, help each other in your quests or not, as you choose. You may find people you recognize from your own world living entirely different lives on another. They will not know you.

There are realms you will find full of crimes, others built on lies. In some worlds you will find yourselves in the midst of war ... you'll be searching for feathers that could be anywhere — the depths of the sea or the hands of a stranger. And these feathers have a power of their own that others will covet — it will be a long, long journey." As the four key characters undertake their epic voyage, motivated by different objectives yet bound by a shared destiny, the past and the future mingle in a multifaceted present consisting of a galaxy of parallel worlds. Across these alternate dimensions, history meets legend, and magic meshes with frankly real human emotions.

Before embarking on an exploration of the alternate universes portrayed in the show's narrative arcs, the protagonists' own homelands deserve some attention. Clow, Sakura's and Syaoran's country, consists mainly of a desert surrounding for miles a city situated on a lush oasis. The archaeologist is said to have come to Clow with his late adoptive father Fujitaka, also an archaeologist, to study the mysterious ruins buried beneath the sand, and to have discovered a chamber in their innermost depths bearing an enigmatic crest on its walls. This same symbol is also perceived in a vision by Sakura as her powers begin to quicken, and instinctively sought by her body when she enters the archaeological site. It is an eerie tune issuing from the ruins that stirs the princess's hidden ability and draws her to the place that will witness her tragic mnemonic scrambling. The cause of Sakura's mishap, it transpires, is the arch-villain extraordinaire Fei Wong Reed, who is keen on reactivating a submerged transdimensional power — though the parts played within his grand scheme by the princess and by the ruins are at first quite unclear. Using a band of implacable warriors as his emissaries to trigger Sakura's transformation, Fei Wong Reed operates from a hidden location referred to as the "Secret Base."

Hosted therein is a glowing liquid chamber containing the floating shape of a young man very much like Syaoran: as to the true nature of this entity, this will be disclosed in the three-part OVA series *Tsubasa Tokyo Revelations* (dir. Shunsuke Tada, 2007–2008) examined in the next chapter. Fei Wong Reed's comments on Sakura's metamorphosis and his personal goals in the game are worthy of notice at this stage: "The moment has come," he portentously declares. "The convergence we awaited begins." He then waxes lyrical about the princess's "power to pass through dimensions" and her possession of the "wings of a gifted heart to guide the way." When Syaoran interferes, the rogue's assistant, namely the Goth beauty Xing-Huo, opines that in interrupting the intended "process," the youth has caused Sakura's "awakening" to fail. However, Fei Wong Reed remains unshakably confident: "Not so. We got what we needed from it. Events have been set into motion and when they are finished, the power to cross time and space will be mine."

Clow is currently ruled by Sakura's brother, King Touya, a benevolent monarch who relies assiduously on Yukito's council. Prior to Touya's ascent to the throne, the Kingdom's ruler was his and Sakura's father, Clow Reed: a character that only features sporadically in flashbacks since he is held to have died in unknown circumstances well before the beginning of the adventure dramatized in *Tsubasa*'s main body. Despite his marginal role, however, Clow Reed is an important character because he connects several of the key personae. A magician endowed with tremendous powers recognized by myriad wizards across the dimensions, including the ability to predict the future and to heal wounds by infusing their sufferers with his preternatural energy, Clow Reed is genetically linked not only to Sakura and Touya but also to the Syaoran lookalike held at the Secret Base and — more disturbingly still—to the villain of the piece. Clow Reed was responsible for bringing Sakura and Syaoran together in the first place and there are strong intimations that he was also well-acquainted with Yuuko. Since the character also appears in two other manga created by *Tsubasa*'s own authors, an adequate amount of information about Clow Reed can only be effectively gleaned through intertextual analysis. It is thus possible to find out that Clow Reed and Yuuko created the white Mokona accompanying the protagonists in their journey and the black twin kept by the Dimensional Witch to chart their progress. This creation was motivated by their shared foreknowledge of the terrible fate awaiting Sakura and of the need for an instrument capable of enabling interdimensional travel as her only means of facing it and, hopefully, overcoming it.

Fai's homeland, Celes, is ruled by the aforementioned King Ashura and little is known about this world except, as intimated earlier, that Fai at one point imprisoned its ruler into an enchanted sleep and placed him into a pool. Since the wizard thereafter fled Celes, it would seem that he had no intention of usurping the throne. Fai remains deeply fearful throughout the series of the prospect of King Ashura's eventual awakening. (The fairy-like Chii is under strict instructions to inform Fai of the monarch's arousal the moment this may occur.) Echoing the motif associated with Sakura's initial discovery of her preternatural powers, the intricate architecture of Celes Castle is surrounded by translucent wings. Kurogane's own place of origin is Japan. The show's version of the country recalls its situation during the Warring States Period (fifteenth and sixteenth centuries), when Japan was torn by unceasing civil war and bloody feuds involving countless factions. Employed as a ninja by Princess Tomoyo, Kurogane arrogantly disobeys his master's policy by leaving a far greater number of corpses in his wake than she deems necessary. It is for this very reason, as noted, that Kurogane is eventually banished from his homeland.

The multiple dimensions visited by the actors are extraordinarily varied, and inspired by settings and characters from previous artistic productions by CLAMP, the team of manga artists behind *Tsubasa*'s prismatic universe.[3] Each of the arcs covered by the show's two seasons inserts the group into a new world posing specific challenges and threats.[4] The first dimension reached by Syaoran and his companions in the early part of the adventure is the Hanshin Republic. Hanshin is an island in the shape of a tiger where people possess animal spirits (*kudan*). One such entity also becomes attached to each visitor to their world. Syaoran's *kudan* assumes the shape of a horned fox, Fai's that of a green phoenix, and Kurogane's that of a blue dragon. In terms of architecture and decor, Hanshin offers an intriguing admixture of the old and the new, juxtaposing an ancient castle with neon lights, funky shops and metallic structures. In this dimension, Syaoran manages to retrieve just one of his beloved's feathers.

Shortly after the team's arrival in the Hanshin Republic, Yuuko's admonition regarding parallel lives is confirmed by the scene where Syaoran and Fai visit a humble *okonomiyaki* joint whose staff look exactly like King Touya of Clow and his chief advisor Yukito. Baffled, the hero instinctively addresses the owner as "His Majesty," to which the bloke jovially ripostes that he has no authority over anything other than pancakes. Two more endearing characters that also recur in *Tsubasa*'s multiverse are Arashi and Sorata, a couple sustained by a deep love for each other and thereby able to extend their warmth to strangers with utter selflessness. They are first introduced in the Hanshin arc, and when their lookalikes make their appearance in the succeeding arc, Syaoran explains to Sakura that "they're parallels with the same appearance and they seem to have the same essence but their lives and memories are different." Notably, "lives" and "memories" are concepts that *Tsubasa* treats as inextricable from each other at all times, even in the context of ostensibly peripheral occurrences.

Tsubasa's next arc takes the company to the town of Ryonfi in the country of Nayutaya (Koryo in the original manga), where Syaoran and his companions take it upon themselves to unite an abused people and incite them to topple their ruthless rulers. Nayutaya is a feudal nation routinely patrolled by the *mitteishu*, an elite rank of top-secret agents envoyed by the government to spy on the local lords and ensure they do not abuse their authority. Regrettably, Ryionfi's vicious ruler, Tambal, has managed to elude the *mitteishu*'s surveillance by gaining possession of one of Sakura's feathers and harnessing its power to the erection of magical shields that render not only his fortress but also the rest of the town utterly impenetrable. The feather has also enabled the oppressor to endow his brutish son Bullgal with superhuman muscles and to destroy the mighty sorceress Cyenyan, the sole person capable of resisting his ascent to power. In the process, Tambal has appropriated Cyenyan's *hijutsu*. This designates the ability to manipulate both natural forces, such as the wind, and human will. The art's legitimate goal is to bring happiness, yet *hijutsu* may be deployed to nefarious ends if it falls into the wrong hands.

By means of *hijutsu*, Ryonfi's despot relentlessly terrorizes his subjects and morphs an entire host of brave rebels into hideous beasts. Last but not least, the feather has given Tambal the power to capture Kishimu, the most proficient *hijutsu* practitioner in the land, and to exploit her skills to his own villainous purpose. Kishimu is eventually vanquished and released from her bondage by Kurogane and Fai following one of *Tsubasa*'s most tantalizing displays of magic, as well as a flurry of top-notch martial moves impeccably executed by both the ninja, despite the loss of his precious blade, and the mage, although he is determined not to resort to wizardry in combat as long as he lacks the restraining tattoo. The most charismatic persona in this segment of the saga is undoubtedly the young Chu'nyan, Cyenyan's daughter. Though merely a kid, Chu'nyan is a valiant freedom fighter and unflinchingly strives to sow the seeds of rebellion among her compatriots even after they have grown disinclined to oppose Tambal in the wake of their fellows' tragic defeat.

The Nayutaya arc plays a vital part in gradually taking Sakura out of the zombie-like daze that has beset her since the baleful incident dramatized in the introductory installment and in revealing her submerged powers. This is most spectacularly demonstrated by the scenes where Sakura penetrates Tambal's bastion (followed, needless to say, by the unwaveringly loyal Syaoran), survives the portentous spells cast by the tyrant to hinder her, and instinctively realizes that the monsters unleashed against the interlopers are actually casualties of necromancy. (These are the aforementioned rebels from Ryonfi.) When Sakura and Syaoran effortlessly emerge from the citadel unscathed and share these disquieting truth with the townsfolk, the latter rediscover their lurking desire to rise against their persecutor once and for all. Sakura is not only instrumental to the advancement of a political drama, however. She also helps Chu'nyan come to terms with her personal loss and learn at last how to master her own *hijutsu* by unwittingly lending her own body to the girl's mother and hence enabling the deceased parent to see her child again and give her some truly life-transforming advice.

It is thanks to Chu'nyan's deployment of her freshly awakened *hijutsu* that Tambal is finally overthrown and the feather he has so avidly treasured is returned to its rightful owner.

The culmination of these events offers an especially memorable flashback: as Sakura incorporates the rescued feather, the reminiscence that instantly visits her is that of a birthday party from her early childhood. The princess remembers feeling intensely happy due to the presence of one particular guest but is powerless to recall the person's name or appearance. As the reawakened memory plays before her mind's eye, she can clearly visualize her brother Touya (at the time just an adolescent prince) and his friend Yukito but the only other guest — the one that truly mattered to her — features merely as an empty chair. As the girl tearfully wonders, "Why was I happy? Who was there?" *Tsubasa* reaches one of its most genuinely affecting peaks.

Flashbacks go on playing a pivotal role in the stand-alone segment of the adventure where the company is briefly relocated to an interstitial world seemingly consisting solely of a deserted forest and a lake. The latter turns out to house at its very bottom a miniature city exuding neoclassical radiance, guarded by a glowing fish of mastodontic dimensions that functions as its "Sun." This is a good example of *Tsubasa*'s occasional indulgence in detours that do not serve to advance the main plot in any obvious way but resplendently attest to its creators' passion for worldbuilding as a worthy pursuit in its own right. Furthermore, although no mnemonic fragment is descried in this dimension, the episode devoted to its portrayal is thematically crucial. As intimated, this is largely due to its sustained use of flashbacks.

In one of these, Sakura returns to the birthday scene presented earlier as she recounts the retrospective vision to Syaoran — who, obviously, knows only too well who the invisible guest was. In a further flashback, Sakura recalls being introduced to Syaoran as a little kid and being told by her father that the boy had endured painful experiences and part of his heart remained, as a result, hard and cold, concluding that Sakura's warm smile had the power to heal his inner wounds. This is confirmed by another flashback in which the princess revisits the moment when she was first able to make the boy smile by showing him a flock of doves flying over the royal palace. At this stage in the story, Sakura has a fleeting sensation that there might be a link between the small boy and her current guide and protector but has no means of translating it into anything tangible or intelligible.

Sakura also appears to apprehend subliminally the existence of a link between Syaoran and her identity crisis in the course of her telepathic conversation with the giant fish (which in itself provides further evidence for her preternatural abilities). In response to the creature's exhortation to state what has brought her to this world, she indeed observes: "I am here because he [i.e., Syaoran] brought me. And I seek to know who I am." Scenes such as this suggest that the bond between Sakura and Syaoran is magically indissoluble and hence capable of transcending the dictates of both memory and its loss. Sakura hopes in vain that one day she might remember the identity of the person so important to her prior to the shattering of her soul. Syaoran, for his part, seems resigned to the idea that the girl simply cannot remember him and seems surprised when she expresses concern about his safety. Yet, neither the princess's hopefulness nor her protector's pragmatism can impair the spellbinding grace of their relationship.

The story's retrospective tenor gains momentum from its disclosure of part of Syaoran's nebulous background. We thus learn through flashbacks that upon meeting Sakura, the boy had no memories of any events predating his adoption. The princess reassures him by proposing that they "make a lot of new memories instead," and further suggesting that since Syaoran cannot remember the date of his birthday, he could just as well share hers — in this way, they will always be able to celebrate the anniversary together. Considering the girl's predicament in the present, this recollection posits an intriguingly ironical reversal of roles. In another important flashback, Syaoran recalls Sakura stating, as a child, that even though she was aware there was much she still needed to discover about the world, she was already determined to act in order to "help people." This anticipates the present-day scene in which the girl ardently declares that she knows "there is still a lot more" she must "learn," yet intends to do her best to help her companions whenever possible. This leads Syaoran to aver that despite the loss of her memories, "she is the same."

Even though the action sequences showing Syaoran as he dives into the lake in search of a possible feather and then of both the youth and his beloved exploring the pygmy metropolis in its depths are nothing short of effervescent, the overall tempo of this portion of the adventure is exquisitely slow. The admixture of vibrant dynamism and methodical pacing parallels the operations of memory itself. Indeed, memory has no scruples in taking a careening plunge into the psyche's eerie backwaters one moment, and torpidly meandering over time and space, the next. The agile alternation of rapid action sequences and deliberately unfolding reflections is axial to the entire show's cinematographical cachet.

Whereas in the Nayutaya arc the saga engages with the mythical dimension of the memory topos, in the segment set in the picturesque world of Jade, it is the folkloric element that comes most prominently to the fore. Children are mysteriously disappearing from Jade's chief town, Spirit, amidst snow-blanketed lands redolent of medieval Europe, and rumors are spreading about their abduction by a royal specter, Princess Emeraude. As far as the memory theme is specifically concerned, this world dramatizes the conflict between inherited memories bequeathed by superstition and lore and empirical memories founded on analytical observation and rational deduction. Thus, while most of the locals tend to explain the endemic vanishing of kids on the grounds of hazy legends, Syaoran believes that to "get to the truth, we need evidence ... not town gossip," and channels his skills as a thorough researcher into ascertaining the mundane causes of the phenomenon. Hence, he eventually discovers that something far more sinister than an old wives' tale lies behind it.

This tension between discordant versions of the "truth" elliptically encourages the audience to doubt all fossilized accounts of the past and its secrets, historiographical ones included. When Syaoran and company arrive in Jade, they discover that local history attaches great significance to the legend of a golden-haired princess reputed to have lived three-hundred years earlier and to have obtained a magical feather that enabled her to draw children to her castle and transform them in inscrutable ways, before returning them to their homes. The recent spate of vanishings have led many to conclude that "the old curse has returned." From a stylistic point of view, this aspect of the story is made particularly intriguing by the exposition of the legend by means of voiceovers accompanying still images executed so as to resemble stained-glass panels. These emanate a fairytale feel, on the one hand, and an aura of timeless wonder, on the other. Moreover, the visuals' connection with the Gothic style aptly complements the arc's emphasis on the haunting motif.

The physician Kyle Rondato, who provides the protagonists with accommodation during their sojourn, circuitously induces them to suspect Glosum, a supposedly compassionless landowner, as the likely culprit behind the abductions. However, the doctor himself is eventually exposed as the power-hungry maniac at the root of the crisis. Before delving further into the causes and aims of the villain's agenda, some attention must be paid to Sakura's personal part in this segment of the adventure and to the remarkable abilities she incrementally exhibits. These prove critical to the resolution of the Jade mystery. By no stretch of the imagination is Sakura a stereotypical "damsel in distress" in this arc. Not only is she the first person ever to see the "legendary ghost come to life," which confirms her preternatural powers, she is also plucky enough to follow the apparition to her derelict haunt and then flee the dungeon in which Kyle has thrown her. Thus, she is able to use her powers to put an end to centuries of strife resulting from the malefic influence of one of her feathers.

In the climactic moments, Princess Emeraude also discloses to the heroine the real events underlying indigenous lore. The feather acquired by Emeraude had disastrous effects on her land, causing whole armies to perish in successive waves of atrocious wars in order to possess it and a lethal epidemic affecting only children to break out. Emeraude was able to cure these innocent souls as long as she could attract them to the castle and expose them to the feather's other side — its healing force — and finally resolved to use Jade's entire reservoir of magic to seal the talisman in a crystal and hence prevent people from fighting over it. As to the part of the old legend claiming that upon their return to their families, the children appeared inexplicably changed, this element was inserted into the story to lend it a dark twist, since the people of Jade have always believed that explicitly voicing one's good fortune is a recipe for disaster.

This time around, Kyle has magnetized Spirit's kids to the castle in the conviction that their "pure hearts" would "slowly unseal the feather" and thus grant him limitless powers. Sakura alone has the authority to release the object and reclaim it as her own legitimate possession, which she does with both aplomb and ceremonial solemnity in an admirable display of strength which one could never have expected of the limp and barely conscious victim seen in earlier frames. As often in *Tsubasa*, Sakura's feathers are posited as concurrently baneful and benevolent agents. This bears witness to the show's inherent aversion to crude binary oppositions in the apportioning of good and evil, a propensity paralleled by the Jade arc's portrayal of its potential heroes and villains. Emeraude is clearly motivated by noble intentions despite her notoriety and Glosum himself is a principled gentleman despite his apparent callousness, whereas the suave Kyle is ultimately no less unscrupulous a hunter for power than Tambal was in the Nayutaya arc. Although Kyle is dealt a poetically just punishment, as he is crushed by a statue of Princess Emeraude within the castle itself, the sense of menace associated with the duplicitous doctor does not evaporate with his demise. In fact, the realization that he already knew about Sakura's feather prior to the travelers' arrival in Spirit suggests that there are other dark forces at large. This is forbiddingly reinforced by the spectral princess's parting words to Sakura: "Please be careful. There is one who watches every step you take."

Syaoran's knack of unearthing the earthbound causes of phenomena traditionally regarded as supernatural occurrences is reinforced by one of the second season's standalone mini-adventures. While the island where he washes up following a direful storm is held to be infested by malevolent ghosts as a result of its tendency to resonate with a bloodcurdling din, Syaoran establishes that the sound is actually triggered by the wind as its direction alters and it blows through a cave-like shrine. His talent as an archaeologist, which enables him to decipher an ancient inscription, assists him greatly in the unraveling of the time-honored mystery.

With the move to the next world, *Tsubasa* offers a subtle variation on the theme of parallel lives. In the standalone mini-adventure herein set, we encounter doubles not in the guise of literal lookalikes but in that of characters linked by thematic and metaphorical analogies to the protagonists. Syaoran's quest to retrieve Sakura's memory shards is here replicated by the task undertaken by Keepha to save his beloved Shalme. The latter has been cursed by a potent spirit upon entering against its desire the ruins of its temple (please note the parallel with Sakura's ordeal) and is doomed to die unless Keepha obtains the "sacred treasure": the prize reserved for the winner of a tournament whose participants are allowed to deploy all manner of magical weapons. Hoping that the treasure might consist of one of Sakura's feathers, Syaoran, Fai and Kurogane enter the contest and Syaoran succeeds in laying his hands on the prize only to discover that it bears no resemblance whatsoever to the hoped-for reward.

Even though by the time Keepha reaches the ring the tournament is already over, he is still determined to win the key to his girlfriend's survival. Following a thrilling duel, Syaoran willingly forsakes the treasure, showing that in his heart, generosity is far more crucial a virtue than sheer vim, thereby enabling Shalme's recovery. While the drama's happy ending provides a genuinely endearing narrative gem, the finale is rendered most effective by Fai's remarks on another hypothetical conclusion where the treasure might indeed have turned out to be one of Sakura's feathers, and a very unpalatable choice would therefore have been forced on the protagonists. Through this ploy, the show offers a self-reflexive commentary on the nature of its diegesis that eloquently attests to director Kouichi Mashimo's acute orchestration of the materials at his disposal and preparedness to make room for might-have-beens no less than for empirically realized facts.

Complementing the exploration undertaken in the preceding segments, where memory is posited as a mental phenomenon imbricated with fantasy and myth, the adventures presented in the first season's final arc underscore memory's inextricability from the realm of illusion. This is set in Outo, where all visitors are required to register their names and get jobs. In order to be allowed to stay in the hope of garnering further clues to the location of Sakura's feathers, Syaoran and Kurogane indeed take on posts as demon hunters, while Sakura and Fai open a café. The valiant slayers Yuzuriha and Kusanagi explain the logistics of their profession to the newcomers in ways that bring to mind the rules of role-playing adventure games: the monsters are strictly classified according to their strength and their hunters gain points with each defeat, thereby progressively ascending the martial hierarchy. The most valued prey is the "A1 demon," a creature whose abilities surpass by far those of other fiends.

The ludic element presages later disclosures regarding the nature of Outo as a whole as a sophisticated simulation. The adventure's RPG feel at this stage of its unfolding reaches a climax in the sequence where Syaoran and Kurogane must infiltrate a tower and win their way to the top — where important secrets might be unearthed — by overcoming legion attackers along a succession of caves, treacherous stairways and subterranean pools steeped in impenetrable gloom. The deceptive quality of the Outo dimension is presciently grasped by Fai when he opines that although this world first presented itself as a welcoming society, it might actually turn out to be the most viciously and surreptitiously hostile of the realms the travelers have visited so far.

In Outo, a particularly important role is played by the character of Seishirou. Although he, too, is a world-hopper, Seishirou can only cross dimensions a limited number of time as a result of having surrendered his right eye to the Dimensional Witch. From his very first appearance, Seishirou emanates a chilling sense of foreboding, heightened by his association with demons endowed with unusual powers. "I know your weakness and I'll never forget, Syaoran," he ominously announces while spying on his addressee from high above, before receding into the nocturnal sky. His heavily cloaked and hooded figure is here set against the sinister backdrop of a glacially effulgent moon and accompanied by a flurry of drifting *sakura* (a recurring fixture in the Outo dimension) that feels eerily incongruous with the brooding sobriety of the scene. Through flashbacks, it is revealed that Seishirou was already acquainted with Syaoran in Clow and introduced him to the kicking techniques at which the youth excels. Possessing one of Sakura's feathers, Seishirou intends to work his magic to achieve eternal life.

This part of the adventure also contributes vitally to the elaboration of the complex relationship, gradually built up throughout the adventure, between Kurogane and Fai. With its jocular banter and sarcastic wit, this infuses welcome moments of comic relief into the drama even in the context of potentially tragic situations. A case in point is the exchange where the two characters confront the rain of corrosive globules conjured by Kishimu:

> FAI: These spheres are quick and can change shape, too. It's taking all my concentration not to get burnt.
> KUROGANE: Good. You won't have any time to think of any more dumb nicknames.

The adoption on the wizard's part of varyingly distorted versions of the fighter's name is indeed a key component of the progressive portrayal of their interaction. The use of Quixotic designations such as "Kuropon," "Kurorin," "Kurotan" and "Kurosama" is one of Fai's trademarks and a vital means of keeping up a smiling façade to conceal what is actually a frail and lonely kernel. On countless occasions, Fai relies on Mokona as an ideal sidekick to poke fun at the warrior, aware that she can sense Kurogane's inherent generosity no less keenly than he himself does.

As a uniquely competent fighter, Kurogane can clearly see that in his confrontation with the Outo demons, the wizard has made no serious effort to dodge their lethal moves, as though he wished to be hit. Kurogane tempestuously expresses his opinions and one feels that Fai is not altogether unresponsive to his words even though he chooses, once more, to circumvent the attack. This impression is confirmed by the following exchange:

> KUROGANE: Is this what you call living? You were a magician. What are you now? You gave up your magic, your life, to the Witch like it was nothing. And now — now you fight somebody else's battle and try to forget something of your own's missing. Coward. I'm sure you'll live, too, but I don't know why you bother if you don't fight for what you've lost. Unlike you, I never intend to give up. Not ever. I'll fight for what's mine, and if I lose, well, there are worse things than being defeated. At least, I won't end up like you, running away from my problems.
> FAI: Lovely speech. You do really have me all figured out, don't you.

The ninja is quick to read through Fai's cheery veneer and instinctively seeks to puncture it, guided by the firm conviction that no matter how dark one's past may be, it is always possible to look ahead. Kurogane simply detests those who have forsaken hope, for he sees this attitude as coterminous with the loss of the will to live. He is not alone in realizing that at his core, Fai is a sad and isolated person. At one point, in fact, Mokona also points out that the magician's cheerfulness is not genuine since the smiles he insistently regales are merely attempts to cover up his real thoughts — which are always elsewhere.

Kurogane rebukes Fai even more sternly in the OVA *Tokyo Revelations*, where he urges the wizard to admit that he does care deeply for his traveling companions. This, the ninja maintains, has been unequivocally demonstrated by Fai's resolve to use magic in Rekord (Season 2) to protect his friends — even though he knows that whenever he resorts to his powers, he risks triggering Ashura'a awakening — while in Nayutaya, Fai seemed more prepared to lose his life than to invoke sorcery. The magician, Kurogane concludes, has been hiding behind the mask of a jovial smile to prevent anyone from getting too close to him, yet has allowed himself to become so involved with Sakura and Syaoran's quest that he can no longer follow unequivocally his initial agenda. (Ironically, it is precisely in relation to Kurogane that Fai has dared breach his vow of reserve, precisely by showering all sorts of unwelcome nicknames onto the warrior.) It is in scenes such as this that the *Tsubasa* saga exhibits most generously its stature as a mature drama coursed by tortuous character interaction, thus transcending the boundaries of standard fantasy anime.

Outo is rendered especially intriguing by the disclosure that its rigidly rule-bound society is actually a game world designed according to codes that clearly delimit the tasks and properties peculiar to both demons and their pursuers. This revelation crowns a series of inexplicable occurrences. Firstly, the monsters begin to behave in an unaccustomed fashion and to assail ordinary civilians although they are supposed to be programmed to attack only slayers. This indicates that they are no longer unproblematically subject to "governmental control" and that an external force must be tampering with Outo's laws. Secondly, the charismatic singer and composer Oruha reveals that her world is now haunted by a brand-new prodigy endowed with the power to assume the shape of a handsome man, as well as the ability to control other demons. This disclosure induces some of the hunters to assume that the A1 demon and the newcomer may well be same entity. Moreover, Syaoran and his companions at first suspect that Seishirou himself fits the bill as an appropriate candidate for the role. The A1 demon, however, turns out to be a presence that the Outo world requires for its proper functioning (its pursuit constituting something of a game-within-the-game), whereas game orchestrators are only too eager to get rid of Syaoran's former trainer, and are aware that he is not a demon but possesses a secret weapon of disruptive potential.

There are also indications that Seishirou may actually be attempting to make contact with the entity supposedly endowed with unmatched powers. This suspicion is corroborated by his declaration that his intention is to find the creature and use it to obtain the gift of immortality which it is held to possess. He is therefore determined to destroy anybody potentially able to eliminate the portentous breed and Fai becomes, at least ostensibly, his first victim. Little by little, Outo's ludic world begins to dissolve as a "system overload" causes its hitherto photorealistic façade to deteriorate into unequivocally digitized swathes of pixels. Following a suspenseful duel between Syaoran and Seishirou intercut with a flashback to their first encounter (where the older man agrees to train the boy in exchange for his services in the translation of a tome on vampire lore), Syaoran and Sakura themselves disintegrate into bits and bytes and seemingly leave not merely this world but all human worlds.

The illusory nature of Outo is fully disclosed with the revelation that the Outo world is inextricable from the Country of Edonis and its popular amusement venue, Fairy Park, which contains egg-shaped capsules through which visitors access the virtual reality of Outo. As Syaoran and Sakura wake up inside their respective game pods, an offstage voice announces: "You're now leaving Outo." As Fai, who has already been "dead" for a while in the logic of the game and has had time to grasp the nature of the ludic dimension, observes, it is not quite correct to state that the characters have "left" Outo since this is a world where they "never were to begin with because Outo doesn't actually exist." Everything that appeared to take place in the Outo domain, the mage adds, "happened inside our heads, collectively." This proposition is vividly redolent of William Gibson's famous definition of cyberspace as a "consensual hallucination" (Gibson, p. 67).

What puzzles Syaoran most is that he has no recollection of traveling to Edonis on the way to Outo. Chitose, one of the game's chief designers, explains: "When you arrived here and entered Outo, all your memories of coming here were suppressed." (It would seem that *Tsubasa* does not miss a single opportunity to foreground the trope of mnemonic repression.) Syaoran is not quite satisfied with the explanations proffered by Fai and Chitose— for one thing, he cannot figure out why he should still be in possession of the sword acquired in Outo. Chitose speculates that the reason for this uncanny migration of the virtual into the actual is that some unknown force is endeavoring to bring the simulation into reality. Sure enough, while the characters from the game are transposed back to the real world, Seishirou endeavors to turn Outo itself into a reality by deploying the power of the feather in his possession. The demon sought by Seishirou, meanwhile, turns out to be none other than Oruha. The singer is indeed the mightiest creature ever to have inhabited the game world. Unluckily for Seishirou, the power to grant eternal life held by Oruha is merely a "programming code"— a rule of the game (of which Oruha herself is a key architect) decreeing that if a player manages to vanquish the special demon she represents, the player's own character will become invincible within the virtual realm. In the real world, Oruha's power amounts to nothing. There is no alternative left for Seishirou other than to quit Edonis— with Sakura's feather, alas, still in his hands.

Although it is in the Outo arc that the tenuousness of the dividing line between reality and virtuality is most blatantly exposed, there are several other instances throughout the anime of the real world's imbrication with the realm of illusion. A case in point is the sequence in which Tambal conjures up phantasms of Sakura and Chun'yan in order to confuse and disable Syaoran. The hero realizes that the Sakura he sees trapped in a floating sphere with the Nayutaya girl is an apparition created by the villain out of his own thoughts when the princess addresses him using the shortened version of his name which she adopted in childhood to break the barrier of formality. Syaoran knows only too well that since losing her memories, Sakura has never called him any names other than his full given one.

The first season does not end with the Outo/Edonis arc, however, but rather with a standalone adventure in which the travelers are inserted into a realm— the Principality of Zarastra—where one of the feathers is tied to a local deity. The feather allows the god to grant a wish to anybody who is able to reach its temple. Since this is fiercely guarded by lethal warriors in Fei Wong Reed's service, scores of questors have thus far met a dismal fate. Sakura now has a chance to regain all her lost memories but this is not the path she chooses. The final installment is markedly open-ended, and while this may be seen as a purely utilitarian move intended to create scope for a second season, it is also, more importantly, a corollary of the show's ethical lesson. Indeed, the primary reason for the story's eschewal of neat resolutions at this stage is that when the heroine is given the opportunity to have her memories restored, she chooses to shelve her private wish for the sake of others, whom she deems far more unfortunate than herself. Feeling at least partly responsible for the misfortune that has befallen each and every supplicant, since their desires could only have been fulfilled through the power of one of her feathers, she entreats the divinity to bring the victims back to life.

This provisional ending does not only bear witness to Sakura's selflessness: it also foregrounds Fai's and Kurogane's sacrificial commitment to the advancement of the princess's and her protector's cause. Indeed, while both know that were they to enter the temple first, they could have their own wishes granted, they choose to stay behind in the belief that their fellow travelers' mission deserves priority. Moreover, they dauntlessly fight the "strange soldiers" sent by Fei Wong Reed to protect the temple in his effort to prevent Syaoran from being the first to access it and ask for Sakura's memories to be restored — which is the last thing in the vast multidimensional universe the villain would want to see happen.

The travelers return the principality in the second season, where it transpires that the effect of the portent pulled off by the Zarastran deity in response to Sakura's prayer is not permanent and that the resurrected humans, therefore, are doomed to die again — and this time irrevocably — by the following new moon. The natives reckon that the only way of averting this calamity is to obtain another magical feather and have the princess renew her wish with the feather's assistance within the temple. Syaoran does succeed in rescuing the available memory shard, somewhat preposterously nested in the nasal horn of a Godzilla-ish dragon, and Sakura once more begs the spirit to lift the curse hanging over the hapless Zarastrans. Yet, the god adamantly refuses to comply, stating that a lost life cannot be conclusively restored in any world. By the next new moon, accordingly, the victims vanish one by one, dotting the otherwise desolate landscape with preternaturally beautiful silver-green sparks.

The deity's philosophy is reinforced by the power of memory, as Sakura regains the recollection of her father's words in response to her grief at the loss of a cherished pet, a sand rabbit given her by Syaoran, and gentle request that he ask Yukito to use his magic to resuscitate it: "Lives that are lost cannot be returned. That is why lives are precious, and living is wonderful." The tragic irony implicit in this dramatic twist is that Sakura might as well have wished for her memories to be mended at the end of Season 1 — although this would have detrimentally curtailed the character's moral stature and, no less inauspiciously, both provided rather a simplistic rounding off and precluded the progression to the follow-up show.

From world to world, it becomes incrementally clear that Sakura's memories, peaceful when left in her possession, hold dark potentialities if claimed by unscrupulous agents keen on advancing their quest for global dominance, for the control of both space and time and, ultimately, for immortality. At the same time, Sakura herself gradually perceives clues to the resolution of her and her friends' seemingly intractable task. When Sakura is first dispossessed of her memories, she is concurrently robbed of any clear sense of her very identity. Turned into a vacuous vessel, her body is the only extant vestige of the girl Syaoran once knew and loved. Not even her uniquely engaging smile initially appears to have managed to survive the malefic spell. The enduring hope, in this otherwise bleak scenario, is that Sakura and Syaoran might build a fresh relationship from scratch. The past and its memories may have been erased and yet, the show intimates, as long as there is a future, new connections and hence new memories can be positively forged. This idea is lyrically brought home by the first ending theme for the series, "Loop," where the central proposition is the idea that separations are never conclusive but actually anticipate novel encounters. The director has overtly stressed the axial significance of this aspect of the story: "when I read the original manga, I felt the message was about the importance of making new memories.... I want to make that the most important part of the anime adaptation" (Mashimo, p. 48).

The suggestion that Sakura and Syaoran might develop a novel relationship based on mutual affection and respect just like the old one is foreshadowed by Fai's observations regarding parallel universes at an early stage in the narrative. Reflecting on the presence of seemingly identical people in radically different dimensions, the mage opines that in "altered surroundings," humans are not likely to "act differently" but rather to "create the same friendships" and "make the same mistakes.... Where it counts, we'd end up the same, no matter what we'd done — or remembered." The validity of this contention is, at least potentially, confirmed by the climax of the Hanshin arc. When Sakura regains consciousness just after the second feather has been found and reabsorbed by her being, she has no recollection of Syaoran, which greatly torments him. However, when the travelers are removed by Mokona from the Republic, she reaches out for the boy's hand in search for reassurance, as though she were instinctively drawn to Syaoran.

Commenting on the protagonists' affective — and, by extension, mnemonic — development, Mika Kikuchi (Mokona's voice actress) emphasizes that Syaoran and Sakura grow "closer to each other" as their journey progresses. By the time the saga reaches the Outo Kingdom arc, and about two thirds of the events covered in the first season have taken place, "Sakura is beginning to sense Syaoran's sincerity, which comes from Syaoran's memory of their old relationship. If he didn't have that, he wouldn't still be enamored of Sakura, and there wouldn't have been any chance of a new relationship developing between them. That connection between them was there all along, but to Sakura it's all new" (Kikuchi, p.42). While this aspect of *Tsubasa* renders it painfully touching insofar as it underscores the magnitude of Sakura's loss, it also inaugurates propitious openings for maturation and self-renewal.

While Sakura's memories have ostensibly dissolved beyond repair, Syaoran never loses sight of the vital bond that has tied him to the princess since childhood. It is this enduring faith that keeps his resolve unscathed throughout the action and even enables him, though he is not a professional fighter, to match both Kurogane's and Fai's superb strength. Concomitantly, the richness of the youth's personality is attested to by the psychological development he undergoes when, in losing the most valuable relationship he has ever had, he learns to value deeply his connections with all sorts of other people. Protecting his traveling companions and fighting on behalf of the oppressed in various dimensions incrementally assert themselves as priorities almost as vital as the injunction to restore Sakura's mnemonic integrity.

Throughout the saga, matters are problematized by temporal, and hence mnemonic, discrepancies across the various realms. Time indeed appears to pass at a different rate in each of them. This is explicitly brought home by the arc set in the world of Nayutaya, whose vicious overlord has been relying on one of Sakura's feathers to keep the populace under his heel for several years by the time the protagonists reach his town even though in their own temporal scale, the princess has only been deprived of her memories for a few days. A further displacement occurs in the arc set in Jade, where one of Sakura's feathers is supposed to have reached the place a few hundred years prior to the present adventure and to have spawned the aforementioned legend surrounding Princess Emeraude and Jade's kids.

The concept of temporal displacement is also evoked by discrepancies between the protagonists' discourse and the speech patterns used in some of the worlds they visit. For example, at various points in the Outo arc, the young demon slayer Ryuuoh accuses Syaoran of expressing himself in an excessively formal fashion. Likewise, in the second season, Tomoyo encourages Sakura to drop the ceremonious register and speak in the way that feels most natural to her. The point is that Syaoran and Sakura come from an older world, so to speak, and know no other linguistic style than the one in which they customarily couch their thoughts. Sakura seems well aware that this is the case but cleverly dodges the issue of temporal incongruity by candidly stating that she feels quite comfortable with her regular mode of speech.

Although it is far from unusual for an anime series to be orchestrated in terms of relatively discrete arcs, *Tsubasa*'s narrative organization is refreshingly innovative. As Tasha Robinson notes, "It's good that the series doesn't follow a predictable pattern of one feather or one new dimension per episode, which would get dull fast—instead, it takes the time to focus on and develop the first world the stars visit, with worthwhile results.... That unhurried vibe stretches into the direction, as well, with long lyrical sequences simply depicting Sakura flying, or Syaoran contemplating his memories of her" (Robinson 2007). Panned stills and placidly drawn-out flashbacks, emblematic of Mashimo's directorial style, abound and contribute to consolidate the series' intentionally methodical pace. The rendition of Sakura's memories themselves in the form of scattered feathers—forever frail, partial and drifting—relates Mashimo's tale to the poetics of *wabi* as a paean to the beauty exuded by imperfection.

Flashbacks are especially useful in underscoring the *wabi*-like friability of Sakura's memories even once the feather-recovery operation has yielded some results. They indeed show that when she is able to recall certain events from the past, these do not offer coherent pictures because they do not quite fit together. At the same time, flashbacks help Mashimo develop aspects of the heroine's personality and past experiences, thereby imparting her with a more fully rounded narrative identity. From a structural point of view, flashbacks are also instrumental to the injection of the narrative's markedly episodic (and hence potentially choppy) nature with a cumulative sense of diegetic continuity.

Two of the entire show's most touching flashbacks are offered in the early part of the Outo arc. The first occurs when Sakura observes that she feels deeply happy whenever she hears Syaoran say "thank you," even though she has no idea why this should be the case. It is interesting to compare, in this regard, the dubbed and subbed versions of the girl's expression of her feelings. The dub states: "Just words but whenever I hear them, I feel like I'm home again." The subtitles—preferably, perhaps—use this wording instead: "It sort of tickles my memories." A flashback playing through Syaoran's mind follows, explaining the origins of Sakura's emotion. Through this retrospective sequence, we learn that as a child, Syaoran always apologized profusely whenever he hurt himself for he was loath to cause others to worry on his account. Sakura was eventually able to cure him of this self-persecutory tendency by teaching him that people worried because they cared about him and instead of apologizing, Syaoran should just thank them.

In the second flashback, Sakura partially emerges from her amnesia, and the enormity of the price Syaoran has had to pay for the recovery of her memories is thrown starkly into relief. The princess begins to suspect that she knew her protector prior to her memory-disintegrating misfortune and that they might even have met as kids — yet, she has no means of ascertaining the veracity of this sensation. Just as she tentatively speculates that Syaoran is "someone very important" to her, she is beset by a hallucination in which a blurred image of the cloaked Syaoran from the Clow days spirals backwards against the background of a cut-out of Sakura's head flooded in psychedelic hues as though her recollection of the boy were being sucked into a black hole. (A shot of a cryptically smirking Yuuko follows). It is as though Sakura's submerged, yet undying, feelings for Syaoran were struggling to break through a titanic barrier, only to be pushed back by the unrescindable authority of the conditions accepted by the boy in order to obtain the Dimensional Witch's assistance. Fai somberly comments on the situation thus: "Even when [Sakura] regains feathers that carry memories of [Syaoran], he'll be immediately removed. Like a story written on paper filled with holes because every mention of him has been cut out."

An inspired variation on the flashback device occurs when Oruha visits Sakura at the café with the intention of gathering information about the girl's origins and induces her to sing, claiming that "Songs are mirrors that reflect what you are, what you need. Songs answer questions, like 'Where did you come from?' 'Why are you here?' Songs look at the future and tell you where you're planning to go. To sing, all you must do is tell me what you care about most." As though hypnotized, Sakura embarks effortlessly on a mesmerizingly beautiful melody and as she sings, old memories of Syaoran flood her mind. The song itself, where the phrase "lost memories" appositely contributes the refrain, portrays the boy as "the traveler with the gentlest of eyes." In the sequence, the heroine seemingly bypasses the mnemonic proscription sanctioned by Yuuko via her unconscious, thereby retrieving abeyant reminiscences of her childhood moments with Syaoran without actually knowing that she is doing it.

Oruha herself emerges from the experience reckoning that she has learnt a lot about Sakura and wishes to find out more, even though the reasons behind her interest in the foreign girl are as yet unfathomable. (Oruha appears to register Sakura's melody and related recollections as digitally encoded data, which offers an important clue to Outo's virtual constitution.) The full import of the singer's journey into Sakura's psyche emerges in the crowning moments of the Outo arc, where she urges the heroine to recognize the immensity of Syaoran's significance in her current life regardless of the trauma she has suffered, suggesting that truly important feelings embedded in a person's heart bypass the limitations of conscious memory. The relevant part of the script is so deeply pertinent to the evolution of *Tsubasa*'s entire psychological trajectory as to deserve full citation: "After hearing your song, I was able to see everything you'd gone through to get here. In your heart, I saw the boy clearly. He's a very important part of your life, isn't he? You don't need memories to know that. The feelings the boy has for you, they're a perfect mirror to your own heart."

Another key flashback occurs in the opening part of the first season's last segment, where Syaoran, shattered by recent exertions, swoons and is taken back to a scene set in some archaeological ruins in Clow where he grows gorgeous flowers to honor the venue's original status as a "sacred garden." Sakura surprises him as he lovingly tends to his crop, and asks him for permission to tell her brother King Touya that he is the unknown gardener responsible for the creation of this beautiful spot, since the monarch is aware that his subjects flock to it quotidianly to admire the flowers and seeks to reward the person who planted them. The boy, however, would rather this information were not divulged to anyone other than the princess. She agrees with alacrity, reckoning that "it will be fun this way." The exchange pithily attests to the intimate bond enjoyed by the protagonists in childhood, as well as to their moving — and utterly convincing — desire to nourish it by sharing innocent secrets.

After reabsorbing the last feather rescued by Syaoran in the show's first season, Sakura herself experiences a flashback that takes her back to the "sacred garden." As in the birthday party sequence discussed earlier, the girl appears to feel enormously happy but Syaoran remains invisible to her and the source of her feeling remains, therefore, obscure. An analogous experience is dramatized in the second season in the sequence where Sakura recovers the memory of her first encounter with the sand rabbit and subsequent adoption of the little creature as a pet. Once again, she can sense that the event made her deeply joyous but has no recollection of the person who gave her the animal. In Sakura's retrospective vision, the space that ought to be filled by Syaoran remains unforgivingly vacant.

An equally touching moment is provided by the scene in which the heroine enters what used to be Syaoran's house in Clow and ingenuously remarks: "I remember this place. A very friendly archaeologist professor lived here by himself." Accordingly, the photograph portraying Fujitaka in Syaoran's company only displays the figure of the professor in Sakura's perception. The company later revisits the setting of the last exchange between the protagonists prior to Sakura's metamorphosis, as seen in the first season's inaugural episode. Upon beholding the location once more, the girl can only retrieve lacunary reminiscences: "I remember this place vividly. I was trying to say something very important to someone. But I can't remember who that someone was. I don't even know what it was that I was trying to say."

It should also be noted that numerous characters presented in *Tsubasa* have been imported from previous CLAMP manga. Sakura, Syaoran, Princess Tomoyo, Touya and Yukito have been drawn from *Cardcaptor Sakura* (1996), Ashura from *RG Veda* (1989), Kamui and Fuuma from *X/1999* (1992), Mokona and Princess Emeraude from *Magic Knight Rayearth* (1993–1995), Chii from *Chobits* (2001), and Yuuko from *XXXHOLiC* (2003). With the exception of Yuuko the Dimensional Witch, the recycled characters presented in *Tsubasa* are not actually the same as their predecessors in earlier works but brand-new configurations of those creatures retaining their names and faces but not their narrative and symbolic significance.

For anime viewers familiar with CLAMP's oeuvre, *Tsubasa*'s intertextual nature provides a precious opportunity to observe the group's evolution over time. This does not mean, however, that only CLAMP fans are likely to enjoy the program. In fact, its ubiquitous evocation of supernatural beauty, on the one hand, and human warmth, on the other, makes *Tsubasa* not only enticing but even addictive for virtually any anime audience. CLAMP have commented thus on their decision to incorporate characters from their prior productions in *Tsubasa*'s narrative palimpsest: "It's actually much easier to write a whole new story with new characters. If we use popular characters from our former works, viewers can't help but see them as their previous personas, which makes it harder for us authors. Take Sakura, for example.... Her cute little exclamations in *Cardcaptor Sakura* stuck in fans' minds, but we chose to leave them out of *Tsubasa* as a way of showing that she isn't the same Sakura. We also took the extra precaution of making her lose her memory at the beginning — hitting the reset button, so to speak" (CLAMP 2007a, p. 45).

Reflecting the atmosphere of passionate cooperation characteristic of Mashimo's venture, confirmed by numerous articles and interviews about *Tsubasa*, the viewing experience draws us repeatedly into a collaborative effort, challenging our own imagination to bridge the gap between one dimension and the next, and to deploy our personal memories of the adventure as a means of strengthening its cumulative coherence. While Sakura's memories are scattered feathers and the narrative itself adopts a deliberately multifaceted format, the spectator's individual recollections, accumulating as each step of the protagonists' peregrinations flows by, may hold those discrete elements together in unforeseeable ways. The show's suppleness at the level of diegesis is paralleled by a richly diversified soundtrack: "*Tsubasa*," Robinson aptly maintains, "is one of those series where the music is as important as the visuals; complicated and widely varied, from mournful piano threnodies to big choral belting, [Yuki Kajiura's score] is front and center throughout much of the series" (Robinson 2007).

As shown in Chapter 1 with reference to *Millennium Actress*, director Satoshi Kon has a passion for yarns that imaginatively erode reality's boundaries by infiltrating its seemingly dependable contents with spectral memories of times and situations that might or might not have obtained in equal measures. In this respect, Kon's oeuvre bears a close affinity with *Tsubasa*'s portrayal of the inextricability of memory from visions, mirages and illusions. Kon revisits once more the theme of memory with the movie *Paprika* (2006) by deploying as his narrative premise a revolutionary gadget invented by psychiatric genius Dr. Kosaku Tokita. Named "DC-MINI," this enables psychotherapists to enter directly a patient's unconscious and effortlessly access each and every memory, image or emotion stored therein. Dr. Tokita's intentions are benevolent but the situation gets out of his control when a DC-MINI prototype is purloined and the inventor's assistant goes missing. Furthermore, numerous employees at the research laboratory lose their minds while dreams and the countless mnemonic residues they host erupt before their eyes while they are awake. It is now up to the charismatic Dr. Atsuko Chiba — one of Tokita's colleagues who has already been using the machine in its unpatented form for therapeutic purposes under the dream-state alias of "Paprika" — to beam herself into people's psyches and operate as the ultimate "dream detective." Her objective is to pinpoint the party responsible for the potentially irreversible brain-tampering ruse.

Paprika's investigation reveals that the DC-MINI, if illegitimately deployed, provides a potent means of manipulating "people's heads" by "implanting dreams" into their folds. It is indeed possible, in the logic of the story, to place the dreams of delusional patients into healthy psyches and derange them altogether. Dozens of innocent citizens are thus "assaulted by a collective dream ... one gigantic delusion" combining the oneiric experiences (and underlying mnemonic traces) of various patients who have come into contact with the new technology. In the film's climax, Paprika literally ingests the collective nightmare in a spectacular purging act, allowing polluted memories to be cleansed and submerged ones to awaken. The daunting intimation that dreams and reality have become indistinguishable persists. Yet, a positive message ultimately emerges from Kon's oneiric tangle. *Paprika* is a brave exploration of the endurance of painful, though abeyant, memories, and exhortation to confront them and assimilate them into the present. In Dr. Chiba's own case, the arousal of submerged memories coincides with a no less salutary stirring of suppressed emotions, as a result of which she is able to declare her hitherto concealed affection for Dr. Tokita (whom she will eventually marry).

The psychological block suffered by Detective Toshimi Konakawa, one of Paprika's unofficial clients and a major character in the narrative, offers an especially effective dramatization of submerged memories. Having failed to pursue his youthful ambition to become a film director, the character has developed a pathological aversion to cinema. As it turns out, the actual cause of his phobia is not his shattered dream as such but rather a cluster of lurking recollections concerning a schoolmate with whom he once shot an amateur production. Resentful of the boy's popularity and talent, Konakawa churlishly forsook him without completing the project and was beset by guilt upon discovering that he had fallen terminally ill and passed away. Thereafter, the detective's memories of the hapless youth were relegated to the depths of his subconscious, and his gnawing sense of guilt displaced onto the hatred of movies as an objective correlative for his flawed relationship with the deceased. Paprika's redemptive gesture enables Konakawa to face up to his inner conflicts, as evinced by his ability to visit a cinema without fear in the film's finale.

In *Paprika*, the theme of memory coalesces with the cognate themes of illusion and dreaming in a whimsically poetic psychedelia of images that serve to expose the inherently constructed nature of the real. At the same time, in underscoring the fragmentary, yet endlessly fascinating, character of the perceptions associated with those states, Kon offers a celebration of the beauty emanating from the imperfect in a vein redolent of the concept of *wabi*. Key to the director's imagery is the use of pictorial strategies that cause apparently solid entities to melt and warp, thereby delivering chimeric composites of light and color. The impression of memories, dreams and fantasies run amok is most effectively conveyed by the recurring scene of a phantasmagoric ticker-tape parade of dancing refrigerators, giant frogs, cherubic dummies, traditional Japanese dolls, multicolored parasols, supple Shinto gates and stuffed toys.

No less intriguing is the image, likewise iterative, used to capture the acme of psychotic disturbance: a swarm of iridescent butterflies. The butterfly motif also features conspicuously in the sequence where Paprika is held captive by one of the villains and is pinned to a table as though she were a collectible specimen. The setting, moreover, is a creepy chamber the walls of which are lined with case after case of gorgeous lepidopteral samples. In one of the movie's most dramatic hallucinatory chases, Paprika assumes the form of a fairy-like entity equipped with pearly butterfly wings. *Paprika* concurrently invokes memory by recourse to legion homages to film history and the film industry, including references to Hollywood classics such as *Tarzan the Ape Man* (dir. W. S. Van Dyke, 1932), *The Greatest Show on Earth* (dir. Cecil B. DeMille, 1952) and *Roman Holiday* (dir. William Wyler, 1953). In the closing sequence, adverts for Kon's earlier movies *Millennium Actress* and *Tokyo Godfathers* make prominent cameo appearances.

The entire story dramatized in *The Melancholy of Haruhi Suzumiya* (TV series; dir. Tatsuya Ishihara, 2006) is predicated upon the injunction to keep the protagonist's memories safely submerged. *Haruhi Suzumiya* shares with *Tsubasa* a multi-universe setup wherein a number of parallel dimensions varyingly clash or interact. Haruhi is a pretty and spunky yet peculiar teenage girl nauseated by anything ordinary and hence hell-bent on spotting mysteries and aberrations round every corner. Indulging her passion for the anomalous, the protagonist creates a school club — the "SOS Brigade" ("Spreading Excitement All Over the World with the Haruhi Suzumiya Brigade") — dedicated to the detection of aliens, time travelers, espers and all manner of paranormal activities, thereby plunging her associates into a whirlwind of mesmerizing adventures. To begin with, there is nothing obviously "melancholy" about Haruhi. In fact, she is ebullient, bossy and highly vocal. She may be bored with the humdrum world by which she unrelentingly feels suffocated but once she has set her somewhat one-track mind on the foundation and management of the quirky club, there is no obstacle Haruhi is not determined to bulldoze.

The melancholy worms itself into the yarn as it gradually transpires that the heroine is literally larger than life and that her will, moods and desires could have fateful repercussions for the destiny of the entire universe. Were she to sink into a state of dejection or abulia, Haruhi's disposition would impact so momentously on the equilibrium of the cosmos as to feasibly lead to its annihilation — or drastic reconfiguration at the very least. The world, we are reminded, exists because humans perceive it the way they do. Even a slight change in the universe could engender a situation in which there is simply no place for either the Earth or the human species.

Haruhi's powers exceed those of ordinary people insofar as she is supposedly capable of bringing into being anything and everything she happens to fantasize about. Whenever Haruhi is emotionally unstable or feels antagonized, her superhuman powers give rise to gaps between dimensions: namely, "Sealed Spaces." These fields closely resemble corresponding portions of the real world but are uninhabited and colored exclusively in grayscale. When Haruhi's listlessness gets out of control, it takes the form of giant luminous monsters known as "*Shinjin*" that appear keen on simply wreaking havoc with their surroundings, unfettered by the laws of either physics or logic.

Relatedly, the story revolves on the hypothesis that Haruhi holds a key role in the state of the universe as a vast sea of data. Since the extent and magnitude of the influence she is potentially capable of wielding are unascertainable, her observation and protection are vital priorities for various members of her club. These characters — with the exception of Haruhi's classmate Kyon, who is a perfectly average teenager — are supposed to be secret agents sent to Earth to study Haruhi and keep her at bay in as friendly a fashion as possible. On one level, therefore, the non-human members of the SOS Brigade whom Haruhi has coerced to enter the club would seem to be the emissaries of various intergalactic agencies that know full well of her power to change the world by just thinking about it. On another level, however, these characters may be manifestations of dreams — or even latent cosmic memories — emanating from the formidable girl's own subconscious. This interpretation is bolstered by the fact that the agents pop into existence just as Haruhi is longing for the appearance of extraordinary creatures fit to join her venture.

While Haruhi's human schoolmates simply see her eccentricity as aggravating or inhibiting, the non-human members of her club provide varyingly frothy explanations for her unusual conduct and tastes, opining that she may be some sort of deity, a product of a space-time warp or a form of human self-evolution. Whatever the case, the underlying proposition is that three years prior to the SOS Brigade's establishment, a large burst of information occurred on the Earth's surface. Having engulfed the planet, the information then dispersed into space. Haruhi was apparently at the epicenter of the phenomenon. The show here brings technology and memory together by suggesting that its protagonist is at once the product of a freaky twist in evolutionary technology and of a sustained program of mnemonic regimentation.

The adventure pivots on the implicit assumption that the heroine's psyche holds no conscious memories of her origins and powers. The special creatures whom Haruhi is so eager to encounter are cognizant of her monstrous potential as a unique life force of cosmic proportions and seek to ensure that the girl herself remains oblivious to her true nature. Preventing Haruhi from realizing her full capabilities means keeping her memories nebulous, approximate and incomplete. This ploy evokes a sweeping sense of *wabi* throughout, lending melancholy undertones to an otherwise rumbustious ride. Although it cannot be unequivocally claimed that this outcome was Ishihara's deliberate intention, *Haruhi Suzumiya* ultimately offers an allegorical rendition of a very real predicament. This pertains to the fate of people who are unwilling to accept the ordinary and the average as the sole legitimate reality and, as a result of what others perceive as an abnormality, are then at the receiving end of stigmatization and, worse still, domesticating strategies.[5]

CHAPTER 9

Haunted Memories

Tsubasa: RESERVoir CHRoNiCLE, TV Series: Season 2
(dirs. Kouichi Mashimo and Hiroshi Morioka, 2006)

Tsubasa Tokyo Revelations — OVA
(dir. Shunsuke Tada, 2007–2008)
– and –
*Tsubasa RESERVoir CHRoNiCLE The Movie:
Princess of the Birdcage Kingdom*
(dir. Itsuro Kawasaki, 2005)

> The leaves of memory seemed to make
> A mournful rustling in the dark
> — Henry Wadsworth Longfellow, "The Fire of Drift-Wood,"
> from *The Seaside and the Fireside* (1850)

> Beginning is easy. Continuing is hard.
> — Japanese proverb

The first segment of *Tsubasa*'s second season finds the travelers already established in Piffle World, a futuristic setting pervaded by many of the architectural and dynamic motifs typically associated with sci-fi anime and cinema at large — vertiginously proportioned high rises and aerial traffic lanes included. The company's task in this dimension is to rescue the feather offered as the prize of a race involving "Dragonfly" vehicles: wind-propelled pods endowed with a stunning variety of shapes and designs but almost invariably equipped with appendages redolent of avian or insectile wings. While being highly relevant to the saga's overall iconography and symbolism, this visual element also serves to make the flying machines eminently toylike, which is consonant with Piffle's pervasively playful look. (The roof of the stadium whence the race kicks off, for instance, is adorned with titanic teddy bears.) The version of science fiction embraced by *Tsubasa* in this arc is by no means dominated by spaceships, *mecha* and hard metallic surfaces but rather exudes a gentle feel of softness.

Although Sakura at first appears rather inept at the art of flying the indigenous vehicles, to the point that at one stage in her training she crashes sensationally into Kurogane's and Fai's own machines, she is determined to participate. The Sakura immediately introduced by the second season is an energetic girl that bears scarce resemblance to the helpless zombie seen in the prequel's early stages following her mnemonic fragmentation. This development in the heroine's personality is paralleled by a shift of emphasis in the portrayal of her relationship with Syaoran. Whereas in previous arcs their growing intimacy was invariably understated, in Piffle, there are overt allusions to their mutual feelings. This is succinctly demonstrated by the scene in which Syaoran inadvertently places his hand over Sakura's while giving her some tips about controlling a Dragonfly and Mokona enthusiastically declares that she can sense love stirring in the air. It is through unobtrusive moments such as this, no less than in the openly spectacular and magic-imbued action sequences, that *Tsubasa* proclaims its artistic caliber most resonantly.

The theme of parallel lives is instantly introduced by the second season by recourse to a Princess Tomoyo lookalike who acts as the President of the "Piffle Princess Company," the organization sponsoring the Dragonfly race. Yet, the Piffle arc also offers a couple of subtle variations on that theme. Most importantly, it proposes that the current Tomoyo has actually met the princess from Kurogane's original dimension. Introducing herself as "you, from a different world," the princess alerted her to the true nature of the feather recently discovered in Piffle. This urged the President to stage the race and ensure that Sakura would not only take part in the contest but also win it so as to guarantee the girl's reappropriation of her rightful possession. Tomoyo's resolve is so staunch that she even resorts to downright cheating by interfering with the machines and causing them to malfunction.

When the ships first experience mechanical problems in the course of the qualifying race, Syaoran quickly arrives at the conclusion that the saboteur is one of the qualifiers (among whom many familiar faces from previous arcs can be discerned), and Tomoyo is only too keen to support this hypothesis. Several near fatal accidents occur during the race proper with a mysterious figure operating from an unknown location triggering a series of explosions. Thus, when Tomoyo eventually admits to her intentions, the game is no longer under her control, for an external agency is clearly tampering with the Dragonflies and their moves. Accordingly, the President appears genuinely troubled when it transpires that the source of the signals sent out to undermine the race is located within her company and that the culprit, a close associate, is endeavoring not only to disrupt the contest but also to kill Sakura. Although Syaoran and a Ryuuoh lookalike with whom he has befriended stop the rogue in the nick of time while the princess does go on to win the coveted award, the protagonists ordeal is far from over.

In fact, through a further inspired variation on the theme of parallel existences, *Tsubasa* introduces what would at first appear to be a double of Kyle Rondato from the Jade arc in the capacity of a determined but ultimately unsuccessful feather questor. Yet, this character turns out to be not merely a parallel persona but the original physician from Season 1, as evinced by his admission to having been in Jade and iniquitously sought to obtain a feather in that dimension, too. Hence, not all recurring faces are actually manifestations of parallel lives: some may be the same person, migrating from one world to another by means of transdimensional powers of the kind granted by Yuuko. Addressing Syaoran and company, Kyle himself admonishes: "If you go to different worlds, you'll find different people sharing the same face. However, there is no way of being sure that they really are different people. Remember that well." Fei Wong Reed, whose behind-the-scene presence is ubiquitous in this part of the series, would seem responsible for dispatching Kyle to Piffle in the first place. This hypothesis is consolidated by the villain's own comment on the poor outcome of the doctor's exploits: "It seems direct infiltration doesn't work."

An additional variant of the parallel-existence motif is yielded by the third dimension in which the travelers are dropped in Season 2, following their Piffle exploits and the return to Zarastra (examined in the preceding chapter): the world of the Lagosta ship. Aboard the vessel, Syaoran meets a double of his adoptive father Fujitaka in the person of the exceptionally skilled little boy operating as the engine room's chief mechanic. Memories harking back to Syaoran's interaction with the adult version of Fujitaka, leading to his decision to become an archaeologist, are faithfully replicated by Syaoran's present-day interaction with the kid, down to minute details—for example, the recollection of his guardian encouraging him to brush gently a relic retrieved from an excavation site is mirrored by the image of the young Fujitaka inviting Syaoran to polish an oily cog by analogous means. Most touching is the kid's zealous assertion, just as Syaoran and company are about to world-jump once more, that he has finally discovered his vocation and is hence determined to become an archaeologist himself. Syaoran's parting words are also disarmingly affecting in their simplicity: "Goodbye, Father."

Variations on the theme of multiple personae sharing the same elemental soul also occur in the standalone adventure developed in Season 2's fourth dimension. Imbued with an eminently Parisian feel, and fittingly dominated by a Versailles-style palace, this city-world is inhabited by people that are all capable of magic and deploy their abilities to maximize their performance in a wide range of occupations. The first two citizens met by the protagonists are lookalikes of King Touya and Yukito, who excel as a chef and a taylor respectively. On one level, the version of Touya presented in this world echoes his pancake-making lookalike from the Hanshin Republic. On another, he also parallels Sakura's brother since he once was the king of the land: in this world, monarchs are picked from the ordinary population on the basis of collective dreams pointing to the person deemed appropriate for the role. Linked by a subtle affinity to *Tsubasa*'s main narrative, this dimension also plays with the theme of amnesia. The chosen rulers' memories are erased upon their ascent to the throne to ensure that their hearts are "pure." As to why a person has to be free of recollections to harbor a genuinely unsullied soul, this is left unexplained. What is made clear, however, is that the temporary kings' memories are restored once their term of office is over: their destiny is evidently rosier than Sakura's own fate.

The current monarch, a double of the magical creature Chii from Fai's homeland, is not fulfilling her responsibilities and the entire realm, as a result, is steeped in an eternal night that threatens to erode its inhabitants' special skills beyond repair. It soon becomes obvious that Chii feels lonely, locked up as she is in the royal palace and prevented from going out to play. When Mokona shrewdly diagnoses the ruler's condition, Fai takes it upon himself to show her a good time, thereby unexpectedly experiencing a sense of élan he has not felt in a long time. Chii would like nothing more that a future at the wizard's side, even if this would amount to an endless flight from the ever-looming specter of Fai's archenemy.

However, since Chii is not a human but the artifact of a powerful magician, she cannot leave her world without disappearing altogether the moment she crosses the fortified perimeter.

In one of the most pathos-laden scenes regaled by *Tsubasa*'s whole saga, Fai succeeds in helping Chii accept her royal duties, whereupon daylight returns and the land's magic escapes the threat of extinction. This standalone episode is not only notable by virtue of its elaboration of the theme of parallel lives. In fact, one of its greatest achievements is the ability to demonstrate that an original anime yarn ungrounded in manga antecedents can work very effectively in the hands of sensitive artists and narrators. The European atmosphere, cornucopian profusion of magical tricks, sumptuous costumes and exuberant action sequences no doubt contribute a great deal to the tale's overall appeal. Even more important, however, is its psychological sophistication, especially in the unprecedented deepening of Fai's personality. The mage is accorded a central position with the opening frames, depicting a dream where he is silently confronted by a fully awakened Ashura and struggles to run away from his foe, the terrified look in his eyes in stark contract with the cheery mien he habitually exhibits. Throughout this ancillary adventure, Fai's emotive range is indeed conveyed by a wide variety of facial expressions hitherto unseen in the anime.

It is integral to Kouichi Mashimo's directorial signature to infuse what is otherwise a fundamentally somber drama with carnivalesque moments of playful revelry. Season 1 offers examples of this proclivity in the scenes set in the Hanshin Republic that focus on hyperkinetic confrontations between rival street gangs (and their *kudan*, of course), as well as sequences from the Outo arc emphasizing the RPG flavor of the enterprise. Season 2 provides novel forays into the carnivalesque — most notably, with the fairground visited by Fai and Chii, where all manner of masked actors, puppeteers, clowns and jugglers abound, and with the circus sequences set in Shara Country, the sequel's fifth dimension. Faithfully representing Japan, though not quite in the style of Kurogane's original world, the place causes the warrior to feel both relatively at home and nostalgic, whereas Fai has to face some adjustment hiccups — not least in the handling of chopsticks. The playful element emanates from Sakura's and Syaoran's involvement with an itinerant circus and its all-female "Suzuran troupe." The images of Syaoran dressed up as a girl and equipped with massive plaits (a ploy meant to sustain the troupe's single-sex constitution) beating up a whole band of opponents by means of his lethal kicking techniques are nothing short of hilarious. No less enjoyable are the scenes in which Syaoran's skills are enlisted to the staging of acrobatic numbers, while the princess endeavors to perform as an aerialist — which fulfils a childhood aspiration of hers, as suggested by a flashback to the Clow days experienced by her protector.

The carnivalesque mood is made especially poignant by its interspersal with a darker narrative revolving around the conflict between the deity worshipped by the Suzuran troupe, Ashura, who is traditionally associated with "battle and misfortune," and the god honored by the all-male clan hosting Fai and Kurogane while they are temporarily separated from their companions, Yasha — the spirit of "night" and the "underworld." The tension endangers the well-being of the whole of Shara Country, proving particularly painful for the leaders of the two factions linked with the warring divinities, Suzuran and Souseki, since they happen to be secretly in love. Thus, a doomed romance parallel to the one endured by the protagonists is alluded to in this portion of the saga.

In this arc, *Tsubasa* experiments not only with spatial migration but also with time travel. This strategy is introduced with the protagonists' transposition to the original King Ashura's world, the legendary land of Shura, and to her clan's ongoing war against Yasha's army from the land of Yama—in other words, to Shara's remote past. Ashura and Yasha fight over the floating "Castle of the Moon," reputed to grant the desires of the person capable of laying conclusive claim to it. A dream experienced by Sakura reveals that Ashura and Yasha's personal history foreshadows Suzuran and Souseki's present predicament, since the two rulers were also locked in a forbidden love and doomed never to fulfill their mutual yearning. Whereas Syaoran and Sakura find their places in this dimension as guests at the female monarch Ashura's sumptuous palace, Fai and Kurogane feature as black-eyed members of Yasha's army. (Please note that black eyes are a trademark of Yasha's troops. The wizard's eyes are normally as blue as "sapphire," to quote Sakura, whereas the ninja's are as red as those of a "bunny," according to Mokona.) The new dimension is also associated with one of Sakura's scattered feathers, which now appear to hold time-crossing powers so strong as to allow them to reach back not merely into earlier phases of human history but even into ancient mythology.

Yasha, though long dead, has been enabled to survive as an illusion by the power of the magical feather located in this world. Up until now, Ashura has not been able to bring herself to destroy the phantom but her discovery of Sakura's dire need to reappropriate the drifting force has finally given her the strength to put an end to the mirage. As for Ashura's own desire—namely, to revive the real Yasha—this cannot be fulfilled. As Syaoran tells her, having learned this harsh lesson in Zarastra, lost lives cannot be brought back in any world— nor by any god. The boy's words have a momentous impact on Ashura and induce her to opt for a destiny quite different to the one courted by the version of Ashura underlying the traditions of present-day Shara: that is to say, one of ceaseless strife. Hence, she begs Yuuko (upon whom she herself has bestowed eternal life as a payment for her wish to have Mokona take Sakura and Syaoran to her world) to make her and Yasha the gods of the next generation—gods that can inspire people to enjoy the one life they have without vainly pursuing otherworldly fantasies.

The Shura part of this arc, therefore, does not simply revisit Shara's past. In fact, it also intervenes in its course and thus affects the future. This is conclusively demonstrated by the arc's climax, where it transpires that Syaoran's admonition to Ashura's loyal follower, Kumara, to bury his king and Yasha together with their most precious belongings—proffered upon leaving Shura—has drastically altered the flow of history. Hence, the Suzuran troupe and Souseki's acolytes are now seen to interact in the most amicable of terms, and their alliance is sealed by Suzuran and Souseki's glorious wedding ceremony. Moreover, the versions of Ashura and Yasha worshipped in this reconfigured domain are epiphanically revealed at the close of the nuptials as a pair of gorgeous statues that have never had to endure separation and segregation into distinct shrines. As Fai puts it, "Because the gods became friendly, the people didn't have to fight anymore."

The Shara/Shura arc makes a crucial contribution to *Tsubasa*'s dramatization of the corporeality of memory: an idea, as noted earlier in this study, economically encapsulated by the material representation of Sakura's lost memories. This is borne out by the scenes in which the princess seeks to relieve Syaoran's physical pain. In the first of these, she touches a wound received by her champion in a confrontation with Yasha's hosts, and specifically, Kurogane, to help it heal by instilling her feelings into it. This "treatment," as Clow Reed would term this kind of gesture in Sakura's childhood, suggests that the girl harbors haunted feelings for Syaoran which her body recalls even though her conscious memory has no direct access to that emotional pool. The second relevant scene emphasizes the embodied quality of memory even more explicitly. Here Sakura kisses Syaoran's left eye, which suddenly begins to hurt following an appearance of the trapped Syaoran held at the Secret Base and Fei Wong's remarks regarding the possibility of his imminent arousal. Mokona explains that Sakura has been guided subliminally by memories encoded in her physical frame: "That kiss just now may be a memory from your body. Yuuko said so. That there are two types of memories. The heart's memories and the body's memories. The heart is very important but the body is too. 'At times the heart may forget but the body will remember' is what she said.... Your wanting to kiss his aching eye was because even though you forgot due to losing your feathers, your body probably remembered. So until all your feathers come back, your body's memories will help you out."

As hidden facets of Fei Wong's agenda are gradually disclosed, it turns out that the villain has thus far been able to determine which worlds the travelers would end up in and always ensured that these would be relatively safe so as to avoid putting their lives at risk. With the shift to Shura, a dangerous world where Fei Wong had clearly not planned the protagonists to go, it becomes patent that the Dimensional Witch is interfering with his scheme in unforeseen ways. Deeply annoyed and aware that defeating Yuuko will not be easy since she holds magical powers akin to those of his own ancestor, Clow Reed, the rogue remarks: "There's no point if they die.... In order to get ahold of that thing buried in those ruins, we must have them work." Although his intentions are not yet clear, it is obvious that Fei Wong's plan is intricate and far-reaching.

No less importantly, the portions of *Tsubasa* set in Shara and Shura offer some of the most stunning visuals at the levels of both background art and dynamic effects. These bring forth an impressive variety of scenarios, ranging from brightly hued city scenes to tenebrous battlefields, from lush royal gardens blessed by the gentle sound of waterfalls to baleful night skies dominated by a blood-red moon. The opulent interiors of Ashura's palace are especially notable in their meticulous rendition of a profusion of furnishings, accessories and ornaments exuding an aura of pictorial and textural palpability. Furthermore, the original creators' skills as costume designers (no less proverbial than their unique proficiency as manga artists) comes resplendently to the fore in the depiction of flowing robes, mantles and veils. The scene in which Sakura plays an indigenous instrument that reminds her of a similar piece of musical equipment from Clow, thereby delivering a mesmerizingly melancholy melody, and Ashura dances to the tune provides a unique graphic gem — not least due to the inspired portrayal of the dancing monarch by means of static tableaux redolent of a traditional scroll painting or paper screen. Additionally, the dramatic impact of the lighting and kinetic effects accompanying the dimensional jumps presented in this arc surpass comparable strategies used in earlier transworld migrations. The fight sequences likewise yield a greater sense of both martial vigor and athletic prowess.

Having restored the carnivalesque mood touched upon in earlier sections with the nuptials crowning the Shara/Shura arc, *Tsubasa* enthrones it as an unrivalled dramatic force with the travelers' transferral to a dimension wherein they feature as infantilized caricatures of their former selves (*chibi*, in anime jargon), drawn by a Princess Emeraude lookalike by recourse to a pencil powered by one of Sakura's feathers. It is entirely up to Mokona to unlock the characters from the story in which they have inadvertently plummeted, bring them back to normality and, in the process, also retrieve the memory fragment with the assistance of the preternatural instrument. This she accomplishes with some truly spectacular results, though not without a few world-warping glitches along the way, affectionately invoking a plethora of anime and manga formulae drawn from various subgenres, and especially from the giant-monster and school-romance typologies. One of the mini-adventure's most amusing aspects consists of Mokona's self-reflexive comments on her deliberate adoption of "clichés." (A comparably jocular mood pervades the ancillary tale set in Kero, where the possessor of one of Sakura's feathers, endowed with the power to reduce humans to Lilliputian dimensions, turns out to be a butterfly.)[1]

The ensuing arc follows the protagonists as they travel aboard a hi-tech bus through desert in search of a feather accidentally stuck to a trailer moving rapidly ahead of them, with a gang of motorcycled robbers in hot pursuit. While this arc offers some suspenseful action and a cornucopia of stunning sceneries, it is arguably most significant by virtue of the philosophical message it promulgates. Central to the segment is the idea that a bunch of perfect strangers apparently thrown together by random chance and at first unwilling to have anything to do with one another can gradually discover an unforeseen sense of kinship and solidarity, with each having learned something from the experience by the end of the adventure: above all, the strength to pursue their objectives against all odds. On one level, the lesson advanced by these events recalls Yuuko's pronouncements from Season 1. These are explicitly echoed by the character of an old sage who also happens to be a double of the sword merchant that sold Kurogane and Syaoran their weapons back in Outo: "they do say there must be some sort of tie when sleeves touch. [Please note that the same words are used by a member of the Suzuran troupe in Shara.] There is an invisible link between all encounters. It's not a coincidence on how we all met here. Perhaps it may be a meeting where we are supposed to do something. There's no such thing as coincidences in this world. There is only inevitability."

On a further level, this arc's philosophy mirrors *Tsubasa*'s central lesson as encapsulated primarily by the indefatigable Syaoran. This concerns the importance of never losing sight of one's goals, never indulging in escapist fantasies to avoid facing one's task and, concomitantly, oneself. As the elderly man warns, "Life is all about the repetition of giving up," and it is this endless reenactment of negativity that causes human "dreams and hopes" ineluctably "to deflate." As a result, when people should be developing, they are merely "growing old." Syaoran, as Fai stresses, "is just someone who doesn't give up." This ethical stance by and by influences practically everybody with whom the youth comes into contact. An analogous lesson is conveyed by the flashback experienced by Sakura after introjecting a freshly regained feather, where she travels back to Clow and to an encounter with Yukito in the course of which the priest states: "You must not give up on anything. No matter how embarrassing it may seem."

It is with the arc set in the country of Rekord, a land renowned for its sorcery and its libraries, that *Tsubasa* extends most adventurously its purview of memory's intricacies and quirks. Memory comes explicitly into play as a major diegetic force with Syaoran's perusal of the "Book of Memories," a magical tome that copies the recollections of the first person who touches it and then communicates them to the person that opens it next. By this means, the hero is able to see Kurogane's past and retrace to the warrior's childhood his determination to become stronger and stronger. We thus discover that at the root of Kurogane's mission lies the yearning to avenge the death of his mother, the priestess of the ancient Suwa clan, murdered by a supernatural agent in her very shrine. (The entity, intriguingly, bears the bat emblem that also marks Fei Wong's troops.) Kurogane's resolve is fuelled by the abiding memory of the solemn promise to develop supreme strength to protect others made to his father, the Suwa leader, just before the latter's final fight. Syaoran feels deeply guilt as a result of having "peeked" into the ninja's past without his "permission" and although Kurogane forgives him in the knowledge that the act was not intentional, the youth adamantly maintains that "Your memories belong to you and you alone."

The Book of Memories contains a feather reputed to have reached Rekord 3,004 years earlier and is locked in the heart of the country's Central Library since its power is known to be malefic: the magician who first chanced upon it indeed deployed it to unleash a terrible calamity. Accordingly, the forbidden treasure is guarded by all manner of mighty spells that engage the protagonists in some of *Tsubasa*'s most tantalizing exploits. The dimensional transition that occurs just as the companions are about to reach their goal is radically different from any other shift of the kind seen thus far. The characters find themselves transposed to a land that looks very much like Clow, even though "Mokona has not teleported yet!" Fai soon realizes that this world has been created from Sakura's memory through wizardry.

As to the feather's location, Mokona shrewdly guesses that it is most likely to be buried in a place that the princess considered "mysterious and mystifying" while she lived in her homeland. Sure enough, the ominous excavation site where the whole saga finds inception turns out to be the feather's treacherous receptacle. *Tsubasa*'s experimentation with alternate forms of world-hopping in this arc continues as the characters are reinstated into Rekord and discover that the country's ubiquitous magic is capable of hindering Mokona's teleporting powers: it will take a full additional episode for the creature to regain her strength and move the company to the next dimension. Taken in tandem, the scenes in which the companions revisit Clow (albeit in virtual form) and those in which Syaoran enters Kurogane's history serve to consolidate the group's strength as a closely knit unit. As Fai cogently remarks, their joint mnemonic excursions have "deepened their bond of friendship" by enabling them to learn "about each other's pasts."

Another inspired variation on interdimensional migration is offered by the segment in which the travelers revisit Nayutaya and discover its "mirror world," namely the demonic land ruled by Kishimu, and help the locals overthrow Tambal's son, now the possessor of a feather in his own right. In the course of this arc, Chu'nyan touchingly remarks that compared to the Sakura she met at the time of the company's first visit, the present-day Sakura is much more lively. The girl's diagnosis is fully corroborated by the adventure set in Ragtime, a superficially glamorous metropolis actually beset by recession, unemployment and crime, where the princess exhibits unprecedented levels of resourcefulness and autonomy. Obtaining three jobs in rapid succession despite the hostile economic climate, Sakura plays a key part in raising the money necessary to purchase the feather for sale in a local antiques store as part of an exquisite brooch crafted by an Oruha lookalike.

Tsubasa's sustained dissection of the vicissitudes of memory with reference to its concurrently psychological, physical and mythical connotations reaches its apotheosis in the second season's final arc. This is set in the Country of Tao, a world modeled on the traditional East where everyone is endowed with special powers. This is due to the realm being enveloped by *senriki* (literally, the "power of the hermit"), which affects not only Tao's original inhabitants but also visitors to the land. *Senriki* manifests itself in varying degrees, allowing some people merely to influence earthly objects telekinetically and others even to fly. Syaoran and company find themselves in possession of highly refined versions of *senriki* thanks to which they are able to levitate. This skill affords ample scope for spectacular dynamic ruses in combat sequences, as well as opportunities for the director's camera to engage in daring aerial effects. In this arc, the nomadic crew is presented with its most unforeseeable opponent yet in the person of Tao's ruler, the charismatic King Chaos. The monarch amiably agrees to yield to Sakura a fan seemingly made from a substantial quantity of her feathers, which she instantly proceeds to incorporate, and additionally informs her companions that the mystical phoenix Genkaku contains many of the treasurable feathers in its plumage.

As a result of reabsorbing numerous mnemonic fragments at once, Sakura experiences what could be termed, by recourse to a neologism, a hypno-overdose. In the course of her protracted slumber, she has a flashback recording her childhood encounter with Chaos in her homeland, engineered by the king himself, where he saves her from a giant worm and then vows to protect her with his very life and travel with her once she has grown older. It gradually transpires that Chaos's objective is to manipulate Sakura's mind so as to persuade her to forsake her friends and go traveling with him across countless dimensions. Since the girl refuses to comply, the king resorts to extreme measures and traps her in a transparent column of light while he fights and vanquishes each of her companions.

As Syaoran, having recovered with the help of a potion concocted by Fai, steels himself for the ultimate duel, Sakura increasingly realizes how deeply she cares for her champion, the memories of their time together since the beginning of the adventure bolstering her swelling emotions. Moreover, a flashback in which she finds herself uttering words that are totally incompatible with her disposition alerts her to the dubiousness of the feathers dispensed by Chaos. These turn out to be fake memories as they push their way out of Sakura's body in the form of charred fragments that show none of the ethereal grace normally exuded by the genuine product. The climax of the Tao arc reveals, in a veritable coup de théâtre, that Chaos's "true form" is neither that of a charming ruler nor that of the mystical bird which he occasionally adopts. In fact, he is a bundle of Sakura's feathers that "began to develop a mind of their own somewhere along the way." The reason behind Chaos's obsessive yearning for Sakura is that he is actually a part of her — and, most vitally, of her mnemonic heritage. Given its abiding preoccupation with the memory topos, *Tsubasa* could hardly have selected a more dramatically apposite climax for its second season's dénouement. Having disclosed this disorienting truth to the princess herself by means of a vision during his final fight, Chaos begs her to release him from his curse. The king's desire is fulfilled as Syaoran eventually defeats him through equal measures of martial competence and gutsy passion. Thus, Chaos dissolves into a galaxy of feathers which the travelers could never presume to retrieve in one go and will, in fact, have to go on hunting as their peregrinations continue well beyond the close of the series.

Mokona confirms the heroic scale of the quest ahead of the group by cheerfully remarking: "Lots and lots of feathers are still out there." An offstage comment proffered by Fei Wong lends further weight to the message: "Their journey is far from over." This finale would feel intolerably frustrating if the audience had been led purely by the desire to witness a reparative conclusion. However, by the time the 52nd installment reaches its climax, the show has taught us to appreciate the incomparable value of the journey per se. The guarantee that Syaoran and company will go on traveling for an indeterminate length of time until their mission has been accomplished thus feels consummately rewarding in itself. In a sense, it would be far less satisfying to be regaled with a finale in which the travelers' goals were achieved at the inevitable cost of their going in separate directions. Indeed, beside the journey itself, the endurance of the bond which this has forged is *Tsubasa*'s key priority.

The series' last flashback is of vital significance in communicating the saga's ethical stance. This shows Sakura engaged in an argument with her brother and Yukito where she claims the right to go traveling around the world, asserting that she will be safe as long as her trusted companion (Syaoran, of course) remained by her side. As in previous flashbacks including Syaoran, the boy is invisible — yet, we are now more aware than ever of his irreplaceable, albeit haunted, role in the princess's life. There is a bittersweet element of dramatic irony built into the situation, for traveling far and wide in her trusted friend's company is precisely the destiny Sakura has met — though through utterly unforeseeable complications and twists.

Each of *Tsubasa*'s dimensions is meticulously detailed in terms of both its natural environment and its architectural style. Furthermore, to each location correspond distinctive costumes, accessories, and both magical and prosaic objects associated with specific rituals and customs. The contrast between any two sets of costumes presented in consecutive domains are often quite stark, not only in terms of sartorial styles but also in those of the cultural memories — and related mores — which they summon. Sakura herself, in keeping with her unwaveringly non-hierarchical world view, looks as resplendent in the maid's uniform she dons in Outo as she does in the Clow royal robe — which is in any case quite austere, though graceful, in conformity with Clow's rejection of pomp in favor of pragmatism. The practical approach to fashion favored by the inhabitants of Sakura's homeland is largely a corollary of the country's desert-swamped location, which encourages the adoption of ample hooded cloaks meant to protect their wearers from frequent sandstorms. The dynamic effects afforded by these garments, given their profusion of folds, creases, rucks and rimples, are numerous and visually enticing. The princess's attire is discreetly singled out by exotic hints one could easily associate with the *Arabian Nights*: specifically, the odalisque-style trousers and curled toe shoes.

In stark contrast with Clow's sartorial vogue, the clothing donned in the icy world of Celes features heavy fur-lined coats — which Fai abandons in preference for a Chinese-style white tunic worn over black trousers when he visits a warm dimension. Chii, created by the mage and presumably unaffected by his homeland's frigid climes, is free to wear a short and frilly dress with a trailing appendage. Although this character does not feature prominently in the anime, her costumes are among the most attractive, not only in the flashbacks to Fai's flight from Celes but also in her cameo appearance as the temporary monarch of a magic-imbued country. The costumes associated with Kurogane's ancient Japan are consonant with indigenous fashions of the feudal era, yet enriched by imaginative details ideated purposely for *Tsubasa*'s narrative. Souma, an eminent member of Princess Tomoyo's retinue, wears a black-net garment redolent of the Goth style as part of her ninja apparel.

Tomoyo's appearance, for its part, is distinguished by a multilayered kimono and a crown-like headdress with beautifully detailed pendants. The Hanshin outfits have a casually contemporary feel. Informal pants and tops are predominant and kids typically don school uniforms based on standard Japanese styles but the local street gangs cultivate distinctive looks intended to highlight their subcultural identities, such as biker goggles and copious gloves or accessories inspired by Punk and Mohawk fashions.

The Nayutaya costumes, conversely, are pointedly old-fashioned and overtly influenced by traditional Korean garb, particularly the *hanbok* (a robe characterized by simple lines and vibrant hues). Ample garments and large straw hats of feudal derivation also feature prominently. In Jade, the characters don apparel inspired by various phases of European fashion with an emphasis on Restoration and Victorian motifs. Accessories are especially pervasive in this dimension's vogue, abounding with elaborate hats, sleek stockings, long gloves, mantelets, bonnets, lace trimmings, cravats, shawls and all manner of buttons, buckles, brooches and jewels that exhibit an impressive range of formal and chromatic variations, as well as a pervasive feel of filigree gracefulness.

In Outo, the costumes amalgamate traditional Japanese elements and twentieth-century Western styles, mirroring the climate of the Taisho Era (1912–1926). This phase of indigenous history constitutes a period of cultural transition in which time-honored tenets came to be challenged by modern Western vogues. While Sakura, Syaoran and Fai adopt decidedly European costumes, Kurogane selects the *hakama* ("divided skirt") available from a local store specializing in traditional gear, presumably finding the style more consonant with his original world and its costumes. In Piffle World, the show's evocation of a sci-fi dimension that self-consciously eschews overtly futuristic styles is reinforced by the use of outfits that typically echo the "Jazz Age" as envisioned by F. S. Fitzgerald, with hints of contemporary sports gear and even an homage to the magical-girl genre.

As a dyad of complementary domains, Shara and Shura deliver a sumptuous gallery of costumes, ranging from the overtly theatrical outfits associated with the Suzuran troupe (and temporarily adopted by Sakura and Syaoran as well), through the austere monastic and martial attire characteristic of Souseki's acolytes, to the mythology-imbued feel of the ancient world witnessing Ashura's and Yasha's epic struggle. Punctiliously executed details are once again accorded a privileged position, especially in the representation of the clothes and accessories filling Ashura's palace. Gem-encrusted diadems, necklaces and anklets, opulent fabric decorations, diaphanous veils and exquisite sandals are especially memorable. In Rekord, the dominant style is informed by late nineteenth-century or early twentieth-century European vogues, enhanced by a sprinkling of steampunk motifs consonant with the country's architecture and vehicles (e.g., the flying train with metallic bat wings). In Tao, finally, emphasis is placed on the traditional end of *Tsubasa*'s vestimentary spectrum, in keeping with the overall atmosphere of Chaos's fictive realm, its architecture and interior design. Both clothes and accessories exhibit a marked preference for cuts and patterns of Chinese derivation. The king's endeavor to ensnare Sakura into his deluded fantasy is economically encapsulated by his imposition on the princess of clothes of his own choice.

While costumes play a key role in lending each of *Tsubasa*'s worlds a distinctive atmosphere, the setting is concurrently enriched by a dense iconography of cryptic symbols, at times inspired by emblems enshrined in traditional magic the world over and at others conceived specifically by the saga's creators. The forbidding winglike structure of the Clow ruins provides one of the most daunting leitmotifs and is echoed by other formations seen outside Sakura's homeland, such as the spectral island in the Lagosta-ship world, the rock formations in the realm of Shura and Mount Gourai (Genkaku's putative home) in the Tao arc. The recurrence of that baleful shape alludes to the ubiquity of the dark forces reputed to lurk beneath the archaeological site across disparate dimensions. The bat symbol associated with Fei Wong is also pervasive, not only within the confines of the Secret Base, its costumes and decor but also in apparently quite separate worlds: for example, in Kurogane's ancient Japan (as previously mentioned), where the emblem is flaunted by the killer of the warrior's mother.

The decorative motif characterizing Sakura's feathers — and clearly distinguishing them from ordinary plumage — is in itself highly evocative and likely to abide in the viewer's mind as one of the show's most enduring graphic landmarks. The pentacle, a symbol associated with alchemy and necromancy for time immemorial, adorns the *mitteishu*'s magical pendant, as seen in Nayutaya. One further magical object resonating with cross-cultural significance is that of the mirror — namely, the means by which Fei Wong and his associate keep track of the travelers' moves, as well as the vehicle through which Chu'nyan yields her benevolent *hijutsu* in Nayutaya. Another ancient emblem, the *yin-yang* circle representing the interplay of darkness and light, cold and heat, Moon and Sun, features in the Hanshin arc, where it decorates the costume of a local *kudan*, as well as in the second part of *Tokyo Revelations*, where it overlays the sphere symbolizing the Syaoran clone's heart.

The visual trope of the enchanted circle traditionally used by magicians to move through space and time recurs as the image accompanying Mokona's world transfers, having been ushered in by the very first episode through the scene where Yukito conveys the protagonists to the Dimensional Witch. An intricate pattern of esoteric signs redolent of some archaic pictographic script is summoned by Fai to create the magic circle that allows him to travel to Yuuko's world at the start of the saga. The tattoo surrendered by the wizard in exchange for the power to traverse dimensions is also exquisitely elaborate and its overall shape recalls, in a stylized fashion, that of a phoenix: the bird whose distinctive form is adopted by Fai's *kudan* in Hanshin. In Kurogane's case, symbolic images are used as a succinct way of evoking his transformation as Tomoyo, before sending him to Yuuko, places him under a curse that will cause him to become enfeebled whenever he kills unnecessarily: the ornate emblem habitually decorating his ninja helmet is altered to encapsulate graphically his inner metamorphosis to the simple shape of a crescent moon. (This figure also features as a symbolic property of Yukito's staff, and as one of the myriad motifs adorning the circle through which transworld migrations are effected.)

The previous chapter showed that *Tsubasa*'s narrative plays with intertextual memories by means of character-based crossovers. At the same time, as intimated, it also charts an intratextual map of mnemonic correspondences by capitalizing on the notion of parallel lives, which enables the show to reintroduce in some of its later arcs characters presented at previous stages in the saga. Thus, while in Nayutaya the protagonists encounter doubles of personae already seen in the Hanshin Republic, in Outo, variations on characters from the Hanshin arc again show up among the local cast. In Outo, the character of Souma from Kurogane's homeland also appears, this time as a demon hunter. King Touya and Yukito, additionally, feature as patrons of Sakura's and Fai's thriving café. Piffle World abounds with cameo appearances from characters presented in all of the first season's arcs — even in the course of a single installment, as attested to by Season 2's inaugural portion. This strategy helps Mashimo convey the idea that the leads' past experiences — and, with them, the memories in which they are inscribed — are constantly affecting their current circumstances and prospective development.

Several aspects of the manga on which the *Tsubasa* saga is based are not explicitly dramatized in the show. This is barely surprising, considering that the publication started running in May 2003 and is still ongoing, having thus far accrued no less than 219 chapters. One of the most intriguing elements elaborated in the parent text which the show only hints at is the relationship between the active Syaoran and his haunted lookalike, held captive by Fei Wong at the Secret Base. This is elucidated in the aforementioned OVA *Tsubasa Tokyo Revelations*, to which the present analysis now turns. The OVA is far more somber and violent than the TV series: a concomitant not only of its format, which justifies the incorporation of materials which a regular anime program intended for general airing would deem inappropriate but also of the harrowing contents of the arc it dramatizes. This darker atmosphere impacts on all levels of the production: its acting style and dialogue, which are practically devoid of any forays into humor or romance; its settings, where a pervasively postapocalyptic mood punctuated by either bleakly monochromatic or luridly colored townscapes dominates the drama; and its character interactions, through which the life-asserting bond forged by the traveling companions in the series comes under severe threat.

In the OVA, the protagonists reach the Country of Tokyo just after the Rekord arc has come to a close. As the first segment shows, the group lands in a desolate metropolis that is being gradually devoured by highly corrosive rain. Tokyo's entire water supply has been contaminated, with the exception of two underground veins locate underneath the Tokyo Government Office and the city's Tower. As it will later emerge, both veins are protected by the power of the two magical feathers situated therein. Each of the locations still in possession of safe aquatic reservoirs is inhabited by a clan and guided by a formidable leader: the Office's boss is Kamui and the Tower's is Fuuma — both of them CLAMP characters, it will be recalled, that also appear in the film *X* in different incarnations (Please see Chapter 4). Kamui is also one of the vampire twins hunted by Seishirou when Syaoran first meets him. (The character's preternatural constitution is succinctly conveyed by a visual effect that causes his eyes to acquire a yellow coloration, while the pupils contract into feline slits, during fights.)

Syaoran and company are hosted by Kamui's gang in return for their services as mutant hunters. Sakura herself, however, has been unconscious since the crew's arrival in Tokyo and remains so for a long time. While she sleeps, so deeply that at one point her breathing ceases, and dreams of floating underwater, a voice issuing from a giant chrysalis urges her to awaken lest she should be trapped forever in the vision she currently occupies. Moreover, the voice exhorts Sakura to rise from her comatose slumber in order to save the person that is most important to her. Yet, the girl seems powerless to open her eyes. The oneiric element plays an important role in this portion of the narrative, echoing the dreamlike nature of the numerous flashbacks experienced by Sakura in the course of the TV show, yet also aptly complementing the spectacular insertion into the adventure of the Syaoran hitherto held at the Secret Base — another character who, like the princess of Clow, has been imprisoned within a liquid dream and unable to break the spell that keeps him bound to his chamber. The OVA's emphasis on dreams does not, however, render it in the least *dreamy*. In fact, its gritty and at times blood-spattered visuals make it akin to a nightmare unleashed by the unconscious at its brashest in defiance of the ego's policing agency.

When, in the OVA's first part, the Syaoran held by Fei Wong eventually wakes up and breaks free, Xing-Huo enables him to cross dimensions and hence conveys him to Yuuko's world, led by the belief that "the dream must end" (CLAMP 2007b, p. 149), though this will cost Fei Wong's assistant her very life. In the ensuing installment, the recently revived Syaoran begs the Dimensional Witch to send him where his "right eye" is, being determined to recover it at all costs — a wish she readily grants, reckoning that she has already received sufficient payment for him in the form of his "connections," his "freedom" and his "time" (p. 155).

In this portion of the OVA, it is also revealed that the chrysalis from which the spectral voice perceived by Sakura emanates is hosted in the reservoir beneath the Government Office and happens to be Kamui's most treasured possession. Its survival comes under threat as it is enveloped by an intensely radiant sphere which, Kamui discovers upon diving into the waters, appears to contain Sakura in the process of absorbing the magical feather responsible for keeping the area uncontaminated, and hence dissolving the protective barrier. The version of Sakura occupying the luminous globe is her "soul" (p. 172), while the unconscious princess in the upper part of the edifice is merely an inanimate vessel. As Syaoran comes to the rescue, Kamui struggles to drain him of his blood and use it to resuscitate the creature encased within the cocoon: his twin Subaru. (When Subaru eventually surfaces, it transpires that the baleful feather was responsible for his enthrallment.) Though seriously depleted, Syaoran withstands the vampire's onslaught with superhuman strength — which intimates that he is a synthetic being and not an ordinary flesh-and-bone youth.

It is now Fai's turn to intervene: although he is aware that this Syaoran is artificial, he still believes that "he is a good kid" (CLAMP 2008a, p. 55) and is determined, therefore, to preserve his human dimension. Even a "false soul," Fai avers, is "a true soul" to the person that hosts it (p. 74). *Tokyo Revelations* now explains that the version of Syaoran kept in Fei Wong's palace, with his left eye shielded by a piece of cloth and his hands and arms branded with binding tattoos, is the original Syaoran, while the incarnation of the character presented in the anime — namely, the youth committed to the retrieval of Sakura's feathers — is a clone created by the villain specifically for the purpose of hunting the memory fragments. The clone does not originally possess any wizardly powers. The original, conversely, is a competent magician worthy of his progenitor Clow Reed whose abilities Fei Wong seeks to contain (and then possibly even harness to his own dubious ends). Aware of his maker's evil intentions, the real Syaoran has surrendered his left eye and half of his heart to the clone in order to invest the synthetic creature with a human core and, at the same time, to gain the ability to see everything which the clone experiences. Concomitantly, the clone is imbued with magical powers that become embedded in his right eye. (A clue to the right eye's special abilities is given in the TV series' first season when a preternatural light flashes across it in the course of a fight against a mighty Outo demon.)

Due to this symbiotic relationship more than to Fei Wong's cloning skills, the real Syaoran and the manufactured double as seen in the TV series end up being remarkably alike. This is fully borne out by the climactic exchange between the real Syaoran and Fai in the

Tokyo arc, where the wizard intends to go looking for Sakura in the city's nocturnal hell, convinced that she is bound to have got hurt, and the youth stops him by stating that if Fai were to be injured in his effort to rescue her, "the princess would hurt even more.... She'd be hurt many times over the pain that your body would feel" (CLAMP 2008b, pp. 171–172). As though enlightened by an epiphanic flash, the wizard reflects: "You really are the same. You and he [i.e., the clone] are" (p. 173).

Fei Wong states that he attempted to remove the magical eye but quickly realized that the clone would die were he to do so, and resolved to send "the image in the path that would unerringly lead him to a meeting with the princess and to the ruins that would be the key to everything" (CLAMP 2008a, p. 65). Following the villain's revelations, the scene switches to Yuuko, who explains that as a result of bestowing his left eye, the original Syaoran's magical power was "cut in half." All he could do, before being able at last to "break the confinements ... constructed for him" was to wait patiently and silently (p. 68). With the real Syaoran's awakening, the magic hosted by the duplicate rapidly begins to fade, and the heart given him by the original automatically returns to its owner. Fai urges him to recognize that he does, however, have a heart of his own: "It's something you and Sakura-chan, and all the people who love you made together" (p. 78).

The clone is quite unmoved by this plea and, now solely concerned with retrieving Sakura's feathers, coldly resolves to gouge out and incorporate one of Fai's own magical eyes so as to replace his lost wizardly strength. (Kurogane manages to stop him from appropriating both eyes by a hair's breadth.) The familiar Syaoran seen throughout the TV show has given way to a ferocious creature keen only on carrying out the task for which he was initially conceived. His robotic declaration pithily captures the clone's attitude: "I will obtain what I need to get her feathers back, And I will remove anyone in my way" (p. 109). At this very point, the original Syaoran makes his appearance in the underground reservoir and urges his duplicate to appreciate that even though the heart he gave him upon his creation must now return to its legitimate owner, he has developed a heart and feelings of his own over time. The heart that has fallen in love with Sakura and vowed to protect her at any price, most importantly, is the clone's own heart. So is the propensity, incrementally exhibited by the youth as the story progresses, to place the happiness and safety of others always ahead of his own private motives. Had he been merely following Fei Wong's orders, the creature would have had no concern for any aspect of his appointed task other than feather-gathering.

Proving again unresponsive to this plea, the clone simply proceeds to use the magic he now possesses to launch a fierce attack against his original. The latter, having vowed that if his double were to fail to form a heart of his own over time, he would have to kill him, engages in a tense duel, determined to destroy the clone at any price. Somewhat ironically, it is Sakura's passionate entreaty not to carry out his intent that stays his hand. Having finally awakened in response to the recognition that the person most important to her is Syaoran, Sakura cannot automatically accept that the boy she has come to know and cherish in the course of her peregrinations through time and space is not a real human being and is, in fact, so ruthless as to deserve termination. In her legendary generosity, the girl senses that the synthetic double is a victim of circumstances, deprived of his heart by forces well beyond his control, and that it is up to her to restore what he has lost — in much the same way as Syaoran has always believed that it is his sole responsibility to reassemble the princess's dispersed memories. The poetic symmetry evoked by this turn of events is an unparalleled dramatic accomplishments on the OVA's part.

The forcefulness, marginally suggestive of a rapist's brutality, with which the clone returns the feather gathered from Kamui's reservoir to the princess, combined with the callous indifference evinced by his abrupt departure, economically encapsulates the magnitude of the change undergone by the former hero. In the manga, the image of Sakura clinging onto "her" Syaoran when he decides to leave Tokyo to hunt for more feathers, and begging him in vain not to leave, is especially affecting. The old-fashioned doll-like costume from Rekord she still wears contributes greatly to the overall sense of helplessness exuded by the girl's depiction in this frame.

Yuuko makes it possible for Fai to survive and for the Tokyo hydraulic supply to be replenished but not without imposing a Byzantine set of conditions: Kurogane, who wants Fai to live come hell or high water, must ask the Witch to grant him the wish of filling the underground reservoir (which is really the wish voiced by Subaru) and the vampire, in exchange, shall grant Kurogane's own wish by giving his preternatural blood to the injured magician and thus enable his recovery. Kurogane's own blood must be mixed with Subaru's and thenceforth the warrior will be Fai's sole source of sustenance. These intricate arrangements are crowned by Yuuko's assertion that "If Fai can get back his stolen left eye, his magic will return. With it he can reject the vampire blood within him. So once his left eye is returned to Fai, your [i.e., Kurogane's] duty as 'game' will end" (CLAMP 2008b, p. 37). (Please note that the term "game," in this context, is synonymous with "living prey.")

It is up to Sakura, ultimately, to pay the price for the water by journeying alone on a hover bike through a forbidding landscape infested by all manner of portentous creatures, getting badly injured in the process, in order to get hold of a magical egg which Yuuko requests. The OVA's closing installment potently highlights the heroine's psychological and emotional growth over this crucial portion of the tale, tersely confirming her evolution from a relatively conventional princess-in-distress type to a mature and self-determining adult. In the manga, Sakura's maturation is graphically conveyed by close-ups of her face exhibiting unprecedentedly plucky expressions totally devoid of saccharine cuteness, especially in the drawings where she proclaims her firm intention to carry out alone the task required of her by the Dimensional Witch regardless of the hazards it entails. The frames that foreground the sheer physical pain undergone by the girl in the course of her quest offer likewise trenchant character studies.

In the arc following the Tokyo adventures, set in the world of Infinity and its live-action chess tournament, the manga further complicates Sakura's personality by highlighting the psychological and emotional torment she must face in the aftermath of *her* Syaoran's replacement by the original. This aspect of the princess's development is most affectingly brought out by the sequence in which she woefully confesses to Fai that although she is aware that the recently introduced version of Syaoran "may be the basis" for the youth she is "familiar with," she nonetheless knows in her "head that they're two different people." What makes Sakura's trial virtually intractable is the girl's inability — quite understandable, in the circumstances — to reconcile the original's concurrent difference and affinity with her former companion: "It isn't just his face," she tells Fai. "His voice ... and the way he moves ... and those straightforward eyes of his ... as I find places that look alike ... traits that are the same ... as I find more and more of them ... it's just no good! I wonder if the one right in front of me isn't Syaoran-kun after all..." (CLAMP 2008c, pp. 173–174). Sakura's inner conflict, moreover, is aptly paralleled by the original Syaoran's pained awareness that no matter what he does or say, "to the princess, Syaoran will always be *that* Syaoran. The shoulder she leans on is not mine" (p. 108). Additionally, the Infinity arc vividly conveys Sakura's darker side by arraying her in Goth clothing.

The OVA's final segment also reveals (courtesy of Yuuko) that Fei Wong's decision to cause Sakura's feathers to disperse across countless dimensions came from his conviction that the phenomenon would compel the princess to "travel across many universes looking for [her] memories" and to "commit all of those dimensions to memory." As Yuuko explains in the manga, the villain "is not interested in the memories contained within Princess Sakura's mind. But the memories contained in a vessel called her 'body'" (p. 8): namely, instruments necessary to the fulfillment of his own wish. The corporeal dimension of a person's mnemonic storage is again foregrounded as it was in the Shara/Shura arc. Having abducted the original Syaoran, who suspected the villain's nefarious plan, and fashioned a duplicate that would make the retrieval of Sakura's feathers his top priority, Fei Wong also killed Kurogane's mother and destroyed his country so as to induce the warrior to enter Princess Tomoyo's retinue and hence embark on an inevitable journey. It was to enable the princess to cross over many dimensions and accrue her lost memories that the companions were drawn together as partners in her voyage.

While the OVA engages in some depth with the plot strands delineated above, the TV show, as seen, leaves the exact nature of the connection between the two Syaorans effectively unexplained, which makes it impossible to ascertain whether they are enemies or allies. In a sense, for the specific purposes of the TV show's two seasons, it is not absolutely necessary to know that the Syaoran at Sakura's side throughout the adventure is a clone. It is also undeniable, however, that the series clearly indicates that Syaoran's past is shrouded in mystery since he lacks any recollection of his life preceding the meeting with his adoptive father. However, it is suggested that this is a corollary of a traumatic childhood and there are no reasons to speculate about more esoteric reasons for the boy's amnesia. It is also suggested that prior to his exposure to Sakura's warming influence, Syaoran's heart was hard and cold but again, the character's checkered past is sufficient to warrant this condition without bringing into play the concept of cloning.

Kurogane appears to sense Syaoran's mysterious alterity at various points in the saga, and most pointedly in the sequence from Season 1 where he sees the strange light flashing across Syaoran's right eye and concludes that this is sightless, and in the sequence from Season 2 where he observes the boy as he endeavors to capture the feather hidden beneath the Clow ruins and cannot quite grasp quite who or what he truly is. On this occasion, Syaoran is stunned by a winged lion guarding the magical book containing Sakura's feather but quickly regains consciousness as the double in Fei Wong's lair moves a hand. The Syaoran we know suddenly appears to have become possessed by an alien force. His eyes are expressionless and his moves uncharacteristically brutal. More disturbingly still, his respect for all things ancient and venerable, intrinsic to his archaeological vocation, dissolves altogether as he unscrupulously destroys the Book of Memories to get hold of the coveted feather. Kurogane's suspicions regarding Syaoran's real identity do not, however, prevent the ninja from assuming a mentoring or even paternal stance towards the youth. The realization that Syaoran is partially blind, in particular, induces Kurogane to teach him how to wield a sword so as to minimize the drawbacks entailed by his disability and thus abet his quest. Deep down, the surly fighter senses a visceral affinity between his own and Syaoran's resolve to protect at any price the women they love. The magnanimity underlying Kurogane's decision is amplified by the fact that the warrior has never before taken a trainee under his wing, presumably deeming the task unworthy of a man of his caliber.

There are also intimations that King Touya instinctively perceives something disquietingly uncanny about his sister's best friend. In the very first installment of Season 1, for instance, he admits to Yukito that he feels inexplicably uneasy in Syaoran's presence: "I don't know what it is about that kid that bugs me so much." Nonetheless, the monarch does not pursue this lead but factually concedes that perhaps he would "think that about any boy she obsessed over," thus rationalizing his unsettling apprehension as a mere concomitant of brotherly jealousy. Moreover, he does not dispute his advisor's prophecy regarding the youth, which decrees that Syaoran is the "chosen one": the person, in the soothsayer's own words, "destined to be at Sakura's side" and to endure with her "many trials and hardships." Thus, regardless of Syaoran's true nature, his unique stature within the adventure is never questioned. A further allusion to the boy's mysterious origins is supplied by the Season-1 sequence in which Kurogane and Fai admire the boy's unexpected display of martial prowess in the course of a fight involving *kudan* and the mage remarks: "He is no amateur, that's for sure.... From what I gather, he hasn't had much of a warrior's life. Where did he learn moves like that? ... Perhaps he has a livelier past than we realize. Maybe he keeps some secrets, who knows."

The connection between the Syaoran accompanying Sakura on her odyssey and *another* Syaoran is cryptically alluded to at the very start of the Piffle arc. In the opening frames of Season 2 of the TV show, Syaoran is indeed portrayed as the victim of a deeply disquieting nightmare where he is stranded in a vacant liquid space and hears a voice calling his name that seems to be issuing from a youth bearing his own physique and facial traits, with a bandaged left eye. This vision does not make any obvious reference to cloning and, given its oneiric status, could be taken simply to exemplify Syaoran's inner unrest — a condition that would be perfectly congruous with the stress he has been subjected to since that fateful night in Clow where it all began. A haunted identity crisis is likewise alluded to by a subsequent dream experienced by Syaoran at the beginning of the Shara/Shura arc. In this vision, the youth sees himself with the left side of his face bandaged up and as he looks into a mirror that reflects him to infinity, anxiously wonders who he is. Shortly after his arousal from this disorienting experience, Syaoran tentatively reassures himself with this thought: "Even if I don't have any memories before that day [i.e., the day of his rescue by Fujitaka], I am definitely Syaoran." In the same segment, the hero's identity is further problematized by an exchange between King Ashura and Yuuko:

> ASHURA: If they [i.e., Syaoran's companions] haven't noticed, there's no need for me to tell them what Syaoran really is. Right, Witch?
> YUUKO: Indeed.

In an arc of the parent manga situated after the Tokyo-based adventures, it is disclosed that Sakura, too, is a clone. The girl we have been following from world to world in the wake of her traumatic memory loss is only an artificial copy of the real princess, who would seem to be Fei Wong's prisoner in the Kingdom of Clow. Her instinctive attraction to the

Syaoran clone may partly derive from a subliminal perception of her affinity with him. This twist produces a somewhat heady scenario, inviting us to reflect on the following successive transformations in the story's presentation of its protagonists' identities and relationship: apparently real Syaoran/apparently real Sakura; clone Syaoran/apparently real Sakura; real Syaoran/apparently real Sakura; real Syaoran/clone Sakura. (The revelation regarding Sakura's identity is foreshadowed in the OVA by the splitting of the character into a comatose body and a sentient spirit.)

Even the most accomplished storyteller might find the articulation of unforeseeable plot twists such as these quite problematic since they hold the potential to deliver great drama but also cause headaches for viewers encountering them for the first time. Above all, they call for elaborate mnemonic gymnastics, the task laid out before the audience consisting of evaluating not merely the impact of contingent developments but also their temporal and logical relationship with hints that might have been dropped several arcs earlier — and feasibly been neglected or seen as utterly peripheral at the time. Although this may sound like an unpalatable option to spectators in search of straightforward entertainment, it is well worth the effort for those who have followed the saga all the way through and are thus bound to welcome some climactic revelations, disquieting as these doubtlessly are.

Vibrant action and a well-sustained tempo contribute vitally to motivate the audience to embark on this challenging decoding enterprise. Even more importantly, the narrative developments presented in the OVA are made immensely rewarding by their focus on the critical changes undergone by each key character in the unfolding of its arc. Not only does Syaoran have to face up to his real identity: Sakura, too, is forced to reassess radically her situation by the disclosure that her champion is not what she believed him to be. Furthermore, Fai is drawn into a genuinely life-changing immolation, while Kurogane must confront an extreme test of his loyalty. The affected characters' memories are concurrently redefined by the imperative to negotiate unforeseen shifts in their personal circumstances and intersubjective connections. These upheavals place *Tokyo Revelations* in the category of psychological drama. The visual style employed in the OVA (as indeed in the manga source) emphasizes this dimension, regularly juxtaposing action-driven effects punctuated by various manifestations of water, fire and lightning with stylized images meant to highlight the story's affective import in a symbolic fashion: e.g., through a profusion of swirling, arcing, swishing and curling lines.

As to whether fans of the TV show would necessarily derive pleasure from the OVA, this remains a moot point. On the one hand, *Tokyo Revelations* offers an awesome viewing experience that spares no effort in the rendition of both meticulously executed details and magisterially choreographed kinetic spectacle. On the other, it is often so raw, uncompromising and painful to behold as to threaten the mellow fantasy element at the heart of the TV show's cinematic range. Where the series' dominant mood is nostalgic, the OVA's verges on the tragic. Any viewer devoted to the exploration of the *Tsubasa* universe will not hesitate to watch the direct-to-video supplement to the TV program. Yet, the encounter with *Tokyo Revelations* may have to come with something of a health warning to those who do not wish to see the original show's wistful gentleness unsentimentally punctured at virtually every turn of the OVA's dark ride.

The *Tsubasa* TV series is also complemented by the film *Tsubasa RESERVoir CHRoNiCLE The Movie: Princess of the Birdcage Kingdom* (dir. Itsuro Kawasaki, 2005). This maximizes *Tsubasa*'s kinetic dimension, exuding energy, dynamism and passion at each turn of its thirty-minute breakneck ride. At times, the action's tempo is so snappy as to dispense with any segue between two scenes, let alone pauses to document character development. This is an entirely pardonable strategy, given that the film's likely viewers would be already familiar with the saga to some extent. Indeed, presuming to enter *Tsubasa*'s world by means of this relatively short piece would be quite preposterous. Kawasaki could hardly have created more radically different an accompaniment to the *Tsubasa* TV show from *Tokyo Revelations* than this movie. Where Tada's OVA, as argued, intensifies the saga's somber dimension to disquieting extremes, *Princess of the Birdcage Kingdom* intersperses the central exploit it dramatizes with frequent forays into humor, romance and martial flamboyance, thus softening the story's potentially baleful connotations.

Using the power of one of Sakura's feather-shaped memories as his weapon, the titular realm's ruler has enclosed the land within a magical birdcage barrier and enslaved his subjects by capturing the bird spirits to whom each of them is connected. The villain's ultimate goal is to plunge the realm into eternal darkness to achieve uncontested dominance. The most severely affected victim of the monarch's vicious tyranny is his niece Princess Tomoyo, who has been deprived not only of her avian companion but also of her voice. Tomoyo is intended to serve as the ultimate "sacrifice" through which the rogue will ensure the cooperation of the sinister forces capable of granting his perverse wish. The princess is secretly sheltered by a young boy, Koruri, who turns to Syaoran and Sakura for help in the protection of the hapless royal girl. With characteristic selflessness, the protagonists do not hesitate to channel all of their energies into the mission, generously shelving their personal quest.

In discussing the *Tsubasa movie*, it is also worth considering salient links between this production and the companion piece with which it has been recently released on DVD: *XXXHOLiC the Movie: A Midsummer Night's Dream* (dir. Tsutomu Mizushima, 2005). Like the *Tsubasa* feature, *A Midsummer Night's Dream* accompanies a more extensive version of the anime. This comprises two TV series directed by Tsutomu Mizushima, *XXXHolic* (2006) and *XXXHolic: Kei* (2008). The film revolves around Kimihiro Watanuki, a young man afflicted by the ability to see spirits, and Yuuko Ichihara, a charismatic witch willing to help him overcome his problem in return for his services as a part-time employee in her shop. Beside Kimihiro and Yuuko, three further key characters are the youth's classmate Shizuka Doumeki, who has the power to dispel spirits as efficiently as the protagonist is capable of sensing them, and the childlike Marudashi ("Streaking") and Morodashi ("Flashing")— a.k.a. Maru and Moro—who have been created by the witch, are tied to the store and are responsible for beckoning people in need of Yuuko's help. Without Maru's and Moro's mediation, the business remains invisible.

Pivotal to the story is the day a girl unable to access her house visits Yuuko's outfit begging assistance and proffers a magical-looking key as her payment. (This is very key which Yuuko conveys to the Birdcage Kingdom in the *Tsubasa* movie to abet the protagonists' quest. This intertextual link connects the two movies in the form of a shared memory.) The girl's visit coincides with the witch's invitation to an auction to be held in a mysterious mansion, which turns out to be the very place the supplicant is seeking to enter. Although Yuuko is certain that the invitation is a trap, she takes up the challenge, eager to discover the sender's identity and motives. At the auction site, she meets seven other bidders—all of them collectors of bizarre items such as shoe insoles — who vanish one by one while waiting for the seller to turn up.

Fitted with doors that open and close of their own accord and ribboned with meandering passages, the creepy building wherein this Gothic murder mystery is staged oozes persistently with eerie sounds redolent of buried and forbidden memories. As a classy blend of fantasy and horror, *Midsummer Night's Dream* is connected with the *Tsubasa* saga not only by the character of Yuuko, who features in both (though much more prominently in the *XXXHOLiC* film) but also by a shared emphasis on the invisible dimensions, inchoate dreams and haunted remembrances lying just beneath the surface of the empirically observable. Yuuko's decision to accept the mysterious invitation in the *XXXHOLiC* movie (despite its potentially dangerous implications) proceeds from the character's deeply ingrained belief, asserted in the early part of *Tsubasa*'s first season, that there are no coincidences in life, only the inevitable (*hitsuzen*). This concept also underpins the relationship between the two feature films, insofar as their yarns intersect and collide in a way that evokes a sense of ineluctability rather than random chance. Indeed, the search for truths hidden within a thick skein of haunted memories is pivotal to both productions and discreetly sustains their dialectical interplay as companion pieces.

The importance of memory in the *XXXHOLiC* movie's diegesis is understated until the very end, where the reason for the mysterious invitation and the peculiar events unfolding within the mansion turns out to be an old promise made by its owner, honored for long and then gradually consigned to oblivion. The film's climax also offers a tantalizing instance of temporal compression, as the girl beseeching Yuuko at the beginning reappears as the person to whom the host is bound by his vow both as the elderly lady she now is and as the small child she was at the time the promise was made: this is also the form in which the man perceives her in the present. On the stylistic plane, an engrossing parallel obtains between the uncanny beauty of the *XXXHOLiC* movie's haunted mansion and that of the Birdcage Kingdom. In the former, the visuals' allure stems primarily from a plethora of architectural and ornamental details; in the latter, from the deceptively dreamy nature of the oppressive environment, wherein lush vegetation and manmade structures harmoniously coalesce. Although the *Tsubasa* movie spins a tale based on heroism and fantasy, whereas *Midsummer Night's Dream* veers towards dark surrealism, the two anime form a perfect partnership as complementary facets of a bold stylistic experiment.

An adventurous exploration of the quirks of haunted memories, comparable in tenor to the twin worlds depicted in the *Tsubasa* and the *XXXHolic* films by virtue of its commingling of action and mystery, is supplied by the TV program *Red Garden* (dir. Kou Matsuo, 2006–2007). Offering an original take on the psychological thriller tinged with traces of the dead teenager horror movie, the show revolves around four high-school students: Rose, Rachel, Kate and Claire.[2] All four wake up one morning feeling a bit off-color, either having lost consciousness the night before or else having no recollection whatever of the previous day. Lured by butterflies which they alone can see, the girls are drawn to a vacant lot by a woman named Lula who unnervingly informs them that they are dead. Lula has the power to resurrect them but first they must earn this precious gift by obeying her orders. They are thus allowed to live "borrowed lives" while fulfilling an exacting contract that requires them to engage in nocturnal battles against formidable monsters.

Two parallel sets of memories insistently map themselves onto each other, drastically disrupting the protagonists' quotidian existence: daytime recollections pertaining to the routine activities of ordinary high-school girls and nighttime ones of horror and strife. This mnemonic schism elliptically echoes the ordeal endured by *Tsubasa*'s protagonists: as shown, while Syaoran remembers every single instant spent in Sakura's company, the girl is incapable of regaining permanently even the slightest mnemonic fragment connected with her protector. The rift presented in *Red Garden* gains emotional complexity from the girls' disparate reactions to their predicament, with defensive denial at one end of the spectrum and a brave confrontation of the truth at the opposite end. Additionally, both sets of memories echo the spirit of *wabi* in their touching imperfection. Given *Red Garden*'s somber content, it is quite surprising to see its ambience bathed in colorful luminosity as often as it is. The bouncy design style, influenced by 1960-ish vogues, also contributes to this ironical sense of cheeriness. While in *Haruhi Suzumiya*, as seen in the previous chapter, the heroine's memories are haunted in the sense that she has no obvious mental record of her coming into being, in *Red Garden*, the protagonists' memories are quiescent to the extent that the girls cannot even remember dying. As in *Paprika*, the barrier between reality and dreams is eroded, since the world to which the protagonists painfully endeavor to cling is akin to a vision designed to keep reality at bay.

What ultimately renders *Tsubasa*'s multiverse utterly unique in spite of its adoption of established formulae drawn from the realms of romance, the epic, the fairytale and the videogame (among other typologies) is its alchemical flair for provoking deep, often unconscious and even inchoate emotions through a seamless blend of entertainment and reflection. *Tsubasa* holds a tantalizing power to embody and enact problems that are pivotal to human existence and often, for this very reason, defy solution — without, however, anaesthetizing the desire to speculate and explore. By focusing on a life rent asunder by the obliteration of its mnemonic underpinnings whose solidity must be laboriously reconstituted one step at a time, the story invites reflection on the very processes through which human identity is incrementally constructed. Imagination is more important than knowledge, in the logic of the anime, and the workings of memory provide the template for this preference. Indeed, memory itself is neither formed nor fuelled by rigorous verifications or mechanistic proofs but rather by intuitive (and often arbitrary) leaps — leaps analogous to the world-crossing transitions engineered by Mokona.

Filmography

PRIMARY TITLES

Gilgamesh (2003–2004). ORIGINAL TITLE: *Girugamesshu*. *Status:* TV Series (26 episodes). *Episode Length:* 23 minutes. *Director:* Masahiko Murata. *Scenario:* Akio Satsukawa, Sadayuki Murai, Yasuko Kobayashi. *Original Creator:* Shotaro Ishinomori. *Music:* Kaoru Wada. *Character Conceptual Designer:* Saki Okuse. *Animated Character Designer:* Masahiro Sato. *Mechanical Designer:* Takeyuki Takeya. *Production:* Japan Vistec, Kansai TV. *Animated Production:* Group TAC, Japan Vistec. *Sound Production:* Jinnan Studio.

Kanon (2006–2007). ORIGINAL TITLE: *Kanon*. *Status:* TV Series (24 episodes). *Episode Length:* 24 minutes. *Director:* Tatsuya Ishihara. *Series Composition:* Fumihiko Shimo. *Screenplay:* Fumihiko Shimo. *Storyboard:* Kazuya Sakamoto, Noriyuki Kitanohara, Shinobu Yoshioka, Ishihara, Yasuhiro Takemoto, Yutaka Yamamoto. *Music:* Jun Maeda, OdiakeS, Shinji Orito. *Producers:* Naohiro Futono, Shinichi Nakamura, Yoko Hatta, Yoshihisa Nakayama. *Art Director:* Mutsuo Shinohara. *Art Designer:* Mutsuo Shinohara. *Chief Animation Director:* Kazumi Ikeda. *Animation Directors:* Chiyoko Ueno, Futoshi Nishiya, Hiroyuki Takahashi, Kazumi Ikeda, Mitsuyoshi Yoneda, Satoshi Kadowaki, Shoko Ikeda, Yukiko Horiguchi. *Original Character Designer:* Itaru Hinoue (Visual Art's). *Character Designer:* Kazumi Ikeda. *Director of Photography:* Ryuuta Nakagami. *Sound Director:* Yota Tsuruoka. *Sound Effects:* Eiko Morikawa. *Color Designer:* Akiyo Takeda. *Special Effects:* Rina Miura. *Animated Production:* Kyoto Animation.

Kurau Phantom Memory (2004). ORIGINAL TITLE: *Kurau Fuantomu Memorii*. *Status:* TV Series (24 episodes). *Episode Length:* 24 minutes. *Director:* Yasuhiro Irie. *Series Composiiton:* Aya Yoshinaga. *Screenplay:* Yoshinaga, Shin Yoshida, Tsukasa Sunaga, Tsuyoshi Tamai, Irie, Yasuyuki Suzuki. *Storyboard:* Akitoshi Yokoyama, Jun'ichi Sakata, Katsumi Teratou, Masakazu Hashimoto, Masaki Kitamura, Takao Abo, Tsukasa Sunaga, Irie, Yoshiyuki Takei. *Music:* Yukari Katsuki. *Producers:* Maki Horiuchi, Masahiko Minami, Schreck Hedwick, Shiro Sasaki, Toshihiko Nakajima. *Art Director:* Kei Ichikura. *Animation Directors:* Atsuko Sasaki, Hiroki Kanno, Kana Ishida, Koichi Horikawa, Kumiko Takahashi, Masahiro Koyama, Shinichi Shigematsu, Takahiro Komori, Takeshi Itou, Toshihiro Kawamoto, Tsuneo Ninomiya, Yoshiyuki Kodaira, Yuji Moriyama. *Mecha Animation Directors:* Hiroyuki Kanbe, Nekomataya. *Character Designer:* Tomomi Ozaki. *Mechanical Designer:* Masahisa Suzuki. *Director of Photography:* Youichi Oogami. *Sound Director:* Kazuhiro Wakabayashi. *Set Designer:* Shingo Takeba. *Production:* Big Shot, BONES, Kurau Project, Media Factory, TV Asahi, Victor Entertainment.

Millennium Actress (2001). ORIGINAL TITLE: *Sennen Joyu*. *Status:* Movie. *Length:* 87 minutes. *Director:* Satoshi Kon. *Original Story:* Kon. *Screenplay:* Sadayuki Murai, Kon. *Music:* Susumu Hirasawa. *Producers:* Kou Matsuo, Taro Maki. *Art Director:* Nobutaka Ike. *Art Supervision:* Kenichi Konishi, Toshiyuki Inoue. *Art Designer:* Yasumitsu Suetake. *Animation Directors:* Hideki Hamasu, Takeshi Honda. *Animation Supervisor:* Shougo Furuya. *Character Designers:* Kon, Takeshi Honda. *Director of Photography:* Hisao Shirai. *Sound Director:* Masafumi Mima. *Color Designers:* Kazunori Hashimoto, Satoshi Hashimoto. *Special Effects:* Kumiko Taniguchi, Sachiko Suzuki. *Cinematography:* Hisao Shirai. *Production:* Bandai Visual, GENCO, Kadokawa Shoten, WOWOW. *Animated Production:* Madhouse Studios.

The Place Promised in Our Early Days (2004). ORIGINAL TITLE: *Kumo no Mukou, Yakusoku no Basho*. *Status:* Movie. *Length:* 91 minutes. *Director:* Makoto Shinkai. *Original Creator:* Shinkai. *Screenplay:* Shinkai. *Storyboard:* Shinkai. *Music:* Tenmon. *Art Designers:* Shinkai, Takumi Tanji. *Chief Animation Director:* Ushio Tazawa. *Assistant Animation Director:* Hiromi Suzuki. *Character Designer:* Ushio Tazawa. *Sound Director:* Shinkai. *Color Designer:* Shinkai. *Production:* CoMix Wave Inc.

RahXephon (2002). ORIGINAL TITLE: *Raazefuon*. *Status:* TV Series (26 episodes). *Episode Length:* 23 minutes. *Director:* Yutaka Izubuchi. *Original Creator:* Izubuchi. *Screenplay:* Chiaki J. Konaka, Fumihiko Takayama, Hiroshi Ohnogi, Ichiro Okouchi, Mitsuo Iso, Shou Aikawa Yoji Enokido, Yukari Kiryu, Izubuchi. *Storyboard:* Akitoshi Yokoyama, Go Sakamoto, Masahiro Ando, Mitsuo Iso, Satoru Sakamoto Shoji Kawamori, Soichi Masui, Tensai Okamura, Tetsu Shimaiya, Tomoki Kyoda, Yasushi Muraki, Izubuchi. *Music:* Ichiko Hashimoto. *Producers:* Daisuke Kawakami (Fuji Television Network, Inc.), Go Haruna (Fuji Television Network, Inc), Katsuji Nagata (Media Factory, Inc.), Masahiko Minami (BONES, Inc.), Shiro Sasaki. *Art Director:* Junichi Higashi. *Animation Directors:* Hiroki Kanno, Hiroshi Osaka, Hirotoshi Sano, Ikuo Kuwana, Kenji Mizuhata, Koichi Horikawa, Takahiro Komori, Takashi Tomioka, Tsunenori Saito, Yasuhiro Irie, Yoshiyuki Ito, Yoshiyuki Kodaira. *Character Designer:* Akihiro Yamada. *Animation Character Designer:* Hiroki Kanno. *Mechanical Designers:* Michiaki SATO, Yoshinori Sayama. *Director of Photography:* Naoyuki Ohba. *Sound Director:* Yota Tsuruoka. *Sound Effects:* Shizuo Kurahashi. *Color Designer:* Shihoko Nakayama. *Production:* Asatsu DK, BONES, Fuji TV, Media Factory, RahXephon Project, Victor Entertainment. *Sound Production:* Rakuonsha.

RahXephon: Pluralitas Concentio (2003). ORIGINAL TITLE: *Raazefuon: Tagen Hensoukyoku*. *Status:* Movie. *Length:* 116 minutes. *Directors:* Yutaka Izubuchi, Tomoki Kyoda. *Original Creator:* Izubuchi. *Screenplay:* Chiaki J. Konaka, Fumihiko Takayama, Hiroshi Ohnogi, Ichiro Okouchi, Tomoki Kyoda, Yoji Enokido, Yukari Kiryu, Izubuchi. *Storyboard:* Akitoshi Yokoyama, Masahiro Ando, Satoru Sakamoto, Soichi Masui, Tensai Okamura, Tetsu Shimaiya, Tomoki Kyoda, Yasushi Muraki, Izubuchi. *Music:* Ichiko Hashimoto. *Producers:* Kenji Shimizu, Maki Horiuchi, Masahiko Minami, Shiro Sasaki, Tatsuji Yamazaki. *Art Directors:* Junichi Higashi. *Animation Directors:* Ayumi Kurashima, Hiroshi Osaka, Hirotoshi Sano, Kenji Mizuhata, Koichi Horikawa, Takahiro Komori, Takashi Tomioka, Tsunenori Saito, Yasuhiro Irie, Yoshiyuki Ito, Yoshiyuki Kodaira. *Character Designer:* Akihiro Yamada. Animation *Character Designer:* Hiroki Kanno. *Mechanical Designers:* Michiaki SATO, Yoshinori Sayama. *Director of Photography:* Naoyuki Ohba. *Mechanical Animation Director:* Shiho Takeuchi. *Sound Director:* Yota Tsuruoka. *Sound Effects:* Shizuo Kurahashi. *Set Designers:* Kazutaka Miyatake, Shingo Takeba. *Production:* Asatsu DK, BONES, Fuji TV, Media Factory, RahXephon Project, Shochiku Film, Victor Entertainment. *Sound Production:* Rakuonsha.

Tsubasa: RESERVoir CHRoNiCLE (2005–2006). ORIGINAL TITLE: *Tsubasa Kuronikuru*. *Status:* TV Series (52 episodes). *Episode Length:* 25 minutes. *Directors:* Koichi Mashimo (first season: 2005); Koichi Mashimo and Hiroshi Morioka (second season: 2006). *Original Creator:* CLAMP. *Screenplay:* Hiroyuki Kawasaki. *Storyboard:* Hiroshi Morioka, Koichi Mashimo, Koji Sawai, Masaya Kawa, Tomoyuki Kurokawa. *Music:* Yuki Kajiura. *General Producers:* Shinichi Tominaga, Sou Ichita. *Art Director:* Shin Watanabe. *Animation Directors:* Kaori Higuchi, Minako Shiba, Takao Takegami, Tomoaki Kado, Yoshimitsu Yamashita, Yukiko Ban. *Character Designer:* Minako Shiba. *Director of Photography:* Katsuaki Kamata. *Sound Effects:* Sho Urahata. *Color Designer:* Makiko Kojima. *Animated Production:* Bee Train.

Tsubasa RESERVoir CHRoNiCLE The Movie: Princess of the Birdcage Kingdom (2005), ORIGINAL TITLE: *Tsubasa Kuronikuru—Torikago no Kuni no Himegimi*. *Status:* Movie. *Length:* 35 minutes. *Director:* Itsuro Kawasaki. *Scenario:* Jun'ichi Fujisaku, Midori Gotou. *Original Creator:* CLAMP. *Music:* Yuki Kajiura. *Producers:* Fumiaki Furuya, Ichiro Seki, Masaki Yasuda, Mitsuhisa Ishikawa, Nobuyo Ogawa, Yuuji Shimamoto. *Animation Directors:* Kyoji Asano, Yoko Kikuchi. *3D Animation:* Kazuya Sugiyama, Yuta Seo. *Character Designer:* Yoko Kikuchi. *Director of Photography:* Miki Sakuma. *Sound Director:* Kazuhiro Iwabayashi. *Production:* Dentsu Inc., Kodansha, MOVIC, Nippan, Production I.G, Pyrotechnist, Shochiku Co. Ltd. *Animated Production:* Production I.G.

Tsubasa Tokyo Revelations (2007–2008). ORIGINAL TITLE: *Tsubasa Toukyou Bakuro*. *Status:* OVA series (3 episodes). *Episode Length:* 25 minutes. *Director:* Shunsuke Tada. *Original creator:* CLAMP. *Screenplay:* Ageha Ohkawa. *Music:* Yuki Kajiura. *Executive Producer:* Rui Kuroki. *Art Director:* Masanobu Nomura. *Art Designer:* Tomoyasu Fujise. *Animation Directors:* Akiharu Ishii, Toshihisa Kaiya. *Character Designer:* Yoko Kikuchi. *Monster Designer:* Keigo Sasaki. *Prop Designer:* Kazunori Akiyama. *3D Director:* Makoto Endo. *Director of Photography:* Hiroshi Tanaka. *Sound Director:* Masafumi Mima. *Color Designer:* Yuko Tsumori. *Visual Effects:* Kanta Kamei. *Production:* Kodansha. *Animated Production:* Production I.G. *Background Art:* Biho Co., Ltd. *Sound Production:* Techno Sound.

SECONDARY TITLES

Aria the Animation (TV series [first season]; dir. Junichi Sato, 2005)
Belladonna of Sadness (movie; dir. Eiichi Yamamoto, 1973)
Boogiepop Phantom (TV series; dir. Takashi Watanabe, 2000)
Captain Harlock (TV series; dir. Rintaro, 1978)
Le Chevalier D'Eon (TV series; dir. Kazuhiro Furuhashi, 2006–2007)
Elfen Lied (TV series; dir. Mamoru Kanbe, 2004)
Five Centimeters Per Second (movie; dir. Makoto Shinkai, 2007)
Hell Girl (a.k.a. *Jigoku Shoujo*) (TV series; dir. Takahiro Ohmori, 2005–2006)
Kashimashi—Girl Meets Girl (TV series; dir. Nobuaki Nakanishi, 2006)
Lum the Forever (movie; dir. Kazuo Yamazaki, 1986)
The Melancholy of Haruhi Suzumiya (TV series; dir. Tatsuya Ishihara, 2006)
Memories (omnibus; dirs. Katsuhiro Otomo, Kouji Morimoto and Tensai Okamura, 1994)
MoonPhase (TV series; dir. Akiyuki Shinbo, 2004–2005)
Noir (TV series; dir. Kouichi Mashimo, 2001)
Ocean Waves (movie; dir. Tomomi Mochizuki, 1993)
Only Yesterday (movie; dir. Isao Takahata, 1991)
Origin: Spirits of the Past (movie; dir. Keiichi Sugiyama, 2006)
Paprika (movie; dir. Satoshi Kon, 2006)

Phoenix (TV series; dir. Ryousuke Takahashi, 2004)
Record of Lodoss War (OVA series; dirs. Akinori Nagaoka *et al.*, 1990)
Red Garden (TV series; dir. Kou Matsuo, 2006–2007)
Revolutionary Girl Utena (TV series; dir. Kunihiko Ikuhara, 1997)
Rose of Versailles (TV series; dirs. Tadao Nagahama and Osamu Dezaki, 1979–1980)
Shigofumi: Letters from the Departed (TV series; dir. Tatsuo Sato, 2008)
Spirit Warrior (*The Peacock King*) (OVA series; dir. Rintaro, 1988)
Vision of Escaflowne (TV series; dirs. Kazuki Akane and Shouji Kawamori, 1996)
Voices of a Distant Star (OVA; dir. Makoto Shinkai, 2002)
When They Cry: Higurashi (a.k.a. *When Cicadas Cry*; TV series; dir. Chiaki Kon, 2006 [first season]; 2007 [second season])
X (movie; dir. Rintaro, 1996)
XXXHOLiC the Movie: A Midsummer Night's Dream (movie; dir. Tsutomu Mizushima, 2005)
Zegapain (TV series; dir. Masami Shimoda, 2006)

ADDITIONAL TITLES CITED

Air (TV series; dir. Tatsuya Ishihara, 2004–2005)
Appleseed (movie; dir. Shinji Aramaki, 2004)
Aria the Natural (TV series [second season]; dir. Junichi Sato, 2006)
Aria the OVA—Arietta—(OVA series; dir. Junichi Sato, 2007)
Aria the Origination (TV series [third season]; dir. Junichi Sato, 2008)
Blade Runner (movie; dir. Ridley Scott, 1982)
Blood: The Last Vampire (movie; dir. Hiroyuki Kitakubo, 2000)
Chobits (TV series; dir. Morio Asaka, 2002)
Clannad (TV series; dir. Tatsuya Ishihara, 2007)
D. C.—Da Capo—(TV series; dir. Nagisa Miyazaki, 2003)
ef—a tale of memories (TV series; dir. Shin Oonuma, 2007)
Elemental Gelade (TV series; dir. Shigeru Ueda, 2005)
Elven Bride (OVA series; dir. Hiroshi Yamakawa, 1995)
Emma: A Victorian Romance (TV series; dir. Tsuneo Kobayashi, 2005 [first season]; 2007 [second season])
The End of Evangelion (movie; dirs. Hideaki Anno and Kazuya Tsurumaki, 1997)
Fate/stay Night (TV series; dir. Yuji Yamaguchi, 2006)
The Fifth Element (movie; dir. Luc Besson, 1997)
FLCL (OVA series; dir. Kazuya Tsurumaki, 2000)
Fullmetal Alchemist (TV series; dir. Seiji Mizushima, 2003–2004)
Ghost in the Shell (movie; dir. Mamoru Oshii, 1995)
Grave of the Fireflies (movie; dir. Isao Takahata, 1988)
The Greatest Show on Earth (movie; dir. Cecil B. DeMille, 1952)
Gunbuster (OVA series; dir. Hideaki Anno, 1988)
Gunbuster 2 (OVA series; dir. Kazuya Tsurumaki, 2004–2006)
H2O Footprints in the Sand (TV series; dir. Hideki Tachibana, 2007)
Haruka: Beyond the Stream of Time—A Tale of the Eight Guardians (TV series; dir. Aki Tsunaki, 2004–2005)
Howl's Moving Castle (movie; dir. Hayao Miyazaki, 2004)
Kanon (TV series; dir. Naoyuki Itou, 2002)
Laputa: Castle in the Sky (movie; dir. Hayao Miyazaki, 1986)

Mahoromatic — Automatic Maiden (TV series; dir. Hiroyuki Yamaga, 2001–2002)
The Matrix (movie; dirs. Larry and Andy Wachowski, 1999)
Metropolis (movie; dir. Rintaro, 2001)
Minority Report (movie; dir. Steven Spielberg, 2002)
Mulholland Dr. (movie; dir. David Lynch, 2001)
Nadia: The Secret of Blue Water (TV series; dir. Hideaki Anno, 1990–1991)
Nana (TV series; dir. Morio Asaka, 2006–2007)
Nausicaä of the Valley of the Wind (movie; dir. Hayao Miyazaki, 1984)
Neon Genesis Evangelion (TV series; dir. Hideaki Anno, 1995–1996)
Oh My Goddess! (OVA series; dir. Hiroaki Gouda, 1993)
Paranoia Agent (TV series; dir. Satoshi Kon, 2004)
Patlabor 1: The Mobile Police (movie; dir. Mamoru Oshii, 1989)
Perfect Blue (movie; dir. Satoshi Kon, 1997)
Please Teacher! (TV series; dir. Yasunori Ide, 2002)
Ranma ½ (TV series; dirs. Tomomitsu Mochizuki, Tsutomo Shibayama, Koji Sawai and Junji Nishimura, 1989–1992)
The Ring (movie; dir. Gore Verbinsky, 2002)
Ringu (movie; dir. Hideo Nakata, 1998)
Roman Holiday (movie; dir. William Wyler, 1953)
Rumbling Hearts (TV series; dir. Tetsuya Watanabe, 2003–2004)
Sailor Moon (TV series; dirs. Junichi Sato et al., 1992–1997)
Sakura Wars (TV series; dirs. Ryutaro Nakamura and Takashi Asami, 2000)
School Days (TV series; dir. Keitaro Motonaga, 2007)
Shuffle! (TV series; dir. Naoto Hosoda, 2005–2006)
Solty Rei (TV series; dir. Yoshimasa Hiraike, 2005–2006)
Soul Link (TV series; dir. Toshikatsu Tokoro, 2006)
Space Battleship Yamato (TV series; dir. Leiji Matsumoto, 1974–1975)
Spirited Away (movie; dir. Hayao Miyazaki, 2001)
Steamboy (movie; dir. Katsuhiro Otomo, 2004)
Tarzan the Ape Man (movie; dir. W. S. Van Dyke, 1932)
Tetsuko no Tabi (TV series; dir. Akinori Nagaoka, 2007)
This Ugly Yet Beautiful World (TV series; dir. Shouji Saeki, 2004)
Throne of Blood (movie; dir. Akira Kurosawa, 1957)
ToHeart (TV series; dir. Naohito Takahashi, 1999)
Tokyo Godfathers (movie; dir. Satoshi Kon, 2003)
Touka Gettan (TV series; dir. Yuji Yamaguchi, 2007)
true tears (TV series; dir. Junji Nishimura, 2008)
Tsukihime, Lunar Legend (TV series; dir. Katsushi Sakurabi, 2003)
Tsuyokiss (TV series; dir. Shinichiro Kimura, 2006)
2001: A Space Odyssey (movie; dir. Stanley Kubrick, 1968)
Utawarerumono (TV series; dir. Tomoki Kobayashi, 2006)
Vampire Princess Miyu (TV series; dir. Toshihiro Hirano, 1997–1998)
Wolf's Rain (TV series; dir. Tensai Okamura, 2003)
XXXHolic (TV series; dir. Tsutomu Mizushima, 2006)
XXXHolic: Kei (TV series; dir. Tsutomu Mizushima, 2008)

Chapter Notes

Chapter 1

1. In the context of Western aesthetics, the concept of *yugen* as an apprehension of the universe's awe-inspiring vastness finds a parallel in the idea of the "sublime" as theorized by the philosopher, statesman and orator Edmund Burke (1729–1797): "whatever is in any sort terrible, or is conversant about terrible objects, or operates in a manner analogous to terror, is a source of the *sublime*; that is, it is productive of the strongest emotion which the mind is capable of feeling."

Chapter 2

1. The film's title carries a double meaning. On the one hand, it refers to the time span covered by the movies in which the heroine has starred in the course of her prolific career, which indeed stretches from ancient Japan to the distant future. On the other, it is consonant with the work's status as Satoshi Kon's first feature-length production of this millennium.
2. For a detailed analysis of this film, please see: Cavallaro, D. 2007. *Anime Intersections — Tradition and Innovation in Theme and Technique*. Jefferson, NC: McFarland, Chapter Three.
3. It is not unusual for anime to contain more or less explicit references to same-sex relationships of either a carnal or a Platonic kind. As Patrick Drazen observes, "Japanese pop culture" at large portrays homosexuality "more prominently" than its Western counterpart (p. 78), and whether a character is "played for laughs" or "for tragedy," it is noteworthy that "seldom are characters condemned for their sexuality" (p. 79). An ambivalent depiction of same-sex friendships is often favored — in keeping with Japanese art's preference for allusiveness — over character portraits based on clear-cut definitions of their erotic proclivities. A motif used time and again to develop the theme of sexual ambiguity is crossdressing. Prominent in *Revolutionary Girl Utena* (TV series; dir. Kunihiko Ikuhara, 1997) and *Rose of Versailles* (TV series; dirs. Tadao Nagahama and Osamu Dezaki, 1979–1980), here discussed in Chapter 3, the trope finds an illustrious prototype in Osamu Tezuka's manga *Princess Knight* (1953) and is further exemplified by the manga *The Sword of Paros* (1986), illustrated by Yumiko Igarashi and penned by Kaoru Kurimoto.

Chapter 3

1. While *Rose of Versailles* is pervaded by memories of the epoch in which it is set, memories of its heroine resonate in later anime in the guise of intertextual allusions. A case in point is *Ranma ½* (TV series; dirs. Tomomitsu Mochizuki, Tsutomo Shibayama, Koji Sawai and Junji Nishimura, 1989–1992), where the character of Azusa names the panda she treasures (i.e. the protagonist's father in his metamorphic version) "Oscar" and proceeds to deck him out in Oscar-de-Jarjayes gear.
2. Steampunk is a subgenre of alternate-history science fiction, typically set in a pseudo–Victorian culture. The aesthetic divulged by steampunk is essentially retrofuturistic since the time zone it portrays is not the future as we might imagine it today but rather the future as imagined by the technovisionaries of past epochs. This sensibility is associated with the works of the pioneering science-fiction author Jules Verne (1828–1905) and with those of the historian and illustrator Albert Robida (1848–1926). Steampunk was brought back into vogue in 1990 by William Gibson's and Bruce Sterling's novel *The Difference Engine*, a synthesis of cyberpunk motifs and Victorian culture. One of the earliest instances of steampunk in manga is the sci-fi trilogy by Osamu Tezuka comprising *Lost World* (1948), *Metropolis* (1949) and *Next World* (1951). In the realm of anime, notable examples are Leiji Matsumoto's *Space Battleship Yamato* (TV series; 1974–1975), Hayao Miyazaki's feature films *Laputa: Castle in the Sky* (1986) and *Howl's Moving Castle* (2004), *Sakura Wars* (TV series; dirs. Ryutaro Nakamura and

Takashi Asami, 2000), *Metropolis* (movie; dir. Rintaro, 2001), *Fullmetal Alchemist* (TV series; dir. Seiji Mizushima, 2003–2004), *Steamboy* (movie; dir. Katsuhiro Otomo, 2004) and *Elemental Gelade* (TV series; dir. Shigeru Ueda, 2005).

3. The meticulous depiction of nineteenth-century England offered by the television show *Emma: A Victorian Romance* is a further remarkable instance of anime's handling of the aesthetics of *sabi* in conjunction with the principle of *akogare no Paris*. The series was directed by Tsuneo Kobayashi, with a first season broadcast in 2005 and a second season in 2007.

4. The *Anime News Network*'s "Lexicon" offers the following definition of the term *"bento,"* the Japanese word for this distinctive local product:
   1. Japanese-style boxed lunch, served cold. Often consists of rice and various side items arranged in a very visually appealing manner.
   2. Train stations usually have a unique version of this, each with its own particular taste, called *ekiben* (from *eki* for train station, and *ben* as a short form of *bento*).
   3. Lovers and devoted wives will make a particularly intricately arranged version of this for their male partner (often to the embarrassment of the recipient), called *aisobento*.

Chapter 4

1. A quest comparable to Kamui's is dramatized in the TV series *Haruka: Beyond the Stream of Time—A Tale of the Eight Guardians* (dir. Aki Tsunaki, 2004–2005). Its heroine, Akane Motomiya, is wrenched away from her ordinary life, told that she has inherited the powers of the "priestess of the Dragon God," and enjoined to prevent the "Demons" from gaining control over the entire world, by deploying special abilities to which she has hitherto been oblivious. In pursuing this quest, the heroine is abetted by the "Eight Guardians." Like Kamui, Akane is thus trapped between two adversarial cultures. The topos of memory is brought into play by the story's transposition of its protagonist from present-day Japan to a fantasy version of the Heian era (794–1192) and its customs. What lends *Haruka* an original twist is the displacement of the pivotal quest from the task assigned to Akane by external agents to a goal of her own choice: searching for her friends Tenma and Shimon who have, like the protagonist herself, been plucked away from her normal routine.

2. Fictionalized versions of these scientific propositions are effectively elaborated in the OVAs *Gunbuster* (dir. Hideaki Anno, 1988) and *Gunbuster 2* (a.k.a. *Diebuster*; dir. Kazuya Tsurumaki, 2004–2006).

Chapter 5

1. An analogous situation is dramatized in Mamoru Oshii's seminal film *Ghost in the Shell* (1995): its protagonist, Major Motoko Kusanagi, is a cyborg and therefore, like Kurau, something of an alien entity. Yet, also like Kurau, she carries potently human affects and memories that are ultimately no less integral to her identity than her technologically constructed side. It is also noteworthy that Kurau and the Major are visually connected by the two shots in which each of them makes her first screen appearance in adult form. Both display an athletic, short-haired and blue-eyed woman crouched atop a skyscraper and scanning silently the urbanscape below. Further instances of human/other syntheses are the female leads in the following anime:

Blood: The Last Vampire (movie; dir. Hiroyuki Kitakubo, 2000): *Saya*
Chobits (TV series; dir. Morio Asaka, 2002): *Chii*
Fate/stay Night (TV series; dir. Yuji Yamaguchi, 2006): *Saber*
FLCL (OVA series; dir. Kazuya Tsurumaki, 2000): *Haruko*
Gunbuster 2 (OVA series; dir. Kazuya Tsurumaki, 2004–2006): *Nono*
Mahoromatic—Automatic Maiden (TV series; dir. Hiroyuki Yamaga, 2001–2002): *Mahoro*
Metropolis (movie; dir. Rintaro, 2001): *Tima*
Nadia: The Secret of Blue Water (TV series; dir. Hideaki Anno, 1990–1991): *Nadia*
Oh My Goddess! (OVA series; dir. Hiroaki Gouda, 1993): *Belldandy*
Solty Rei (TV series; dir. Yoshimasa Hiraike, 2005–2006): *Solty*
This Ugly Yet Beautiful World (TV series; dir. Shouji Saeki, 2004): *Hikari and Akari*
Vampire Princess Miyu (TV series; dir. Toshihiro Hirano, 1997–1998): *Miyu*

The above list is by no means exhaustive but will hopefully offer the reader apposite pointers to additional treatments of the topos.

While *Ghost in the Shell* is an explicit point of reference for Irie, other titles are simultaneously alluded to in a more oblique fashion. The architecture is occasionally redolent of the anime *Appleseed* (movie; dir. Shinji Aramaki, 2004), while the multilayered traffic system recalls sequences from the live-action films *The Fifth Element* (dir. Luc Besson, 1997) and *Minority Report* (dir. Steven Spielberg, 2002). These citations never come across as gratuitous ripoffs, for *Kurau*'s world is very much its own in terms of both the show's panoramic vision and its attention to aesthetic and affective details.

2. Saito's iniquity is subtly captured by the name of the vintage wine consumed by the Commissioner over a tense meeting with Ayaka, *"Palus Putredinis,"* which translates literally from Latin as "marsh of decay." Although the phrase designates an area of the Moon's surface and could be taken to refer to the wine's place of origin (quite consonant with *Kurau*'s ambience), its underlying association with concepts of deterioration and corruption also makes it a fitting comment on Saito's ethics.

3. Another recent release in which the theme of

split identities, and hence memories, plays a key role is *Nana* (TV series; dir. Morio Asaka, 2006–2007). Like the anime discussed in Chapter 5, this show revolves around a pair of characters whose experiences bring them intimately together as two facets of one single narrative. These are the naive Nana Komatsu, a small-town girl, and the worldly-wise Nana Osaki, a punk-rock singer. The two meet on a train journey to Tokyo where the former intends to join her boyfriend and the latter to make a major debut with her band, "Blast." Despite the two Nanas' radically different backgrounds and objectives, they gradually forge a deep connection as both their love lives and their careers bring them closer and closer. Their respective memories accordingly coalesce. Although they remain separate individuals, the two Nanas are bound by shared experiences as complementary sides of one composite personality.

Chapter 6

1. The theme of the young man visiting a remote town in which buried childhood memories are progressively reactivated by his encounters with various female characters is also dramatized in *H2O Footprints in the Sand* (TV series; dir. Hideki Tachibana, 2007).

2. Please note that *Kanon* is a major instance of a burgeoning anime format based on "visual novels": namely, interactive role-playing games distinguished by highly refined visuals, subtly nuanced characterization, complex storylines and an emphasis on textuality designed to maximize the player's participation in the shaping of the narrative. Other notable examples include:

Air (TV series; dir. Tatsuya Ishihara, 2004–2005)
Clannad (TV series; dir. Tatsuya Ishihara, 2007)
D.C.— Da Capo —(TV series; dir. Nagisa Miyazaki, 2003)
ef— a tale of memories (TV series; dir. Shin Oonuma, 2007)
Fate/stay Night (TV series; dir. Yuji Yamaguchi, 2006)
H2O Footprints in the Sand (TV series; dir. Hideki Tachibana, 2007)
Rumbling Hearts (TV series; dir. Tetsuya Watanabe, 2003–2004)
School Days (TV series; dir. Keitaro Motonaga, 2007)
Shuffle! (TV series; dir. Naoto Hosoda, 2005–2006)
Soul Link (TV series, dir. Toshikatsu Tokoro, 2006)
ToHeart (TV series; dir. Naohito Takahashi, 1999)
Touka Gettan (TV series; dir. Yuji Yamaguchi, 2007)
true tears (TV series; dir. Junji Nishimura, 2008)
Tsukihime, Lunar Legend (TV series; dir. Katsushi Sakurabi, 2003)
Tsuyokiss (TV series; dir. Shinichiro Kimura, 2006)
Utawarerumono (TV series; dir. Tomoki Kobayashi, 2006)
When They Cry: Higurashi (TV series; dir. Chiaki Kon, 2006 [first season]; 2007 [second season])

Chapter 7

1. The studio behind *RahXephon* is BONES, also responsible for the execution of *Kurau Phantom Memory*. In both series, the company's legendary flair for amalgamating highly detailed static art with fluid dynamics asserts itself unequivocally. Other very popular productions issuing from BONES are *Wolf's Rain* (TV series; dir. Tensai Okamura, 2003) and *Fullmetal Alchemist* (TV series; dir. Seiji Mizushima, 2003–2004). In *RahXephon*, specifically, the studio's technical excellence is confirmed by the smooth blend of digital effects and 2D animation coordinated by Mitsuo Iso: notable examples include the Dolem's self-regeneration in the first Movement, the mud doll creeping out of the gloom in the fifteenth Movement, the titular creature's climactic morph and the old world's dissolution. The integration of cel illustrations and digitized colours, for which Shihoko Nakayama must be credited, is also remarkable. So is the meticulous presentation of industrial designs (executed by Shingo Takeba) meant to impart the futuristic ambience with a solid sense of everyday life.

2. As the *RahXephon Bible* explains, the term "quantum" designates "the smallest possible physical unit that can be represented only by integer multiples, and not continuous changes, of a given unit quantity. The start of quantum theory came in 1900 when [Max] Planck suggested the idea of energy quanta (the quantum hypothesis)" (Hikawa, Kubo and Kaneko, p. 75).

3. In the film, Maya is portrayed as Ayato's biological mother and is said to have been already pregnant by the time of her awakening as a Mu, at which point she supposedly murdered her husband and fled to Tokyo.

4. Useful reviews assessing parallels between *RahXephon* and *Neon Genesis Evangelion* have been penned by Mioko Matsuda and Claude J. Pelletier, Martin Ouellette, En Hong, Zac Bertschy and John Huxley. (Please see Bibliography.) Additionally, an interesting frame-based comparative evaluation is supplied by the online dossier *EvaXephon* available at the following address: <http://evaxephon.com/gallery1.html>

The view underlying the analysis of *RahXephon* offered in this book is that Izubuchi'a allusions to *Evangelion* are so explicit that they should be regarded as an admiring homage to Anno's seminal work and not as mere borrowings.

5. The concept of parallel universes so central to *RahXephon*'s diegesis also finds a correlative in the mu-

sical realm. As the *RahXephon Bible* explains, "There is a musical term, heterophony, that describes a kind of musical form found in musical styles such as *gagaku* (ancient Japanese court music). It originally referred to an arrangement where a single principal melody is wrapped with several different ornamental variations on that melodic theme, or perhaps even by different modified melodic transformations. It could be called a two-dimensional, multi-part musical form whose purpose is to achieve a single overlapping resonance that is both heterogeneous and ironically unified at the same time. That's also a good description of a phase-space" (Hikawa, Kubo and Kaneko, p. 63).

Chapter 8

1. Feathers play a pivotal ceremonial role in numerous cultures, and are often used as healing implements endowed with talismanic powers and symbolic associations with the spirit world. In the context of Japanese mythology, feathers feature most prominently in the legend "The Robe of Feathers," a version of a tale also found in Native American and Celtic traditions. A fisherman finds a magnificent robe of feathers and resolves to keep it at all costs. Confronted by the heavenly maiden to whom the garment originally belonged, and without which she is powerless to return to her celestial home, the man eventually consents to yield his treasure on condition that the deity will dance for him. As she does so, she gently rises into the dawn surrounded by a rainbow-colored halo emitted by the gleaming array. Several of the anime here examined adopt feather-based symbolism in varyingly explicit fashions, most notably *RahXephon*, *Kanon*, *Gilgamesh* and *Phoenix*.

2. Please note that the alternative spelling "Fay" is used by numerous reviewers. The spelling here adopted is consonant with the English translation of the parent manga.

3. Having started life in the late 1980s as a group of *doujinshi* (fan artists), CLAMP has risen to the status of one of the most popular, original and accomplished teams of *mangaka* (manga authors), scriptwriters, character designers and costume designers. CLAMP's international reputation is attested to by the sale of nearly 100 million copies of their volumes to date throughout the world. The first volume of the *Tsubasa* manga was published in *Weekly Shounen Magazine* in May 2003. The series is still ongoing and this makes it CLAMP's longest-running manga to date. According to Dallas Middaugh, associate publisher of the Del Rey Manga division of Random House responsible for the English-language release of the *Tsubasa* manga, as well as several other CLAMP publications, the artists "have been an integral part of the manga explosion that's occurred in the U.S. over the past several years. Their fluid, dramatic artwork and storytelling style struck a strong chord with male and female manga readers" (Solomon).

4. The table below offers a schematic recapitulation of the worlds visited by the protagonists throughout the *Tsubasa* series.

SEASON 1		
World	World Type	Episodes Covered
Clow & Yuuko's World	Saga's Foundations	1
Hanshin Republic	Contemporary City	2–6
Nayutaya	Feudal East	7–11
Standalone Episode	Submerged Realm	12
Jade	Mediaeval Europe	13–15
Standalone Episode	Tournament	16
Outo/Edonis	Japan's Taisho Era	17–25
Zarastra	Rural Principality	26

SEASON 2		
World	World Type	Episodes Covered
Piffle World	Futuristic City	1–3
Standalone Episode	Zarastra	4
Standalone Episode	Lagosta Ship	5
Standalone Episode	Wizards' Kingdom	6
Shara/Shura	Modern and Mythical Japan	7–10
Standalone Episode	Chibi World	11
Highway	Road Narrative	12–13
Rekord	Magical Libraries	14–17
Standalone Episode	Lilliputian Kero	18
Nayutaya/Kishimu Country	Feudal East/Otherworld	19–20
Standalone Episode	Ragtime	21
Country of Tao	Traditional Japan	22–26

OVA SERIES		
World	World Type	Episodes Covered
Country of Tokyo	Postapocalyptic	1–3

In the parent manga, the principal arcs articulated in the TV and OVA series occur in the following order: Clow & Yuuko's World; Hanshin Republic; Koryio (i.e., Nayutaya); Jade; Outo/Edonis; Shara/Shura; Piffle World; Rekord; Country of Tokyo.

5. The show was first aired in Japan in a non-consecutive episode order that contributed significantly to its instant appeal as a groundbreaking venture. However, its chronological rearrangement for the purpose of the DVD releases (in both Japan and the U.S.) makes it a lot easier to follow, as it refrains from taxing the audience's mnemonic faculties in any radical fashion.

Chapter 9

1. As a cultural emblem, the butterfly typifies the transience of pleasure and beauty: a concept, as seen in Chapter 1, of pivotal significance in the context of Japanese aesthetics. Moreover, butterflies have been

employed as symbols of metamorphosis and rebirth all over the world for time immemorial. Unlike the phoenix, examined in Chapter 3, whose transformation and cyclical phases of death and resurrection are ideated as ongoing processes, the butterfly encapsulates the inexorable ephemerality of the fleeting moment. The butterfly is a ubiquitous visual symbol in anime, and Japanese art generally. This is clearly indicated by three other titles examined in this study: *Boogiepop Phantom*, *Paprika* and *Red Garden*.

2. Horror has featured with a certain regularity in anime, often in conjunction with other genres, such as humour, romance or erotica. The most common visual tropes include grotesque creatures, supernatural occurrences, Gothic mansions and underground haunts. As Patrick Drazen notes, whereas the "Western formula" tends to use horror to "express sexual anxiety" (p. 70), anime shows grounded in the horror genre often deploy it as "the subtext of a sexually explicit story" (p. 71).

Bibliography

Ando, T. "What is *Wabi-Sabi*?" <http://nobleharbor.com/tea/chado/WhatIsWabi-Sabi.htm>

Arnold, M. 2002. "Review: *Millennium Actress*." *MidnightEye*. <http://www.midnighteye.com/reviews/millactr.shtml>

Ashford, B. 2008. "I got new brain in kidney swap." *The Sun*. Wednesday, May 21. <http://www.thesun.co.uk/sol/homepage/news/article919964.ece>

Banks, P. R. "*RahXephon* Timeline." *Khantazi*. <http://www.khantazi.org/Rec/Anime/MuTimeline.html>

Barrow, J. D. 1990a. "Strings." In *The Fontana Dictionary of Modern Thought*, second edition, edited by A. Bullock, O. Stallybrass and S. Trombley. London: Fontana Press.

Barrow, J. D. 1990b. "Superstrings." In *The Fontana Dictionary of Modern Thought*, second edition, edited by A. Bullock, O. Stallybrass and S. Trombley. London: Fontana Press.

Bashou, M. 2004. *Bashou's Haiku: Selected Poems of Matsuo Bashou*. Trans. D. Landis Barnhill. Albany: State University of New York Press.

Benjamin, W. 1985. "Central Park." *New German Critique* 34, Winter: 32–58.

"Bento." *Anime News Network*. <http://www.animenewsnetwork.com/encyclopedia/lexicon.php?id=7>

Bertschy, Z. 2003. "Review—*RahXephon* DVD 2." *Anime News Network*. <http://www.animenewsnetwork.com/review/rahxephon/dvd-2>

Bertschy, Z. 2004. "Review—*RahXephon* DVD 7." *Anime News Network*. <http://www.animenewsnetwork.com/review/rahxephon/dvd-7>

Burke, E. 1909–1914. *On the Sublime and Beautiful*. Vol. XXIV, Part 2. The Harvard Classics. New York: P. F. Collier & Son.

Calvino, I. 1997. [1972.] *Invisible Cities*. Trans. W. Weaver. London: Vintage.

Calvino, I. 1993. [1981.] *If on a winter's night a traveler*. Trans. W. Weaver. London: David Campbell Publishers.

"Carpe Diem—an *Aria the Animation* review." 2008. <http://natsuneko.animeblogger.net/2008/01/24/carpe-diem-an-aria-the-animation-review/>

Carroll, L. 2003. [1871.] *Alice's Adventures in Wonderland: AND Through the Looking-Glass, and What Alice Found There*. London: Penguin.

Cavallaro, D. 2007. *Anime Intersections: Tradition and Innovation in Theme and Technique*. Jefferson, NC: McFarland.

de Certeau, M. 1984. *The Practice of Everyday Life*. Trans. S. Rendall. Berkeley and London: University of California Press.

Churchward, J. 1987. [1926.] *The Lost Continent of Mu*. St. Albans, UK: C. W. Daniel Co.

CLAMP. 2007a. "Different worlds, different pleasures." *Newtype USA*, vol. 6, no. 11.

CLAMP 2007b. *Tsubasa Reservoir Chronicle*, vol. 15. Trans. W. Flanagan. New York: Ballantine Books.

CLAMP 2008a. *Tsubasa Reservoir Chronicle*, vol. 16. Trans. W. Flanagan. New York: Ballantine Books.

CLAMP 2008b. *Tsubasa Reservoir Chronicle*, vol. 17. Trans. W. Flanagan. New York: Ballantine Books.

CLAMP 2008c. *Tsubasa Reservoir Chronicle*, vol. 18. Trans. W. Flanagan. New York: Ballantine Books.

Clarke, J. 2004. *Animated Films*. London: Virgin Books.

Couser, G. T. 1989. *Alter Egos: Authority in American Autobiography*. New York: Oxford University Press.

Dalí, S. 2007. [1942.] *The Secret Life of Salvador Dalí*. Trans. H. M. Chevalier. Whitefish, MT: Kessinger Publishing.

Dickinson, E. 1988. *The Complete Poems*. London: Little, Brown.

Dohgen. 1988. *Dohgen, Shohbohgenzoh: Zen Essays by Dohgen*. Trans. T. Cleary. Honolulu: University of Hawaii Press.

Drazen, P. 2003. *Anime Explosion: The What? Why? & Wow! of Japanese Animation*. Berkeley, CA: Stone Bridge Press.

Ekuan, K. 2000. *The Aesthetics of the Japanese Lunchbox*. Trans. D. Kenny. Cambridge, Mass.: MIT Press.

Eliot, T. S. 2002. *Collected Poems*. London: Faber &

Faber. *EvaXephon*. <http://evaxephon.com/gallery1.html>

Faulkner, W. 1951. *Requiem for a Nun*. New York: Random House.

Fay, S. 2005. "Promises to Keep." *Animefringe*. <http://www.animefringe.com/magazine/2005/05/feature/01.php>

Foucault, M. 1973. *The Order of Things: An Archaeology of the Human Sciences*. New York: Vintage.

Gibson, W. 1995. [1984.] *Neuromancer*. London: HarperCollins.

Gibson, W., and B. Sterling. 1990. *The Difference Engine*. London: Victor Gollancz.

Gonzalez, E. 2003. "Film Review: *Millennium Actress*." *Slant Magazine*. <http://www.slantmagazine.com/film/film_review.asp?ID=795>

Green, M. B. 1986. "Superstrings." *Scientific American*, September.

Hakuin, E. 1971. *The Zen Master Hakuin: Selected Writings*. Trans. P. Yampolsky. New York: Columbia University Press.

Harlib, A. 2003. "*Millennium Actress* Review." *Frames Per Second Magazine*. <http://www.fpsmagazine.com/review/millactress.php>

Hikawa, R., M. Kubo, and K. Kaneko. 2003. *RahXephon Bible*. Trans. K. Bertrand and J. Wiedrick. Houston: ADV Vision.

Hong, E. 2002. "Feature: *RahXephon*." *Animefringe*. <http://www.animefringe.com/magazine/02.09/feature/4/index.php3>

Hume, N. G. 1995. *Japanese Aesthetics and Culture: A Reader*. Albany: State University of New York Press.

Huxley, J. 2004. "*RahXephon* Anime Reviews: *RahXephon Orchestration 7: Crescendo*." *Anime Boredom*. <http://www.animeboredom.co.uk/anime-reviews/rahxephon/419/>

"Iki." 2003. *Taste of Japan*. <http://global.mitsubishielectric.com/tasteofjapan/imprints/iki/index01_b.html>

Ishihara, T. 2008. Interview in "A Close Look at an Anime Production House Part I." *Kanon* DVD, vol. 1. ADV Films.

James, W. 2006. [1895.] *The Will to Believe and Other Essays in Popular Philosophy*. New York: Cosimo Classics.

"Japanese Aesthetics." 2005. *Stanford Encyclopedia of Philosophy*. <http://plato.stanford.edu/entries/japanese-aesthetics/>

"Japanese Superstitions." *Japan Zone*. <http://www.japan-zone.com/omnibus/superstition.shtml>

Kanon DVD vol. 1 Cover. 2008. ADV Films.

Kanon Visual Memories. 2007. Tokyo: Ichijinsha.

Kikuchi, M. 2007. "At the Crossroads." *Newtype USA*, vol. 6, no. 11.

Kon, S. 2004a. "A Conversation with the Filmmakers." <http:www.www.millenniumactress-themovie.com/>

Kon, S. 2004b. "Interview." <http:www.millenniumactress-themovie.com/>

Larsen, J. L. 2001. "The Inspiration of Japanese Design." *Traditional Japanese Design: Five Tastes*. New York: Japan Society.

Lefebvre, H. 1991. *The Production of Space*. Oxford: Blackwell.

littlejonny100. 2007. "*Kanon* Review." *Minitokyo*. <http://reviews.minitokyo.net/1243/kanon/>

Longfellow, H. W. 1988. *Selected Poems*. London: Penguin.

Lowenthal, D. 1961. "Geography, experience and imagination: towards a geographical epistemology." *Annals of the Association of American Geographers* 51.

MacInnes, D. T. 2006. "*Omohide Poro Poro*." *Conversations on Ghibli*. <http://ghiblicon.blogspot.com/2006/07/omohide-poro-poro.html>

Mannering, D. 1995. *Great Works of Japanese Graphic Art*. Bristol, UK: Parragon.

Manovich, L. 2001. "Digital Cinema and the History of a Moving Image." *The Language of New Media*. Boston: MIT Press. Extracts: <http://www2.unibo.it/parol/articles/manovich.htm>

Mashimo, K. 2008. "*Tsubasa: RESERVoir CHRoNiCLE*." *Newtype USA*, vol. 07, no. 02.

Matsuda, M., and C. J. Pelletier. 2003. "*RahXephon*: Overview." *Protoculture Addicts* (76): 17.

Merleau-Ponty, M. 1969. *The Visible and the Invisible*. Trans. A. Lingus. Evanston, IL.: Northwestern University Press.

Morley, C. 1986. [1922.] *Where the Blue Begins*. Norwich, UK: Telegraph Books.

Murakami, H. 2005. *Kafka on the Shore*. Trans. P. Gabriel. London: Vintage.

Murakami, K. 2008. *One Single Impression: Prompt 9: Flowering*. Sunday, April 27. <http://onesingleimpression.blogspot.com/2008/04/prompt-9-flowering_27.html>

Nakagami, Y. 2007. "Life Is Sweet." *Newtype USA*, vol. 6, no. 1.

Nakagami, Y. 2008. "We Are Family." *Newtype USA*, vol. 6, no. 1.

Nuclear Buddha. 2007. "*The Place Promised in Our Early Days*." *Nuclear Buddha*. <http://nuclearbuddha.blogspot.com/2007/06/place-promised-in-our-youth.html>

Oppliger, J. 2002. "Can You Explain the Ending of *RahXephon*?" *AnimeNation*. <http://animenation.net/news/askjohn.php?id=579>

Ouellette, M. 2003. "Reviews: *RahXephon, Vol. 1*." *Protoculture Addicts* (76): 53.

Ozaki, T. 2006. "Les 24 Chevaliers Part X: Tomomi Ozaki (Character Design)." *Production I.G*. <http://www.production-ig.com/contents/works_sp/44_/s08_/000579.html>

Park, R. E. 1984. "The city: suggestions for investigation of human behavior in the urban environment." In *The City: Suggestions for Investigation of Human Behavior in the Urban Environment*, edited by R. E. Park, R. D. McKenzie and L. Wirth. Chicago and London: Chicago University Press.

Pascal, D. "Japanese Aesthetics and the Nature of Anime." *Unreal City: Literature of the Twenty-first*

Century. <http://www.davidpascal.com/unrealcity/reviews/anime.html>

Pavese, C. 1961. *The Burning Brand: Diaries 1935–1950*. Trans. A. E. Murch. New York: Walker & Company.

Pearce, J. 2005. "*The Place Promised in Our Early Days.*" *DVD Verdict.* <http://www.dvdverdict.com/reviews/placepromised.php>

Pile, S. 1996. *The Body and the City: Psychoanalysis, Space and Subjectivity.* London: Routledge.

Pocock, D. C. D. 1973. "Environmental perception: process and product." *Tijdschrift voor Economische en Sociale Geografie (Journal of Economic and Social Geography).* Utrecht, NL: Royal Dutch Geographical Society.

Raban, J. 1974. *Soft City.* London: Hamish Hamilton.

Rajneesh, B. S. *ThinkExist.com.* <http://thinkexist.com/quotation/when-sadness-comes-just-sit-by-the-side-and-look/350280.html>

Richie, D. "Turning Japanese: An Interview with Donald Richie." <http://www.english.ccsu.edu/barnetts/Richie.htm>

Robinson, T. 2007. "*Tsubasa: RESERVoir CHRoNiCLE*—Vol. 1: Gathering of Fates (eps. #1–5)." *Sci Fi Weekly.* <http://www.scifi.com/sfw/anime/sfw15773.html>

Robinson, T. 2008. "*Kanon.*" *Sci Fi Weekly.* <http://www.scifi.com/sfw/anime/sfw17993.html>

Saito, Y. 2007. "The Moral Dimension of Japanese Aesthetics." *Journal of Aesthetics and Art Criticism* 65 (1), 85–97. Blackwell Publishing: The American Society for Aesthetics.

Santos, C. 2005. "*Gilgamesh*—DVD 1—Orphans of the Apocalypse." *Anime News Network.* <http://www.animenewsnetwork.com/review/gilgamesh/dvd-1>

Schiavo, P. "Discovery Concert: Messiaen's *Turangalîla Symphonie*—Notes on the Program." *Carnegie Hall.* <http://www.carnegiehall.org/article/box_office/events/evt_8118_pn.html?selecteddate=02152008>

Shinkai, M. 2005. "Interview." *Activeanime.* <http://www.activeanime.com/html/component/option,com_alphacontent/section,1/cat,19/task,view/id,1000/Itemid,46/>

Shinkai, M. 2006. "Interview." *The Place Promised in Our Early Days* DVD. ADV Films.

Solomon, C. 2006. "Four Mothers of Manga Gain American Fans with Expertise in a Variety of Visual Styles." *The New York Times.* <http://www.nytimes.com/2006/11/28/arts/design/28clam.html?ex=1322370000&en=915b5385604af201&ei=5090&partner=rssuserland&emc=rss>

Starr, P. 2008. "*Five Centimeters Per Second*—The Precise Speed of Human Longing." *PiQ Magazine* Issue 2.

Steinbeck, C. "The Body as a Medium of Memory." <http://www.ruhr-uni-bochum.de/kbe/Steineck Cambridg.pdf>

Stiegler, B. 1998. *Technics and Time 1: The Fault of Epimetheus.* Stanford: Stanford University Press.

Tanizaki, J. 1933. *In Praise of Shadows.* New Haven, CT: Leete's Island Books.

Turan, K. 2003. "Movie Review: *Millennium Actress.*" *Los Angeles Times.* <http://www.calendarlive.com/movies/reviews/cl-et-kenny12sep12,2,5118759.story?coll=cl-mreview>

Ueda, M. 1967. *Literary and Art Theories in Japan.* Cleveland: Case Western Reserve University Press.

Waldman, H., and A. Levin Becker (2008). "Scientists in State, Worldwide Await Results of Large Hadron Collider." *Courant. com.* Wednesday, September 10. <http://www.courant.com/news/local/hc-cthadron0910.artsep10,0,6923966.story>

Wilde, O. *Quote DB.* <http://www.quotedb.com/quotes/1869>

Winterson, J. 1988. *The Passion.* London: Penguin.

Winterson, J. 1997. *Gut Symmetries.* London: Granta.

Wolf, F. A. 1988. *Parallel Universes: The Search for Other Worlds.* New York: Simon & Schuster.

Wordsworth, W. 1994. *The Collected Poems.* Ware, Hertfordshire: Wordsworth Editions Ltd.

Wright, J. K. 1947. "Terrae Incognitae: The Place of the Imagination in Geography." *Annals of the Association of American Geographers* 37 (1).

Wright, S. "Steven Wright Quotes." *BrainyQuotes.* <http://www.brainyquote.com/quotes/quotes/s/stevenwrigl38064.html>

xenocrisis0153. 2008. "*Kanon*—Volume 1." *AnimeSource.Com* <http://www.anime-source.com/banzai/modules.php?name=Content&pa=showpage&pid=1083>

Index

Air 100–101
Akane, K. 30, 109–110
Ando, T. 19
Anno, H. 58, 81, 127
Aria the Animation 94–96, 106, 107
Aria the Natural 96
Aria the Origination 96
Aria the OVA-Arietta- 96
Arnold, M. 17
Ashford, B. 10

Banks, P. R. 113
Barrow, J. D. 64
Bashou, M. 5, 6, 69
Baudelaire, C. 90
Baum, F. 126
Beardsley, A. 22
Belladonna of Sadness 21–22, 27
Beneath the Wave off Kanagawa 20
Benjamin, W. 119
Berkeley, G. 130
Bertschy, Z. 120, 123
Big Bang 60
Blade Runner 39
Boogiepop Phantom 58, 67, 91–92, 106, 107
Buddhism 28, 128
Byron, G. G. 130

Calvino, I. 7, 8
Captain Harlock 32, 34, 49
Cardcaptor Sakura 150, 151
Carroll, L. 109, 126
Le Chevalier D'Eon 33–34
Chobits 150
Christianity 128
Churchward, J. 114
CLAMP 51, 135, 137, 150–151
Clannad 26

Clarke, J. 11
Couser, G. T. 1

Dalí, S. 1, 127
D. C.-Da Capo- 26
de Certeau, M. 107–108
de Chirico, G. 110
DeMille, C. B. 152
Descartes, R. 130
Dezaki, O. 32
Dohgen 104
Drazen, P. 57
Dulac, E. 22

ef—a tale of memories 58
Einstein, A. 64
Ekuan, K. 48
Elfen Lied 46, 85–87, 88
Eliot, T. S. 51
Elven Bride 109
The End of Evangelion 81

Faulkner, W. 31
Fay, S. 65–66
5 Centimeters Per Second 25–27, 46, 58, 59, 67
Foucault, M. 49–50
Furuhashi, K. 33–34

García Márquez, G. 126
Ghost in the Shell 39, 76
Gibson, W. 39, 145
Gilgamesh 33–49, 67, 102
Grave of the Fireflies 58
The Greatest Show on Earth 152
Green, M. B. 64
Gonzalez, E. 18
Gunbuster 127
Gunbuster 2 25, 58, 67

Hakuin, E. 104
Harlib, A. 17

Heisenberg, W. 63
Hell Girl (a.k.a. *Jigoku Shoujo*) 53–54, 57
Hikawa, R. 116, 118, 127
Hokusai, K. 20
Horace 95
Hume, N. G. 7

Ide, Y. 24
Ikeda, R. 32
iki 20–21
Ikuhara, K. 33
Impressionism 22
Irie, Y. 69–85
Ishihara, T. 26, 96–108, 152–154
Ito, N. 96
Izubuchi, Y. 111–129

James, W. 63
Joan of Arc 21

Kahlo, F. 110
Kanbe, M. 85–87
Kaneko, K. 116, 118, 127
Kanon (2002) 96, 100
Kanon (2006) 42, 46, 56, 96–108
Kashimashi—Girl Meets Girl 23–25, 27
Kawamori, S. 30, 109–110
Kawasaki, I. 173–174
Kikuchi, M. 147
kire 2, 7–8, 9, 84, 86, 88–89
kire tsuzuki 2, 7–8, 9, 84, 86, 88–89
Klimt, G. 22
Kon, C. 92–94
Kon, S. 13–21, 25, 58, 151–152
Kubo, M. 116, 118, 127
Kurau Phantom Memory 33, 46, 67, 69–85

Kurosawa, A. 17
Kyoda, T. 125–129

Lao Tzu 119, 130
Laputa: Castle in the Sky 29–30
Large Hadron Collider 60
Larsen, J. L. 48
Lefebvre, H. 106–107
Levin Becker, A. 60
Lewis, C. S. 126
littlejonny100 101
Longfellow, H. W. 155
Lowenthal, D. 105
Lum the Forever 26, 90, 91, 106
Lynch, D. 18

MacInnes, D. T. 57
Magic Knight Rayearth 150
Magritte, R. 110, 127
Mahoromatic — Automatic Maiden 25
Mannering, D. 20
Manovich, L. 11–12
Mashimo, K. 85, 133–151, 155–164
Matsuo, K. 175–176
The Melancholy of Haruhi Suzumiya 67, 100, 152–154
Memories 67, 110–111
Merleau-Ponty, M. 83
Metropolis 39
Michelet, J. 21
Millennium Actress 13–21, 22, 23, 25, 27, 67, 152
Miyazaki, H. 29–30, 58, 81
Miyazaki, N. 26
Mochizuki, T. 22–23, 58
mono no aware 2, 5–6, 9, 26, 76, 85, 91, 95, 103
MoonPhase 87–88, 89
Morimoto, K. 110
Morley, C. 90
Mulholland Dr. 18
Munch, E. 22
Murakami, H. 13
Murakami, K. 5
Murata, M. 34–49

Nagahama, T. 32
Nagaoka, A. 58, 109–110
Nakagami, Y. 99
Nakanishi, N. 23–25
Nakata, H. 53
Nausicaä of the Valley of the Wind 29, 81
Neon Genesis Evangelion 58, 127
Neuromancer 39
Noh theatre 22
Noir 85, 88
Nuclear Buddha 67

Ocean Waves 22–23, 58
Ohmori, T. 53–54
Okamura, T. 110
Okuse, S. 41
Only Yesterday 57–58, 60
Oonuma, S. 58
Oppliger, J. 123–124
Origin: Spirits of the Past 28–30
Oshii, M. 39, 76
Otomo, K. 111
Ozaki, T. 33–34

Paprika 67, 151–152
Park, R. E. 105
Pascal, D. 6
Patlabor 1: The Mobile Police 39
Pavese, C. 13
Paz, O. 128
Pearce, J. 66
Perfect Blue 15, 58
Phoenix 31–32
Pile, S. 107–108
pinku film 21
The Place Promised in Our Early Days 51, 58, 59, 60–68, 112
Please Teacher! 24
Pocock, D. C. D. 107
Princess Mononoke 29
Puccini, G. 110
Puranas 64

quantum physics 60, 63, 112–113, 130–132

Raban, J. 106
RahXephon 26, 29, 42, 61, 67, 102, 111–129
RahXephon: Pluralitas Concentio 61, 125–129
Rajneesh, B. S. 69
Record of Lodoss War 109–110, 127
Red Garden 175–176
Revolutionary Girl Utena 33
RG Veda 150
The Ring 53
Ringu 53
Rintaro 32, 39, 51–53
Robinson, T. 100, 148
Roman Holiday 152
Rose of Versailles 32

sabi 2, 6, 9, 32, 33, 34
Sailor Moon 26
Saito, Y. 48
Santos, C. 47
Sato, J. 26, 94–96
Sato, M. 41
Sato, T. 54–57
Schiavo, P. 39
Schwarz, J. H. 64

Scott, R. 39
Shigofumi: Letters from the Departed 54–57
Shimoda, M. 130–132
Shinbo, A. 87–88
Shinkai, M. 25–27, 58–68, 112
Shinto 29, 81–82, 128–129
La Sorcière 21
Spirit Warrior (The Peacock King) 51, 57, 60
Spirited Away 58
Starr, P. 26
Steinbeck, C. 10
Stiegler, B. 11
String Theory 64
Sugiyama, K. 28–30
Superstring Theory 64

Tada, S. 136
Takahashi, R. 31
Takahata, I. 57–58
Tanizaki, J. 31
Taoism 119
Tarot 22
Tarzan the Ape Man 152
Tetsuko no Tabi 58
Tezuka, O. 31
Throne of Blood 17
Tokyo Godfathers 152
Tolkien, J. R. R. 28, 126
Tsubasa: RESERVoir CHRoNiCLE, TV Series: Season 1 26, 46, 121, 133–151
Tsubasa: RESERVoir CHRoNiCLE, TV Series: Season 2 155–164
Tsubasa RESERVoir CHRoNiCLE The Movie: Princess of the Birdcage Kingdom 135, 173–174
Tsubasa Tokyo Revelations — OVA 136, 167–171, 173–174
Tsurumaki, K. 25, 58, 67
2001: A Space Odyssey 17

ukiyo-e 20–21

Van Dyke, W. S. 152
Verbinsky, G. 53
Verne, J. 64
Vision of Escaflowne 30, 109–110, 127
Voices of a Distant Star 58–60

wabi 2, 6, 9, 17, 18, 19, 20, 23, 26, 148, 154
Waldman, H. 60
Watanabe, Takashi 58, 91–92
Watanabe, Tetsuya 58
When They Cry: Higurashi 91, 92–94, 106, 107

Wilde, O. 109
Winterson, J. 64–65, 95
Wolf, F. A. 63–64
Wordsworth, W. 94
Wright, J. K. 105
Wright, S. 133
Wyler, W. 152

X 51–53, 57, 60
X/1999 150

xenocrisis0153 102
XXXHOLiC 150, 174
XXXHOLiC the Movie: A Midsummer Night's Dream 135, 174–175

Yamaga, H. 25
Yamakawa, H. 109
Yamamoto, E. 21–22
Yamazaki, K. 90

Young, R. F. 126
yugen 2, 6, 9, 32, 62, 67, 129
yuri 24

Zegapain 119, 130–132
Zen 7, 8, 9, 88–89, 103

www.ingramcontent.com/pod-product-compliance
Ingram Content Group UK Ltd.
Pitfield, Milton Keynes, MK11 3LW, UK
UKHW050524150426
5217IPUK00026B/1791